"Here are the voices that South Africa's famous Truth and Reconciliation Commission (TRC) failed to hear—yet they are crucial to understanding how it was the young, on the streets of small townships, who out-fought, out-stayed their government's repression in the 1980s. The reader is offered not just the tortures (the 14 young men are reticent and modest in retrospect) but also the young men's responses to betrayals and their underlying codes of ethics. Pamela Reynolds involves the reader in her actual fieldwork—its personal dilemmas and doubts, its sensitivities, and physical senses; lame academic anthro-speak is not for her. The book ends with a vehement, angry critique of the way the TRC's Report deliberately omitted the young: Because they refused to categorize themselves as 'victims,' the young were given no recompense for their woundedness and their losses in the struggle. Any serious student of contemporary violence (and the realities of being young combatants against a tough state apparatus) must read this—and take to heart how such studies can, despite the odds and the time required, be really well done."

—Murray Last, University College London

"This is an extraordinary book that goes below the surface of master stories of the struggle against the cruel regime through which apartheid was sustained for so long in South Africa. Writing in collaboration with the young who see themselves as engaged in a national struggle for liberation rather than as victims, Pamela Reynolds gives us a book that is methodologically innovative and theoretically sophisticated, yet able to communicate the everyday realities of those who traversed many layers of relationship with swirling emotions of fidelity, betrayal, joy, and grief. This book is indeed a treasure unmatched in its simplicity and integrity."

—Veena Das, Johns Hopkins University

"Dramatizing the role of children and recalling the place of violence in the anti-apartheid struggle, Pamela Reynolds also offers luminous evidence of *imfobe*—the youthful sense that her protagonists generated both to guide and to understand their acts. For an age that honors only nonviolent struggle in the face of oppression and views youth solely as victims when it acknowledges their distinctive experience at all, this book is doubly thought-provoking."

—Samuel Moyn, Columbia University,
author of *The Last Utopia: Human Rights in History*

War in Worcester

forms of living

Stefanos Geroulanos and Todd Meyers, *series editors*

With
Nana Charity Khohlokoane
Amos Monde Khomba
Eric Ndoyisile Tshandu
Xolile Dyabooi
Paulos Mnyuka
Zandisile Leonard Ntsomi
Mawethu Bikani
Vuyisile Malangeni
Zingisile Yabo
Nation Andile March
Edwin Mnyamana Rasmeni
Isaac Lehlohonolo Tshabile
Sonwabo Sitsili
Ntando Pringle Mrubata

War in Worcester

Youth and the Apartheid State

Pamela Reynolds

FORDHAM UNIVERSITY PRESS
NEW YORK 2013

Fordham University Press has no responsibility for the persistence or accuracy of URLs for external or third-party Internet
websites referred to in this publication and does not guarantee
that any content on such websites is, or will remain, accurate or
appropriate.

Fordham University Press also publishes its books in a variety of
electronic formats. Some content that appears in print may not
be available in electronic books.

Library of Congress Cataloging-in-Publication Data

Reynolds, Pamela, 1944–
    War in Worcester : youth and the apartheid state / Pamela
Reynolds ; in collaboration with Nana Charity Khohlokoane . . .
[et al.].— 1st ed.
        p. cm. — (Forms of living)
    Includes bibliographical references and index.
    ISBN 978-0-8232-4309-9 (cloth : alk. paper) —
ISBN 978-0-8232-4310-5 (pbk. : alk. paper)
        1. South Africa. Truth and Reconciliation Commission.
2. Youth—South Africa—Worcester.   3. Anti-apartheid
activists—Violence against—South Africa—Worcester.
4. Anti-apartheid movements—South Africa—Worcester.
5. Worcester (South Africa)—Race relations.   I. Title.
II. Series: Forms of living.
    HQ799.S5R496 2013
    323.1196'068733—dc23

                                                    2012012388

Printed in the United States of America
15 14 13   5 4 3 2 1
First edition

We dedicate the book to the memory of
Paulos Mnyuka
Zingisile Yabo
Sonwabo Sitsili
Pringle Ntando Mrubata

In addition, I acknowledge my gratitude
to my fourteen collaborators
and
to the continuing support and patience I received
from my daughters,
Talitha, Portia, Sabaa, and Abigail,
despite the Savonarola tendency they began to show
toward the manuscript.

CONTENTS

x   *Contents*

Photographs follow page 132

ACKNOWLEDGMENTS

I acknowledge the tact and imagination with which Rasna Dhillon edited the initial draft. I thank the participants of a series of Writing Groups we held at Johns Hopkins University, especially Todd Meyers, Aaron Goodfellow, and Sylvain Perdigon, for companionship and intellectual engagement. I am beholden to Colleen Crawford Cousins, Fiona Ross, Patti Henderson, and Thomas Cousins for commenting on a late draft of the manuscript. I deeply appreciate Geoff Grundlingh's generosity in giving me permission to print his photographs and Barbra Wright's allowing the use of hers. Lindy Wilson and Fiona Ross permitted me to quote from the interviews they conducted with Charity Nana Khohlokoane. I thank Alana De Kock, Nyami Mhlauli, and M. Thabang for completing small projects adjacent to the research, Andrew Alexander for assistance with formatting, and Megan Greenwood for contributing to the compilation of the endnotes.

Marlene Dumas has honored my collaborators and me in giving us permission to use her wonderful painting *The Witness*, on the cover. The generosity of Zeno X Gallery in Antwerp, Belgium, the gallery that represents her, is acknowledged.

The research was conducted during my tenure from 1991 to 2002 in the department of Social Anthropology, University of Cape Town, and I am indebted to my colleagues for their support and to graduates for contributing their field reports on Worcester. I am grateful for the stimulating collegiality I enjoyed as a Visiting Fellow in 1999 among the Fellows of All Souls College, Oxford, where I began to write the book. As a Visiting Professor at the University of California, Berkeley, in 2000–1; as a Mellon Presidential Visiting Professor in 2001–2 at the International Centre at the University of Michigan, Ann Arbor; and as a Professor in the Department of Anthropology, Johns Hopkins University from 2002 to 2009 I learned from and enjoyed the companionship of faculty members, especially Veena Das and Jane Guyer, and graduate students. In 2010 the University of Cape Town conferred on me an Honorary Professorship in the Department of Social Anthropology, and it is fitting that the project has, at last, come to fruition in the place where it began.

The following institutions are gratefully acknowledged for having granted funds to support the project: I received a Harry F. Guggenheim Foundation Award in 1997 for an Ethnographic Study of the Truth and Reconciliation Commission; an Anglo-American Chairman's Fund Award in 1996; an Ernest Oppenheimer Memorial Trust Award in 1996; and a Centre for Science Development Award in 1995 for the Study of the Truth and Reconciliation Commission.

Colleen Crawford Cousins has been a loyal, uncompromising partisan in focusing her intellect, wit, and will on the project and on me; Fiona Ross has continued to give me unstinting support; Todd Meyers and Stefanos Geroulanos have complemented me in adding my work to the list of distinguished writers in their series; and Helen Tartar and Tom Lay of Fordham University Press have made the production a joyful experience of finely tuned expertise. I thank each one as well as the two reviewers of the manuscript.

Finally I thank the people of Zwelethemba for their hospitality, particularly for the welcome extended to me by the families of the men whose stories are told here.

A portion of Chapter 2 of this book was published as "Mapping the Conflict," in *anthropologies*, ed. Richard Baxstrom and Todd Meyers (Baltimore: Creative Capitalism, 2008), 56–80. A portion of Chapter 6 was published as "On Leaving the Young Out of History," *The Journal of the History of Childhood and Youth* 1.1 (2008): 150–56. An earlier version of Chapter 5 appeared as "Neutralizing the Young: The South African Truth and Reconciliation Commission and Youth," in *On Knowing and Not Knowing in the Anthropology of Medicine*, ed. Roland Littlewood (Walnut Creek, Calif.: Left Coast Press. 2007) and appears with permission of Left Coast Press, Inc. An earlier version of Chapter 4 appeared as "Imfobe: Self-knowledge and the Reach for Ethics among Former, Young, Anti-Apartheid Activists," *Anthropology Southern Africa Journal* 28 (2005): 62–72.

Introduction

> i cannot think of tears, lonely geographies
> and the third world, without the urge to cry or to sit down
>
> — MXOLISI NYEZWA

Boyhood in Worcester

The book is about youth fighting for freedom and a state's retaliation. It is about the young not consenting to the kind of adulthood on offer under a particular political dispensation. It is about the character of revolt under conditions of tight surveillance. It is about negative forms of governance of children and about the violence of the state. It is about government-sanctioned cruelty. It is about the labor of youth in the work of war and about their reach for ethics despite experiences of pain and betrayal. It is, in part, about the attempts by the Truth and Reconciliation Commission (henceforth, the Commission or the TRC) to document the past and its shortcomings in recording the role of the young and in securing a fair dispensation for them. Finally, it is a description of the relationships between young men of Zwelethemba, a suburb of Worcester, who were brought together as local leaders during the struggle, who led the fight together, and who, in retrospect, examined it microscopically once it had ended. It represents an anthropology that takes on the intimacies of warfare.

John M. Coetzee's book *Boyhood: Scenes from Provincial Life* (1997) is taken to be autobiographical and is set in the small, rural town of Worcester, in which Coetzee spent much of his childhood and in which my ethnography was situated. He says of the town: "But perhaps Worcester is a purgatory one must pass through. Perhaps Worcester is where people are sent to be tested" (1997, 34).

Worcester lies in a dip in the mountains where the Hex River Valley leads into the valley carved out by the Breede River, some 110 kilometers north of Cape Town. It falls in the region called the Boland ("the land above"), which is made up of a series of fertile valleys behind the Hottentot-Hollandse Mountains, which separate the valleys from the sandy isthmus, colloquially called "The Flats," that stretches across to the mountain range that includes Table Mountain, around the base of which the city of Cape Town took root. The Boland is a beautiful area where wine is produced and fruit, including table grapes, grown. Worcester is a center for farmers and the municipal administration of four towns. The region had, prior to the election of a democratic government in 1994, been demarcated as a "Coloured labour preference" area, which made it difficult for Africans to live and work there, because preference was given to people designated "Coloured" in terms of employment and other rights, including the right to live in urban areas.[1] Most jobs available to Africans in the Boland were on farms.

A Double-Edged Study

I set out to do an ethnographic study of the TRC as an institution. My focus was on learning more about the part the young had played in securing the end of oppression. Having worked on a separate study in 1991 and 1992 with young political activists, both men and women, who had recently been released from prison, where some had been incarcerated for many years for their engagement in the antiapartheid struggle,[2] I sought to discover from the Commission's deliberations more about young activists' commitment over time, their political consciousness, their development, their ethics, their actions, and the consequences of their involvement. I was interested in the character of urban conflict and the relationships between command-ers and foot soldiers (or leaders and protesters), and whether those ties held up over time and whether they were forged around rhetoric, contact, ac-tion, accountability, or responsibility. I was interested in a particular layer of leadership among the young—those recognized within communities as local leaders. I anticipated that the Commission would document the activi-ties of those who, while still at school, had begun to protest against their oppressors and who, through processes of self-selection and induction, had become leaders. It soon became clear that the Commission was structured in a way that precluded it from gathering information systematically, which could have led to that kind of analysis of the recent past. That the Commis-sion's focus was split by the binary notion of perpetrator or victim, leading to the award of amnesty or reparations, determined its pursuit and its meth-ods. The emphasis for "victims" was on the descriptions of violations. The young who fought inside the country were classified in accord with the Ge-neva Conventions and Protocols as "civilians," not "warriors," and therefore the platform they were given related to victimization and not to resistance or revolt. There is, Emmanuel Levinas says, no "transparency possible in method" (1996, 33). I take from this the suggestion that an approach to ethnographic fieldwork cannot be made completely explicit or justified as to why certain ways of proceeding were chosen. My ambition in this eth-nography was to account for the fullness of some young men's experiences in standing against the apartheid state to the extent that that is possible and that I am able to achieve it within the loose confines of the discipline of an-thropology. I sought to depict their fight as they described it in retrospect. The question is, of course: what is description? Is it a chronicle or a product of reflection? Under what circumstances, in what place, across what span of time, and before whom is it made? The conversations on which this writ-ing draws are different from those recorded at the Commission's hearings and from those within the African National Congress (ANC) now: there are many ways of talking about the past. Any description of major conflicts has an elliptical relationship to what actually happened. Veena Das says that the most compelling moments for her in ethnography have occurred when she found someone responding to events that put his or her entire life into question. She is fascinated by the process of seeing, particularly in scenes of forgetfulness, how one is drawn into an examination of one's life. She observes that "there is something resistant to thought when we try to imagine the condition of being wounded . . . something else than rational argument is called for in the face of this condition—not simply emotion or empathy but 'wakefulness to one's life'" (spoken at a Sawyer Seminar 2010, University of Cape Town). In Zwelethemba, the scene was a request to remember. The invitation to remember in conjunction with others was an invitation to each of the men to examine his life. In the process of our meetings, the men seemed to be engaged in a retrieval of the condition of being wounded, so that a certain balance of reason and emotion could be achieved in the service of remembering. Mxolisi Nyezwa (2000, 87) writes in his poem "i won't forget" the following lines:

> at night I won't forget to remember
> . . .
> i won't forget that we were men on this earth
> with numbed emotions,
> nabbing at shadows
> hidden from sight.

It was, in part, to avoid becoming an "ethnographer of victimization" (Said 2006, 139) in the process of attending a slew of the Human Rights Violation hearings (HRV hearings—not to be confused with the Human Rights Committee, an independent nongovernmental institute) that I resolved to add a parallel ethnographic project to the study of the TRC. After the first few months of acting like a peripatetic groupie of the Commission, it became clear to me that its deliberations were not plumbing the experiences of young activists and that there was more to be learned through a different kind of ethnographic exploration. Theodor Adorno said, "Social analysis can learn incomparably more from individual experience . . . while conversely the large historical categories . . . are no longer above suspicion of fraud" (1974, 17). Edward Said uses this quote to observe that the force of protest lies in the performance of unreconciled individuals' critical thinking (2006, 15). He values Adorno's notion of tension in what he, Said, calls "irreconcilabilities" (2006, xv). Reconciliation is not necessarily what we need, he felt, for its worth depends on how it is pursued (2006, xvii). I attended almost every Human Rights Violation Committee Hearing in the Western and Northern Cape and heard extraordinary accounts from young people who had fought for change in the small towns. The Boland Hearing was held from June 24 to 26, 1996, in Worcester, and it was while listening to the testimonies of the young that I decided to work in Zwelethemba ("place of hope"), the municipal area to which, in 1952, Africans had been forcibly relocated by the Worcester Council (see appendix 1 on Worcester). Thereafter, I studied both the TRC and the community of black African activists in Zwelethemba: the former a multisited project and the latter firmly situated in a single community. Fiona Ross worked with young women activists in Zwelethemba and I with the young men. On the basis of our joint work tracing the process of the TRC's deliberations, especially the HRV hearings, we had become aware of differences in the accounts given by women and men. According to our notes, more women than men were giving testimony in public, and they were frequently testifying on behalf of fathers, brothers, husbands, or sons, and, sometimes, they did not talk about their own experiences even when they had been activists themselves (see Ross 2001). This may have influenced our decision for one of us to work with young women and the other with young men. However, I recall that Fiona quickly had made important contact with women, and our division of labor began then (see her wonderful book, *Bearing Witness: Women and the Truth and Reconciliation Commission in South Africa*, 2003). We continued to work alongside each other and share our thoughts.

The Truth and Reconciliation Commission

The establishment of the Truth and Reconciliation Commission was an extraordinary experiment, part of a twentieth-century rash of similar attempts to end conflict. It contributed to the documentation of the depth and breadth of terror and destruction under apartheid. The TRC of South Africa originated in the agreement on amnesty reached in 1993 between representatives of the South African government, political parties, and some liberation organizations. The proposal for the Commission drew on work done by similar commissions established elsewhere, especially in South American countries. It was established in 1994 under the auspices of a democratically elected government led by President Nelson Mandela. In 1996, it described its creation as follows:

The Truth and Reconciliation Commission has been established by an Act of Parliament; *The Promotion of National Unity and Reconciliation Act, number 34*. It was passed into law on 27th July, 1995. The preamble of the Act states that,

. . . it is deemed necessary to establish the truth in relation to past events as well as the motives for and circumstances in which gross violations of human rights have occurred and to make the findings known in order to prevent a repetition of such events in the future.

(Promotion of National Unity and Reconciliation Act, number 34 of 1995, 2)

In addition, the Act states that the aim of the Commission will be reconciliation based on "a need for understanding but not for vengeance, a need for reparation but not retaliation, a need for *ubuntu* but not for victimization" (ibid.). Finally, the Act makes provision for the granting of amnesty "in respect of acts, omissions and offences associated with political objectives committed in the course of the conflicts of the past" (ibid.). The full announcement is given in appendix 2, and it is followed in appendix 3 by a description of the Boland Hearing at which the people from Worcester gave testimony.

The Act's preamble recognizes apartheid as having comprised more than one form of violence and imagines a future founded on peaceful coexistence, human rights, and democracy. To achieve its aim to "promote national unity and reconciliation in a spirit of understanding which transcends the conflicts and divisions of the past," the Act created three committees: one on amnesty, one on human rights violations, and one on reparation and rehabilitation. It also provided for an investigative unit, a research unit, and a limited witness protection program, and it granted the Commission considerable powers, including rights of search, seizure, and subpoena.

A vast amount of the documentation of the past under apartheid was systematically erased, between 1990 and 1994, from social memory when the state engaged in the large-scale destruction of its memory resources. Verne Harris, who was from 1988 to 1994 an archivist with the State Archive Service, called the destruction "a purge on social memory in South Africa" (1999, 14). In his opinion, the Commission successfully depicted (with significant assistance from him) the broader processes of records destruction, and it provided evidence that suggests that the obliteration of swathes of official documentary memory, particularly around the inner workings of the apartheid state's security apparatus, has had a considerable and lasting impact on social memory. He continues,

> Moreover, the apparent complete destruction of records confiscated from individuals and organizations over many years by the Security Police has removed from our heritage arguably the country's richest accumulation of records documenting the struggles against apartheid. The overall work of the TRC suffered substantially as a result. . . . As the TRC itself indicated, "the destruction of state documentation probably did more to undermine the investigative work of the Commission than did any other single factor." For the most part the big picture, the fundamental shape and pattern of process, was as clear as any interrogation of the past can be clear. *But so often the details, the nuances, the texture, the activities and experiences of individuals, was absent.*
>
> *(1999, 14; emphasis mine)*

It is toward this absence that this book gestures.

A major concern of the Commission was with "gross violations of human rights," which are defined in the Act as killing, torture, abduction, and/ or severe ill treatment, or the conspiracy or attempt to commit such acts.[3] The period of apartheid rule that was under examination fell between the years 1960 and 1994. The Human Rights Violation Committee (HRVC) took 21,298 statements concerning 37,859 violations (sometimes the figure is given as 37,672) from people who had experienced harm that fitted the definition, and 10 percent of those who made statements were heard at public hearings held between April 1996 and June 1997 (*Truth and Reconciliation Commission Report* 1998, 1:166; hereafter, the *Report*). One of the seventy-six public hearings was conducted from June 24 to 26, 1996, in Worcester, at which three of the young men from Zwelethemba with whom I worked gave testimony (see appendix 4, on the Commission's findings on violence in the Western Cape). It was on the basis of the statements collected by the HRVC that testifiers were declared to be "victims" and thus deserving of reparations. The Commission received 7,115 applications for amnesty. Amnesty was granted to a relatively small number of applicants: 1,167, with a further 145 granted partial amnesty (see Sanders 2007, 216n3; Sarkin 2004, 108–148). The Commission declared that more than 19,050 persons were found, on the basis of their statements, to be victims of gross violations of human rights, and more than 2,975 victims emerged from the amnesty process (*Report*, foreword to volume 7). Interim reparations, totaling about R42 million, were distributed to some sixteen thousand victims, with payments ranging from R1,400 to R4,200. There was slow delivery of full reparations, and the amount did not meet the Commission's recommendations. The "recognized" victims were allocated a lump sum of compensatory money—R30,000 (in 2003 about US$3,900; Thompson 2003). The Commission published its *Report* in seven volumes, five of which were presented in October 1998 to President Nelson Mandela and the sixth and seventh on March 21, 2003, when the chairman, Archbishop Desmond Tutu, delivered them to President Thabo Mbeki, marking the formal end of the Commission's work.[4] A wide variety of books have been written on the Commission, and I shall attempt no coverage of it except as it relates to the question of documenting the role of the young (a selection of writings on the Commission and the situation of South Africa under apartheid is given in this note).[5]

I acknowledge the fascination that many people have for truth commissions, including South Africa's. I am cognizant of reminders to me by readers of early drafts of the book that the very institution of the Commission represents the success of those who fought to end apartheid and that both its establishment and its procedures exist as beacons for people mired in states of oppression in various parts of the world. The critique I give of the Commission refers specifically to my search for documentation and recording of the role of the young.

Neither the Promotion of National Unity and Reconciliation Act nor the Commission recognized young fighters inside the country as formal, legitimate combatants for the purposes of the HRV hearings. The Act categorized them as "victims," and it was as "victims" that they were heard by the Commission's Human Rights Committee and awarded victim status, giving them the right to claim reparations. In terms of pensions and formal recognition, the ANC only recognized those who could prove that they had been members of the organization and active within it for five or more years. (The government's Special Pensions Bill of 1996 took, according to Villa-Vicencio and Verwoerd [2000, 248–249] a "step of 'rewarding' or recompensing those who fought for freedom . . . but one that excluded thousands of people who may not have been formal members of a liberation movement or who were excluded by the stipulations of the bill, for example that a recipient had to be 35 or older in 1996.") That bill has, since the end of this project, been altered.[6] Neither the ANC nor any other liberation organization had been able to keep records of membership during the conflict—the nature of the struggle precluded that—and possession of evidence of membership or of literature relating to a banned organization could, and often did, result in imprisonment. It was difficult for many activists, especially young activists, to prove that they had fought on behalf of liberation as members of one of those organizations. The Act established and, thereafter, the Commission drew on the binary notion of victim and perpetrator. Those seen to have been soldiers in formal armies or who were members of the armed forces of a "party to the conflict" (see the Commission's definition in chapter 5) were not included in the Commission's deliberations, although this was not rigidly adhered to. Special hearings were held on conscription within South Africa to the South African Defence Force (SADF)[7] and on abuses in liberation organization camps. The question of the recognition of young fighters touched on here is closely examined in chapter 5. Disgruntlement was stirred by the fact that amnesty, when granted to an applicant who testified before the Amnesty Committee, took immediate effect, whereas an applicant to the HRVC had to wait for over a year before he or she was granted or refused the status of a victim and some years before he or she was awarded final reparations.

War Was Being Waged

The definition of war is at issue because it determines who is recognized as a legitimate fighter. In South Africa and in other conflicts, many an individual fought in relation to his or her understanding that he or she was a member of a liberation organization (one that he or she had formally joined) with a structure that attempted to coordinate efforts to achieve specified ends.[8] The understanding affected the person's sense of participating in the pursuit of a larger cause, one for which there was little point in fighting in isolation or even with a small, local group. The nature of the fight was amorphous, one might say organic, in its origins, growth, and spread. It was multipronged, and it is difficult to designate which efforts contributed significantly to the final achievement of its goal. Command was dispersed, secrecy vital, and action channeled through cells that purposely obscured identities and tasks. On the one hand, it was not possible or even desirable to track membership, but, on the other hand, the loyalty and labor of individuals was donated in the name of organizations to which they saw themselves as belonging. A conundrum?

It is to be regretted, I believe, that an efficient, broadly based effort was not instituted to record, once the fight was over, the names of those who were recognized in communities and liberation structures as having been engaged in political activities within the country. Membership lists have been, after 1994, compiled, but they are incomplete, and, not surprisingly, they have left out many who contributed significantly to the fight, and the consequences in terms of lack of acknowledgment or support (whether monetary, access to education or skills training, or job opportunities) distress many. In 1996, I made enquiries from the liberation organizations about their membership and was told by each of them that they had no comprehensive lists and very little information on those who fought inside the country. The executive of one organization invited me to write their history. I regret not having been able, at that time, to contribute to the task.

The ANC and its armed wing, Umkhonto weSizwe (MK),[9] in a Declaration at the Headquarters of the International Committee of the Red Cross, November 28, 1980, referred to the fact that the international community had legally denounced apartheid as a crime against humanity, which led to an International Convention for the Suppression and Punishment of the Crime of Apartheid. The Declaration interprets this as a recognition that a "war [was being] waged by this nefarious system against the vast majority of its population" (Asmal, Chidester, and Lubisi 2005, 65). It continues:

> The state of war, which exists in South Africa, is a war of national liberation, for self-determination on the basis of the Freedom Charter,[10] of whose adoption we are celebrating the 25th anniversary this year [1980]. It is, as Article 1 of Protocol 1 of 1977 recognises, an armed conflict in which peoples are fighting against colonial domination and alien occupation and against racist regimes in the exercise of their right of self-determination.
>
> *(ibid.)*

With regard to the experiences of those who stood against the state inside South Africa, people argued as to whether they were engaged in a war, a struggle, a conflict, or even a fight for liberation. Recently, the term "asymmetric war" is being widely used to describe certain forms of internal eruptions. Later in this book, I discuss the various terms that were used, but here I want to note that it was seen as a war by the liberation organizations.

Once the conflict had been declared to be a war, liberation organizations could draw on the Geneva Conventions and the additional Protocol 1 and humanitarian international law. The Declaration called on the South African regime to stop treating the combatants of the liberation organizations as common criminals and to stop executing them, imposing savage sentences of imprisonment on them, or torturing and generally poorly treating them contrary to international law (Asmal et al. 2005, 66). The South African government did not desist. It was important to call the conflict a war to secure international condemnation of the regime, to gain support in imposing sanctions on it, and to fund efforts toward liberation. It mattered, too, for the drive to ensure prisoner-of-war status for combatants. The South African government did not formally grant that it was a war but rather characterized the conflict as the result of sustained terrorist activities. The Commission had an international orientation, and its pronouncements had performative effects, as did the ANC declaration on war.

Nigel Penn calls the colonization of the northern frontier zone, in which Worcester now lies, a zone of warfare. He identifies the initial clashes as "the first Khoikhoi-Dutch war (1659–1660)" followed by "the second Khoikhoi-Dutch war (1673–1677)" (2005, 32). His book details "the magnitude and ferocity of Khoikhoi and San resistance" that continued into the eighteenth century (2005, 60). There followed, he says, nearly two centuries of violence. That period includes the violence recorded in this book.

The Work of War

The South African government gave the young who joined the struggle inside the country no quarter; indeed, they targeted them. In this book, I write about children and youth identified by the apartheid system as "African," although those who joined the fight and who fell under other categories defined according to set notions of racial difference were met with the same wrath (see note 1). The government's security forces meted out cruel treatment to them, incarcerated even the very young under dreadful conditions, and used torture frequently and over long periods of time.[11] Many of the local leaders among the young were imprisoned again and again and ill treated even before any formal charges or court appearances were made. All of this is well known. Many organizations were careful and courageous in keeping track of abuses and in caring for those harmed (for example, the Black Sash, the Human Rights Committee of South Africa, the Detainees' Parents Support Committee, the Legal Resources Centre, the Black Lawyers Association, the Catholic Welfare and Development Organization, and the Centre for Applied Legal Studies),[12] many lawyers represented the young in court, and many people took great risks in protecting the young. The men gratefully acknowledged the support of three people in particular—Di Bishop (a member of the Black Sash), Leslie London (a physician), and Dumisa Buhle Ntsebeza (a human rights lawyer and former head of the Commission's investigative unit). The activists with whom I worked acknowledged people of all races in Worcester and other towns in the Boland who had given them aid and support. The Commission's work has added to the record, and so has the research being done within the former liberation organizations and in institutions such as the Centre for the Study of Violence and Reconciliation, the Institute for Justice and Reconciliation, and the Khulumani Support Group (see note 12). The writings of people who were closely involved as well as those of academics continue to contribute to the documentation of the past (see a selected list of references in note 5).

However, little is known about the efforts the young made to sustain the momentum of the fight or about the stretches of time during which many were active; what they endured on an everyday basis; the nature of the battlefield; how much they depended on relationships with families, peers, and community members; how their commitment was tried; what the stakes were of success and failure; and what was achieved in terms of growth and what paid in terms of harm. These matters are examined in the chapters that follow.

There is a strong genealogy to the revolt by the young against apartheid. The ANC was founded in 1912, and its Youth League was formed in 1944—its manifesto was issued that year under the impetus of Nelson Mandela, O. R. Tambo, Walter Sisulu, and others (Asmal et al. 2005, 2).[13] The three men became leaders of the organization. The trigger for a widespread revolt among the youth occurred on June 16, 1976, in Soweto.[14] The apartheid state unleashed its brutality against the children who gathered in an unarmed and peaceful protest against new directives in education that ruled that Africans would henceforth be taught certain subjects in the medium of Afrikaans rather than in English (the latter was seen as the language of access). Many people, including children, were killed that day, and, as the violence spread, more died that week (the numbers are contested). As many as one thousand people were injured. It was the start of violence against the young on a massive and persistent scale behind which lay the technologies of war. The protest among the young gathered force and, between 1976 and 1987, some twenty-four thousand children under the age of eighteen were imprisoned, and many (or most) were tortured or severely ill treated (see chapter 5).

The Violence of the State

Emmanuel Levinas (1996, 23) describes the oppression of the individual by the state:

> For me, the negative element, the element of violence in the State, in the hierarchy, appears even when the hierarchy functions perfectly, when everyone submits to universal ideas. There are cruelties which are terrible because they proceed from the necessity of the reasonable Order. They are, if you like, . . . the tears of the Other (*Autrui*).

The violence of the state in South Africa was crafted into a hierarchy of dominance, control, and limitations over the majority of the population. It was terrifying in its reach and durability, and it was founded on over three hundred years of Dutch and then British dominance that carried over into self-governance (see Wilson 2009 for a very short history of South Africa). In 1948, a general election, in which people of African or Indian origin were not allowed to vote, was won by the National Party (NP), which entrenched racism and segregation into a form of governance that operated in accord with a policy of segregation and discrimination on the grounds of race. It came to be called apartheid. The NP ruled until 1994, when the first democratic elections were held and won by the ANC. The ANC was against the formal, institutional, and governmental racism promulgated and put into effect by the apartheid regime that came into power in 1948 and that extended and entrenched a form of rule established by the British, which was the form of rule that the liberation organizations fought.

The way the state treated African children under apartheid enables us to look closely at how the governance of children in one country was separated out: it allows us to see which children—whose children—were set aside as not deemed worthy of good governance, or any governance, or of only destructive governance. It is the isolation of the child who protested under apartheid that is startling. He or she was targeted as a threat to law and order, as being a terrorist or potentially one. But the system of governance had already isolated the child by undermining the abilities of families or communities to care for them as they saw fit: it did so through a panoply of laws having to do with the denial of, or restrictions on, rights to citizenship and ownership of land and assets, demand for tax and therefore participation in a cash economy, undermining the agricultural base, insidious migration policies, denial of rights to live outside designated areas except under stringent terms involving employment and housing, the separation of heads of household (initially men but later increasingly women, too) from homes, and low wages. This is not to say that the child was not held and nurtured by parents and kin but that the state nestled white children in layers of care and protection, as a state interested in its own reproduction must, while it peeled away such layers for children identified as "nonwhite," leaving them vulnerable before the forces of the state.

Michel Foucault describes as a fundamental phenomenon in Western history the "governmentalization of the state" as bearing on the mass of the population. Foucault identifies in the great preoccupation about the way to govern and the search for the ways to govern, which exploded from the fifteenth century in Western Europe, a perpetual question: "how not to be governed *like that*, by that, in the name of those principles, with such and such an objective in mind and by means of such procedures not like that, not for that, not by them" (2003a, 265). He locates a critical attitude in this movement of governmentalization of both society and individuals. Those governed would then act

> as both partner and adversary to the arts of governing, as an act of defiance, as a challenge, as a way of limiting these acts of governing and sizing them

up, transforming them, of finding a way to escape from them or, in any case, a way to displace them, with a basic distrust, but also and by the same token, as a line of development of the arts of governing . . . a kind of general cultural form, both a political and moral attitude, a way of thinking etc., and which I would very simply call the art of not being governed . . . like that and at that cost. I would therefore propose, as a very definition of critique, this general characterization: the art of not being governed quite so much.

(ibid.)

Not to want to be governed "like that" means not wanting to accept these laws because they are unjust and hide a fundamental illegitimacy. Critique, for Foucault, means putting forth universal and indefeasible rights to which every government, including a *paterfamilias*, will have to submit. He is talking about the limits of the right to govern. And, finally, "not to want to be governed" means to question authority, and it raises "the problem of certainty in its confrontation with authority" (2003a, 265–266). The description matches the initial thorough critique that the liberation organizations made of their governance and their eventual confrontation with the state. The refusal to be governed under apartheid laws was a fundamental reason for the revolt by the young. The question for today and tomorrow is the governance of children, how it fits into current notions of obligations and responsibilities of the state, and how it is theorized and acted upon by citizens.

Stanley Cavell lays emphasis on the remarkable fact of the presence of the figure of the child in the opening scene of Wittgenstein's *Philosophical Investigations*, which quotes Augustine on the instruction of the child. In it, Cavell is struck by "how isolated the child appears, training its own mouth to form signs"—something you might expect of a figure in a Beckett play. Cavell calls the child "the unobserved observer of the culture" (1995, 169). That is, for me, a moving depiction of the child. It is a theme in this book: how the child comes to a political and ethical understanding, however immature and imperfect, through observing its culture and acting in accord with that understanding. Cavell continues: "The scene portrays language as an inheritance but also one that has, as it were, to be stolen, anyway in which the capacity and perhaps the motivation to take it is altogether greater than the capacity and perhaps the motivation to give it." A question being raised is: when and under what conditions does the inheritance of a culture—the process of cultivation (of a child into a mature, social being)—end? Cavell suggests that it does not come "to a natural end, or rather its own end, but to one ended, by poor resources, or by power." I take from him, for my own purposes, the notion that control over what was taught to the child protesting against apartheid after 1976 moved its locus, on the initiative of the child and at the prompting of the retaliation of the state. In so doing, the child moved into an even greater position of isolation—from family and community and even within the law as it was practiced. I am borrowing from Cavell "the idea of the child as a necessary figure, however obscure and untheorized, for philosophy's stake (or repression of the stake) in the ordinary" (1995, 167). I do that not for philosophy's stake but for the sake of clear analysis of what the children did against a system of governance they did not like and how isolated they were in the certainty of confrontation with authority.

On Studying the Commission

The Commission was launched eighteen months after the first democratic elections in April 1994. It was hurried into being without, in my opinion, sufficient thought or due preparation. A sense of rush was derived from a perceived danger of civil conflict, a need to encourage people to speak out about the pain of the recent past, have it publicly acknowledged, begin the move toward reconciliation, and so launch the new national project. The Act defined, the Commissioners often asserted, much of the structure and activities of the Commission, and it was formulated and promulgated during a time of delicate political negotiations, when many leaders feared the outbreak of armed dissension. An issue that has been brought to our attention most forcefully by the writings on the Holocaust relates to the relationships between truth, memory, and time: how soon after a period of deep conflict and horror can those who have been embroiled in it describe their experiences and articulate its meanings? I have in mind the experiences of the young who led the fight within their communities inside the country, suffering dire consequences. How difficult it must have been for them to conceive of the particulars within the sweep of history (the long battle, the eventual victory, the personal loss in relation to their brief lives thus far). Did it help them to tell their stories that the Commission characterized them as "victims" at that time? Did the asking preempt other forms of listening? "There are," writes Adam Phillips, "surprisingly few occasions—or rituals—in which people are expected or invited to tell the story of their lives" (1994, 75).

The stretch of time that the Commission examined (1960 to 1994) was—had to be—arbitrarily selected. Clearly, a commission must have limits to its sweep through the past, but there are implications in the choice of beginnings and endings. While the shooting of protesters in 1960 in Sharpeville marked the start of a brutal form of oppression of public protest, it really represents no more than a glottal stop in the history of racial oppression in South Africa. In the process it adopted, testimonies often seemed to have been set free from context and history.

We see, then, the lineaments of time, including those that formed each "victim's" appearance at a public hearing on "Gross Human Rights Violations," during which the Commissioners were to examine a specified chunk of the recent past. They were to hear over a period of a year (stretched to eighteen months) "ordinary" people talk about what they had suffered. The 10 percent who were heard in public were selected by the Commissioners and their staff to reflect the range of violations experienced. The slot allowed each person testifying was circumscribed by time (to, on average, half an hour). This was intentional, for the focus was on victimhood and, therefore, on events or incidents of trauma. Every applicant filled in circumscribed forms. (They are described in chapter 2). Of necessity, much was left out, including, very often, political allegiance, activity, and commitment *across time*; the iteration of violations; the subtlety with which fear was instilled; and the sheer brutality of the terror and suffering endured over and over again.

On an Ethnography in Zwelethemba

I worked with young men on the periphery of the ANC: an edge from which they and their comrades across the country sometimes led. I studied the Commission's search for reconciliation and the fourteen young men's reach for it among those with whom they had lived and operated and within themselves. It was an astringent ethnography that I undertook in Zwelethemba:

one that made high demands on each of us as we trod with care across egg-shell terrain.

The two strands of the study offered a number of ways to triangulate the analysis. Three were of particular use to me: the triangulation between the Commission, the activist, and the State; between a truth commission, a small town, and fourteen individuals; and between the individual, the group, and the community. The study of the Commission offered a background against which to place the close-grained study: it offered a breadth, varieties of context, the findings of the Commission's Research Team, and hearings on famous cases including young activists such as Siphiwe Mthimkeulu, James Moeketsi Seipei (known as Stompie), Hector Pieterson, and the Gugulethu Seven.[15] The Commission was public, authoritative, official, and in possession of legal force, although it operated in the light of an inheritance from the former government of secrets, lies, mass shredding of data, and a refusal to cooperate by many sectors, especially the SADF. By contrast, the study in Zwelethemba was on a microscopic scale. It could only provide a mininarrative that entailed a search for depth in time unfolding: it could trace how young activists built support and sustained it, renewed their own and others' commitment, regained composure when time stopped (for example, under torture), reflected on failure and humiliation, and nourished networks. It could look at the substance of a life devoted to a cause fraught with dangers that threatened self, family, and community.

Sifting the evidence drawn from parallel studies for the book has meant leaving out a great deal, especially on the Commission. Nevertheless, I suggest that the analysis of a public institution and an ethnographic study of a single community yielded rich material—each strand gaining immeasurably from understandings gathered through the labor on the other.

The core of the study relies on the evidence I gathered from fourteen young men of Zwelethemba. I worked with each of them individually, and we met in groups of three or four and, often, all together. We met frequently during the first year, 1996, while I was on sabbatical, and then often, from 1997 to 2000, during weekends and university breaks. From 2000 to 2011, we met about once a year and maintained other forms of contact; over the last year, we have held a number of meetings and have had many exchanges. We met in their homes, in the newly constructed library in Zwelethemba, and in the offices of NGOs and a trade union. In the charming if not always welcoming town of Worcester, we met in fast-food joints, municipal offices, and on the village green, as well as at the police station and prison, and we met at sites where they had been tortured beside the Breede River, in a public nature park on the slopes of a mountain just outside Worcester, and on the pavement of the Sanlam Insurance Building; we even met at the train station when the Blue Train made a special stop to allow President Nelson Mandela to address a small crowd. Sometimes we met in Cape Town in my home, in the university residence where two of them were living, and once at my inaugural lecture. We held weekend workshops at Nekkies Resort, a guest house in the Breede Valley, and at Goedgedacht Trust Farm.

Six features of the ethnography that focuses on Zwelethemba make it particular. It is an account of what it means to do research on youth and conflict, for until recently few studies have given satisfactory descriptions and analyses of the subject.[16] It depicts the activities of young people who voluntarily engaged in a fight for a cause beginning when they were still at school and who had been neither conscripted nor forced to participate. They were not children of the street, nor were they gang members. It is a record of the struggle in a small country town compiled soon after the conflict had ended. It is set within the context of an analysis of a truth commission that had been created to document and examine the same conflict and the recent past, thus offering an elaboration of context that few ethnographers could hope to obtain. And, finally, it is a description of the relationships between young men who were brought together as local leaders during the struggle, who led the fight together, and who, in retrospect, examined it microscopically once it had ended.

While poring over a map of Zwelethemba one afternoon, five of the fourteen men in our group and I were tracking networks relied on by the comrades among the maze of identical houses, and it was suggested, laughingly, that we call our group MAZE, for Male Activists of Zwelethemba. And so we did. The group was composed of the young men who had been leaders in the 1980s of the youth and who were still, in 1996, based in Zwelethemba. Together we set out to make sense of the past using what Bernard Williams calls "the small scale of mini-narratives" that gives structure to matters of interpretation on a larger scale (2002, 244). Making sense of the recent past was no easy matter for the men, ten of whom had been tortured and two shot (resulting in paralysis for one and the loss of a leg for the other) by members of the security forces. Each had been embroiled in direct conflict with the forces of the law. In writing their stories, I recognize that their telling may not have been possible without the opening provided by the Commission.

In anthropology, an array of means to check the truth of what one is told is used. In this ethnography, direct checks were not possible for, for example, the recall of intimate facets of certain experiences, especially of torture and severe ill treatment. My attempts to interview the police were thwarted even with regards to the search for less incendiary information. Veracity was obtained—to the extent it could be about individual memory of an extraordinary phase in the history of the country and in each man's trajectory from childhood to adulthood under dire circumstances—in the interchanges between us all over a significant stretch of time, in the slew of methods that I and others utilized in the community and the town, in the study of the Commission, and in sharing (accompanying and being accompanied through) parts of their everyday lives. The interchanges occurred between each man and me in group meetings, gatherings of a few of us, individual interviews, formal explorations and exercises, three weekends spent together, and attendance at functions, celebrations, and rituals, community meetings, protests, and funerals. On request, I helped people, including men in our group, to fill in the TRC's application forms on human rights violations, once in a group and sometimes with two or three persons engaged in the task. In combination with attendance over eighteen months of HRV hearings, I was able to identify the patterns of torture most commonly found in the Boland area, and I came to know the names of many of those said to have tortured the young, a small coterie of whom traveled the country interrogating activists. I have not included their names in the text because they are in the public realm, having been recorded as spoken by people who gave testimony from the Boland at the Worcester Hearings and at other hearings in the Cape. The Research Team of the Commission examined the veracity of all testimonies in determining who the victims were.

The young men were not equal in status as leaders. Some played much more prominent roles, and some suffered more than did others. There are real differences among them in leadership qualities, skills, education, security at home, and employment opportunities. In 1996, some had full-time employment, others were unemployed, and two were university students; some were married, and some had children; one, the man who had lost a leg, had given up his post as a teacher in Zwelethemba and had become a prison warden in a town a few hundred kilometers away. The one who had been paralyzed was unable to work. Each is an admirable person on many counts, some revealed flaws in their behavior, and a few are hard to know in their fullness, perhaps as a result of what they have been through. They are, in their variety, ordinary men. (Having written that word—ordinary—I read again Mxolisi Nyezwa's poem "day" and am rebuked, for he says, "as an ordinary man, / as a man persecuted i'm easy to know" [2000, 50].) They were not formally trained as soldiers; they did not ascend the ranks of a military hierarchy; they were unarmed, wore no uniforms, and had no recourse to the protection of an army or military legal apparatus, nor could they as warriors expect defense from international law. There were many thousands like them, and the nature of the war they fought is not yet well documented. We worked together in a postconflict situation of social change and readjustment.

I do not, of course, know how the men viewed me—the anthropologist, the outsider: as an older woman, a mother figure, a scholar, a companion? I asked a lot from them in terms of recalling the past but tried not to ask about certain matters or probe into sensitive areas beyond what was offered to me. I hardly ever asked about pain, except for the purposes of helping them, at their request, to fill in the Commission's forms, but it came up, as it must given their history. They quite often characterized me as a "radical," but I am not sure what they meant. We met much more frequently as a group than I had supposed we would. I would often make an appointment with one of them and, on arrival, find that almost all of them had gathered to meet me. It made for a fascinating dynamic: in each meeting there would be a group of three or four men, not always the same ones, who challenged me, always politely and with due decorum but strongly on many issues ranging from my political opinions to my failure to fulfill promises. I tried to meet many of their requests, for example, to have appointments with psychologists or seek funding for business ventures, but I often failed, usually for logistical or bureaucratic reasons. I did things for them, but fieldwork always impresses on me the tight limits of one's power, purse, and influence. There were some for whom I wish I could have done more, like Ntando Mrubata, who died in 1998 as a result of the wound that he had received from a policeman's gun.

The more senior leaders in the group gave the others loose rein in interrogating me but would use tact and acuity in eventually taking control of the conversation, reaching agreement as a group, then focusing on other matters. Another aspect of group dynamics had to do with a gradual evolution in the depth and range of our discussions. There are among certain peoples of South Africa forms of discourse that are bound by rules of respect and avoidance, particularly when people of different age, gender, and status are gathered together—in Xhosa it is called *hlonipha*, and it influenced our early relations. In addition, there was a code among activists that called for silence with regard to many matters, especially pain and suffering. Given that the conflict was over and that the Commission and other institutions were encouraging people to speak out about their difficult experiences under apartheid, constraints slowly fell away, and it helped us to achieve an intimacy that was held within a certain formality and economy of expression.

We spoke, for example, often glancingly, about heroism and cowardice and how difficult it had been to hold onto a sense of pride or virtue after torture or after having experienced the clever, invasive forms of humiliation at which the security force members excelled. The men did not speak in romantic terms about the past, though there had been heady days, nor with much nostalgia, except sometimes for comradeship shared, leadership exercised, and direction assured.

The meetings were marked by courtesy, generosity, seriousness, tact, respect, and humor and by their treatment of me as a source of information about the world, especially about national politics, government policies, liberation organizations' offerings, the Commission, and Western forms of therapy. It was often hard to get a hearing for my research agenda; there was scant interest in questionnaires, surveys, categorization, narrative lines, or chronological order, and I had to accumulate such data in less directed ways. As an ethnographer, I found them seriously wanting in terms of gossip—usually an important source of information in the field. While they demonstrated expertise in conflict resolution, they did not shy away from confrontation, especially around community politics. The group worked together over a number of years that allowed individuals time to decide when to talk about sensitive matters. It provided a nonjudgmental space in which to come to terms with damage done and suffering endured and to reexamine lines of loyalty and betrayal. Remembrances of the past were recast and reconstituted through a process of mutual listening. The retrieval of meaning from a powerful and difficult set of experiences was made possible. The group traversed moral difficulties and delicacies. I have tried, in the writing, to keep the tone of mutuality that characterized the group conversations, to hold the delicacies of the exchanges in trust, and to respect the moral difficulties that arose. My participation may have offered a form of acknowledgment. The group gatherings became the framing device for the exploration and the writing.

I should like to make explicit a certain mode of writing and anticipate a certain way of reading that emerges from the nature of the research, for there is something at stake in restraint. It includes the men's ownership of their stories and their vulnerability before my retelling; the complexity of their fight for liberation—its *longue durée*—and the fact that the strands of the liberation efforts have yet to be crocheted into a story. A form of writing that has acquired a style of bareness is the best way I can answer the problem of description in this work. There are many ways of talking about the recent past. Different conversations record various kinds of recognition, often with an elliptical relationship to what actually happened. Various registers are to be found in the text, and sometimes there are internal interlocutors.

In puzzling over the writing of an ethnography of youth sliding into adulthood, I take from Wittgenstein a wariness of superficial similarities of form that can disguise very important differences of meaning. He discourages the "craving for generality" (Monk 1999, 547)—a desire that seems to pervade the description of youth in conflict. I should like to mark some dissatisfaction with the genre of works on children and youth in armed conflict in relation to the kinds of things I want to accomplish. The focus in writings on a youth in war is more often on his or her stuttered existence than on the graph of his or her life's span. The book does not aim to be a comprehensive text on apartheid or the TRC.

We began to meet two years after the election, on April 27, 1994, of a democratic government and just six years after the cessation of turmoil in Zwelethemba. Emotions were raw. Members of the group had operated together in a context in which they had experienced violence that had breached privacy, security, and the forms of presentation of self that normally shield us from intrusion. Past intimacy and present involution charged the atmosphere of the meetings. It is remarkable that they came together, stayed together, and allowed me to enter. The burden of my task in writing has weighed heavily. Would that I could have dispatched it more quickly in their interests and fulfilled the brief more nearly.

At the end of the project, the group announced that, through our shared interest in documenting their past, they had maintained connections with one another after the struggle was over, enabling them to take joint action and make community contributions in ways that might not have happened otherwise.

Specific Procedures Used in Data Collection

On the Commission: In 1996 and 1997, Fiona Ross and I attended almost all the Human Rights Violation hearings in the Western and Northern Cape, each of which lasted three or four days. We took copious notes and have the tapes of the transcriptions that were aired on the radio to the nation, and we have a stash of background notes from the Commission. We attended many other hearings around the country during the full period that the Commission sat. We attended special hearings and amnesty hearings. I talked on a number of panels organized by the Commission, and Andy Dawes and I prepared a submission on children under apartheid that was read out by children at the Children's Hearing in Cape Town. I attended some of the Commission's committee meetings on reparation and reconciliation, and I was one of the editors of the section on children for the *Final Report* (1998), although I declined an invitation to write it because of the academic restrictions involved. I participated in many conferences, including two on the media and the Commission, and have since given over one hundred talks in fifteen countries.

In Zwelethemba, I worked closely with fourteen young men, the testimonies of three of whom I heard being given at the Boland Human Rights Violations Hearing of June 24 to 26, 1996. Apart from conducting many individual and group interviews, the young men and I filled in questionnaires on the basic data concerning their families, households, and education; recorded their life histories, filled in timelines on local history, including the struggle; made charts of important events, connections, and influences; and drew maps of networks, actions, movements, and players. We held three weekend workshops, once with Fiona and the young women with whom she was working. Geoff Grundlingh photographed the men and women at a site that each had selected as marking an important event in his or her experience of the struggle. The photographs were exhibited in a number of places, including St. Georges Cathedral in Cape Town, and a selection is reproduced in James and van de Vijver (2000, 6ff.). The photographs in the book are his, and some are by Barbra Wright.

In the community of Zwelethemba, I examined, from a variety of angles, the context in which the young men acted. Anthropology graduate students from the University of Cape Town undertook background studies in Worcester on the newspapers, police records, town administration, and other topics. We did a census of Zwelethemba and a household survey of experiences of violence in the 1980s. Barbra Wright compiled a book of photographs of the suburb and donated it to the new library. At the request of the local community statement taker appointed by the Commission, I helped people to fill in the two forms required to document experiences of violations and to claim reparations. I attended community meetings on land, on the elders, on education, and so on. I participated in feasts and funerals, a women's protest march, and the care of child laborers who had been summarily evicted from a farm. Many members of the community generously granted me interviews.

Other work: Nyami Mhlauli, in 1998, undertook a small study of the children of the Cradock Four.[17] In 1997, M. Thabang, then at the University of Cape Town, studied the opinions expressed by fifty-three African students at eight universities in the country of the Commission, the meanings of words frequently used in its deliberations, and the different connotations they can have in the six languages the students speak, including English. Patricia Henderson researched the formal and popular definitions of a similar but extended list of words in Xhosa and in English—words like "betrayal," "forgiveness," "torture," and "complicity." Alana de Kock analyzed the testimonies by and about children and youth from nine of the Western and Northern Cape hearings. In Johannesburg, I interviewed, on a number of occasions, women who had participated in the fight conducted by liberation organizations from within countries on the border of South Africa and two groups of youths who had fought in the Vaal Triangle outside the city.

A Sketch of the Chapters

There are two themes in the book, one sheathed by the other. One is the question of the young men's experience during the struggle against apartheid (their recollection of and reflection on it) and the specific ways in which they were targeted and attacked by the regime; the other is the Commission's approach to the documentation of what happened to people, including the young, and how it handled the questions of activism and victimhood. Chapter 1 takes the reader through a compressed account, told through the retelling on the map, of the fight in the 1980s in Zwelethemba and the excruciating conditions in the area. Chapter 2 shows how pain is borne in such a struggle and what it does to one, that there was bearable and unbearable suffering, and the ways of reckoning or acknowledging such experience and its social meaning, specifically in the Commission. Chapter 3 plunges into the heart of the matter—dependence on one another and the regime's use of betrayal as a weapon, both as conditions as well as outcomes, through torture and the threat of pain. Chapter 4 explores the intangible structures probed and built by some of the men, a seeking of meaning, toward a language and grammar for their actions, and the state's response—the "rejects of history" and the "government of children." This idea of the detritus of history is picked up in chapter 5, which queries, through data and discussion, the Commission's timid approach and its bureaucratic rigidity.

ONE

The Ground on Which They Stood

I am looking for all this with my imprecise,
because nervous, finger on a map—a child's map, I must admit.

— PAUL CELAN

The Ground and Its Context

The chapter is about the work of war (or the labor of revolt), living in the place of war (or on the battlefield), and local fame and local danger—it outlines the battle in a township under close surveillance. The questions that inform it are: What do the young do in war? How do they do it? How are they drawn in? How do they hold through it? Against what odds? It is about commitment and choice, not simply revolt or rebellion, grasping opportunities, taking advantage, settling scores, or even just having fun. Despite the recent concerted interest in the engagement of the young in conflict, there are few publications (apart from autobiographical accounts) on the details of their actions on the ground in relation to the choices they make, the passion that directs them, and their understanding of their predicaments—which is not to deny the reality of the situations in which children have no choice but to participate in war.

The account given here is centered in one place, and it encompasses a decade. The place is a small, cordoned-off patch of ground at the edge of town. My interest lies in the continuity of the effort that local leaders among the young in Zwelethemba made day after day to sustain the revolt. It is the element most disturbingly left out of the TRC exercise. Once embroiled in conflict, the young had to work at paying attention, planning, and acting as well as concentrating on the continuous threat they faced and on keeping command of themselves during intermittent crises that directly threatened them with pain, extreme harm, and even death. At certain times and in certain places in the 1980s, to be, quite simply, a young black person out of place—moving, hanging out, visiting—was to be a target for the security forces. Even to be in place, in the home or in the yard—or in school—was to be unsafe.

There were obvious benefits to engagement in the struggle for a democratic dispensation in South Africa that made the day-after-day effort worthwhile, and they included the accumulation of local power, status, and admiration; excitement; the pleasure of collaborative efforts; the headiness of leadership; and the comfort of belief in a purpose. The labor of involvement day after day had little to do with the routines of traditional forms of fighting; rather, the work involved "moving"—a colloquialism for networking and gathering information in the community. It entailed seeking contact; affirming ties; acquiring news about exiles, national leaders, and actions in the cities; giving and receiving directives on policy and heeding warnings (for example, to watch out for, report on, or capture certain persons); building connections; drawing in recruits; watching those under suspicion; plotting protests; visiting those in mourning; planning funeral tactics; and seeking solace or healing. In the process, knowledge was acquired about the temper of the community, the mood of the young, police movements, and key persons' tolerance of or disdain for young protesters. Moving gave the leaders the opportunity to plan clandestine meetings and to avoid capture. In this way they tested "the proclivities and expectations of the social milieu" (Freud 2003, 234).

In part, the young expressed "real rebellious spontaneity" (Deleuze 1995, 176) as they sought "ways of living with what would otherwise be unendurable" and "of confronting the line" (113–114). The spontaneity can be seen in the humorousness of certain actions. An instance of this occurred when road workers were busy at the edge of the township on the main artery that leads out of Worcester toward Robertson. The workers habitually took a nap at midday, and one day some of the young men crept up and stole the steamroller, driving it into the township, then leaping off to escape through the yards as the workers pursued them in fury. The steamroller rolled on majestically alone.

The Young Seen as Dangerous People

At the height of the revolt, when there was widespread disruption inside the country plus incursions of liberation forces from outside, the South African government had at its command, according to Howard Barrell (1990) four hundred thousand troops, at full stretch; sixty-nine thousand police members; and twenty-two thousand temporary members. Between 1997 and 1987, the liberation organizations, largely the ANC, had 12,500 soldiers with some six months training behind them. About six thousand were deployed in South Africa, of whom, if Barrell is correct, about 30 percent were unable to fulfill their missions. By 1988, some 281 acts of revolutionary armed activity had been recorded. The government commanded vast resources: there was a defense budget of up to R3 billion; the CCB (Civil Cooperation Bureau within the security forces) operated with R29 million annually; and in 1989 and 1990, a huge budget was voted to the Special Defence Fund. It is unclear as to what resources the liberation organizations had, but they certainly were no match for the government's resources. It is not my intention to detail the resources of either side; I simply want to underline the disparity between them.

   It is beyond the scope of this book to describe the full conflict between the government and the liberation organizations. Suffice to refer to the literature and to give a few indications of the nature of the force that the young faced. In the early 1980s, Bell and Ntsebeza write that "massive intimidation, murder, torture and detention confronted the rebellious communities. But for all their brutal and bloody response the police were losing control. The army was drafted in. By late September of 1984, there were more than 32,000 troops in 96 townships around the country. . . . Many townships were clearly becoming ungovernable" (2001, 204). The authors outline the brutal aspects of the internal maintenance of the system of apartheid, one that the TRC examined and on which it reported. Bell and Ntsebeza (2001, 205) elaborate on some of the means the government employed to quell resistance:

> During the security crackdown of the 1980s, suspected opponents were detained in their thousands and most of them were tortured. Of 600 released political detainees examined by a panel of doctors from the National Medical and Dental Association in 1985, 93 percent complained of torture and other physical abuse and 83 percent bore evidence of abuse, sometimes weeks after the abuse had occurred. More than 350 of the people examined were classified by the doctors as "severely injured." This was a pattern that was to continue for years.

By 1986, according to Bell and Ntsebeza (2001, 238), mass resistance had turned the tide against the government. It is with hindsight that some success for mass resistance can be allocated. On the ground, the fight continued, and the government's force neither diminished in presence nor yielded in attack or pursuit.

Members of the South African security forces and others who had no sympathy with the stance and tactics of political activists in "making the country ungovernable" viewed the young as dangerous people undoubtedly seeking trouble, causing mayhem, indulging in sex and alcohol, spying on community members to detect infractions of local rules they had imposed, stirring chaos to force a retaliation by the police who were trying to maintain law and order, burning targeted homes or *shebeens*, destroying property, and ruining the goods of those deemed to have broken boycotts against white-owned businesses or collaborationist dealers.

I shall use the word "police" in describing the measures that were taken to stamp out unrest in Zwelethemba, although members of other branches of the security forces were often actively involved. (The measures were similar to those taken in the towns and in other areas allocated for the domestic occupation by people identified as "Coloureds" or "Africans" in the Boland; see Skinner 1998). Close surveillance was organized by the monitoring of travel and telephone calls; the manning of a roadblock at the sole entry and exit point; the imposition of a curfew after 6:00 p.m.; a check on the ownership of vehicles; control of bus times and routes and the institution of random searches; the maintenance of a network of informers; the occupation of three police stations, including a surveillance tower in the township during the height of the conflict; patrolling on foot and in marked and unmarked vehicles; and the gathering of information on political activists. In quelling crowds that they considered to have gathered illegally or that they thought likely to incite trouble or when conflict had begun, they used *sjamboks* (rubber whips), rubber or live bullets or truncheons, or they set trained dogs on people or sprayed teargas. They caught people and forced them into cars or vans. They spread out into the township ready to catch those who tried to escape. They conducted search-and-seize exercises once the conflict had died down, and they targeted the homes of known activists or political spokespersons. Sometimes they trawled the area and shot or beat or arrested people when there had been no incident to ignite a reaction. The treatment of children who boycotted school was cruel.

The young leaders stood out in a community under surveillance—marked by adulation from those they were leading and by danger in their exposure in a constricted area. Once they had become engaged in conflict with the security forces, it was difficult to retreat, to end involvement. One option was to go into exile, but that was difficult; another was to go underground or merge into the areas demarcated for blacks in Cape Town or in small towns of the Western Cape. Poverty limited some means of escape and strained the resources of kin who gave them shelter. Jobs were hard to find in the area once the attention of the police had been focused on them. Nevertheless, some did find work in fish factories on the western coast and on farms when they had to leave Worcester. Most of the leaders were forced to leave school or dropped out partly because the routine of attendance that it demanded made arrest too easy. Perhaps the single most defining feature of the conflict in South Africa between the local leaders of the youth and the security forces was the fact of their repeated detention and abuse. In Zwelethemba, the young stirred conflict and were arrested mostly in their community, held in police cells and prisons in the town, often released without charge, and then returned to their community. Ground was not gained, battles neither won nor lost: at the beginning of the 1980s, most of them believed that they would defeat the apartheid regime within a few years, but it was only at the end of the decade that signs of change became palpable in Worcester. It was the repetition of that cycle of arrest and return that marked the fight as different from the kind of guerrilla warfare in which surprise attacks could be launched in the countryside, where familiar terrain, a supportive population, and fighter mobility made attacks, retreat, and hiding possible.

For the young men who saw themselves as fighting within the broad ambit of liberation organizations, there was no security in identification by uniform, badge, or base with the protections that in formal wars, as recognized by the Geneva Conventions, are supposed to be accorded a soldier. The possession of symbols of belonging to the ANC, the organization to which most of the young fighters in Zwelethemba belonged, was illegal and offered the opposite of protection. Senior leaders were removed from the district, and contact with national leaders was sporadic; besides, the national leaders had very little to do with local actions. Nevertheless, there was an intricate and important network of communication. Some protection was afforded by being faceless in a crowd, but no leeway was granted to the young in the manner in which the security forces treated them. Legal protections were ignored, although there was a "legalistic façade that cloaked apartheid" (Bell and Ntsebeza 2001, 153), and even in courtrooms, legal recourse was often denied.

Another facet particular to this conflict is that youth were targeted, and in turn, they made themselves a target. The pursuit of youth gave security force members the excuse (or reason) to intrude into their homes. There was, given the structure of colonialism entrenched by apartheid, little institutional support for youth that escaped the imprint of the state. There was scant access to clandestine newspapers, radio programs, or literature. The reversal of roles that occurred when youth took charge of the townships, requiring that their elders obey their authority, made guidance and support of the young by their elders more problematic for some time. Yet another particularity was that the youth took up the cudgels while they were living in the same communities as some who had stood bravely against the state in the 1960s but had been cruelly treated and retreated for many complex reasons. Some of the young suggested that one reason for their elders' defeat then had been that they had not secured a large enough support base. Many of the young stood in defiance of their elders' cautions.

The men with whom I worked were born between 1960 and 1972. At the beginning of 1976, the year that the mass resistance by youth was sparked off in Soweto, they were all under eighteen and thus children under the law.

In 1980, the start of the decade that is the focus of this analysis, three were in their late teens, and eleven were under eighteen (nine of whom were under sixteen). In 1985, the most intense year of the conflict, six were in their early twenties, three in their late teens, and five under eighteen. In 1996, the year we began this study, half were in their thirties and half in their twenties.

Four of the men had between them seven siblings who were political activists: three had brothers (two of whom died in the fray), and two had sisters (two of whom were leaders and suffered greatly in detention, and one had a sister who was arrested and harmed by the police in their search for her brother). The mother of one of the men was a committed activist, and she was jailed for three months when he was a child. A maternal uncle of one of the boys was a renowned political figure, and he had been banished from Zwelethemba for many years. Two of them had close kin who stood against them on the other side of the battle lines, and both of those relatives were instrumental in harming them. Two of the men in MAZE are related: one is the son of the other's mother's mother's brother.

Most of the leaders in the 1980s in Zwelethemba were from families respected in the community, and many were successful school children at the local school, confident in their abilities, sure of their identities, and hopeful for a future of opportunity yet aware of the possible costs in terms of loss of education and training that political activism could entail. They saw their efforts as contributing to a broad, persistent revolt by the young. In the 1980s, the activities of the young were drawn together with other forces by the United Democratic Front (UDF) in alignment with the ANC.

Mapping the Battleground

Five men in their thirties stood utterly absorbed as they leaned over a table on which a map of Zwelethemba lay. They were tracing with colored pens their battle with the security forces on the field of war that was Zwelethemba. The five, Xolile Dyabooi, Amos Khomba, Eric Ndoyisile Tshandu, Paulos Mnyuka, and Vuyisile Malangeni, pooled their memories and marked the battleground in a way that I have never seen done for a struggle of this nature on an encircled, urban terrain. In the 1980s, the five men had been part of the top level of leadership among the youth: each had joined the conflict when very young and had fought for years, each had been detained a number of times, and each had been severely tortured. Each had dropped out of formal education as a consequence of his participation, and only Xolile was then continuing his studies. Three were employed in local government, and one was unemployed but involved in community development. Amos is introduced in interlude 1, Xolile in chapter 3, and the other three in this chapter.

It was April 1998, and we met twice (on April 19 and 26) to complete the map. They had come at my invitation to Zwelethemba's new library. I provided a municipal map that gave the main features of the township—the road along which people entered and left the area, the streets, the houses, the soccer field, and so on. I had brought colored pens and crayons and a tape recorder, but their excitement at sharing memories and recreating the past was beyond the scope of the machine, and I was unable to capture many of the stories that the task called forth. (At an earlier meeting on May 24, six members of MAZE, Zandisile Ntsomi, Ntando Mrubata [profiles of both are in chapter 2], Isaac Tshabile [his profile is in interlude 1], Zingisile Yabo [his profile is in interlude 2], Eric, and Vuyisile, had noted on poster-paper timelines acronyms of local organizations and other data having to do with the struggle between the community, led by the young in the 1980s, and the forces of the apartheid regime.) The five men and I had worked together for almost two years, and they had come to map their fight against the government. The template that formed a rough guide for their operations in the community was derived from the M-Plan, which had been adopted in 1953 by the ANC, prompted by the belief that political conditions at that time were changing toward much greater repression and that the need was to prepare to organize in a way that adapted to new conditions, precluding public activity such as huge rallies and very large branches (Suttner 2008, 18–19). They decided to take one year, 1985, the year in which the youth had caused the most mayhem and suffered the most extreme retaliation, as a focus for the task of mapping, and they sketched in minute detail the struggle for liberation on one small piece of ground. Zwelethemba was X-rayed. It was a privileged briefing a dozen years after the year depicted on the map.

They began with animated conversation about the map and the past and about what they should record on the stark outline of the municipal map. First they made lists of the leaders of the youth, people who had collaborated with government forces, sympathetic policemen, and those who had been "necklaced" (a brutal form of political lynching)[1] and, in the process, discussed each person's name and the merits or demerits of the part he or she had played. The homes of the people they named and the sites where three people had been burned were identified on the map. Together we chose the colors and symbols to represent them. It was their social and cultural knowledge of the community that animated the two-dimensional sketch on the municipal grid of streets and houses printed on the piece of white paper. It was animated by their knowledge of which persons and houses they had to avoid, especially those in which policemen and collaborators stayed; the places where it was safe to take refuge; the homes where doors were kept unlocked, providing quick entry and exit as they evaded the police or a place to sleep when it was not safe to stay at home; and the buildings with hidden nooks in which it was possible to hide for a while. That kind of knowledge had to be constantly updated: they had to estimate people's mood and changes in their attitudes toward them, and they had to sift gossip for information that was being carefully tendered in their interest or cleverly let loose to trap them. In the early 1980s, the men lived at home or in small rooms that they built themselves at the back of their parents' dwellings or other people's houses; they had little access to money or to the unrestricted use of telephones. There were no cell phones then.

The map represented the sort of local history that it is a pity not to have had documented before the TRC began to hear testimonies or judge amnesty applications. It was not just naming and plotting that was important but also the way in which the descriptions of actions and connections enlivened the sketch and the ways in which temporality informed place and was, in turn, influenced by space.

Twelve years after 1985, that year of intense conflict between youth and government forces, and four years after the first democratic election and the installation of Nelson Mandela as president, the men still held an intricate and intimate knowledge of the community. Visible changes in Zwelethemba included the erection of a fine library, the foundations of a community center and gym, and an increase in the provision of council housing. Paulos still knew who owned each house and the name and place of residence of almost every person in the area. He recalled with precision where and when each incident had occurred. The five men contributed names to a list of youth who had played a notable part in leading the revolt, and I wrote down the fifty-one names. Twelve of them were women and thirty-nine men. After careful scrutiny, they crossed out seventeen names and confirmed the significant contribution of others, speaking with care and tact. They ended up with a list of thirty-four names: twenty-five in the top layer of leadership, those at the forefront as leaders of the revolt in Worcester from 1980 to 1986, and nine in the next layer, some of whom were active from 1987 to 1989, during the last three years before apartheid began finally to unravel. Eight women were recognized as leaders in the top layer and four in the next. The names of the fourteen men in MAZE were included.

The details given in the rest of the section refer to the twenty-five leaders identified as having been in the top layer. Their homes were marked on the map. All but four had been held in the cells of police stations and/or prisons, some many times, but they were often released without having been charged.[2] Four had died, and three had gone into exile to join the liberation forces, one of whom had died in an ambush in Angola. (Eight people are said to have died fighting for the MK in Angola.)

Of the eight collaborators named, the homes of seven are marked on the map. The eighth came from Cape Town: he was believed to have informed the security forces about the detailed plans of two groups from Zwelethemba who were caught on the borders of the country as they were attempting to leave in order to join MK in exile (accounts are given in chapters 2 and 3). As they marked the homes of the collaborators, the mapmakers expressed their ambivalence about naming people thus. Although Xolile had helped to compile the list, he continued to express his doubts about the accuracy of the accusations against some of the persons named as collaborators. He said, "It is not always justified to name someone as a collaborator because he or she may have been caught while protecting kin or may have been targeted out of a personal grudge." They talked about an incident in which one of them had accused a neighbor of betrayal, and his comrades had nearly killed the man without checking the evidence. On the insistence of another member of the group, he was given a hearing and exonerated.

The places where three men were necklaced are marked. Of the three, one escaped and two died. One of the two was burned to death on instructions from senior activists in Cape Town after he had escaped an attempt to necklace him there and had sought refuge in Worcester. Heated discussion preceded his death. Three men employed by the police force were named as having been sympathetic to the plight of the young escaping from the police in Zwelethemba. It was said by people in the community that two were subsequently punished and the third lured into a trap and killed. Two of their homes are marked on the map.

Later maps, drawn by other members of the group during a weekend workshop, depicted three war zones, six secure meeting places, three training areas for self-defense units, the place where an older leader had been hidden, the beer hall that was burned, a policeman's house that was razed, the avenue where a number of activists dubbed the "Comrades of Moscow" lived, the three police stations (two of which had since been removed), a shop that supported the activists, the "House of Justice," and nine sites of action that were instigated by the youth to stir confrontations with the police. Each site was described as the map was marked.

Eric, one of the mapmakers, was the judge of the People's Court, and he presided in the "House of Justice," which was no more than a room in someone's home. He was dubbed the "Zwelethemba Magistrate" by the police. The court was set up in accord with the M-Plan to monitor compliance with the rules established in the attempt to form local governance of the township and wrench it from outside control. Under the auspices of the court, he and his colleagues undertook investigations of and negotiations about disturbances in the township. They claim to have helped prevent violence in the community more successfully than in other areas of conflict around Worcester. They held sessions and proclaimed sentences against those found guilty of misdemeanors such as breaking a boycott. Few community members could have welcomed their presumption of authority, but, at the height of the troubles in the mid-1980s, it was difficult to counter the dictates of the activists.

Eric was born on January 28, 1963, to Xhosa parents, and from the early 1980s he was politically active. He became a leader in many local and national structures (a word commonly used by those linked to liberation efforts to refer to organizations established to further the cause), including the ANC, MK, COSAS (he was an organizer in 1982), WOYCO (as a member of the executive committee), and SAYCO. In 1990, he was on the executive committee of the ANC Youth League (ANCYL). In the 1980s, he was well respected in Zwelethemba. When we met, Eric was working in the Tourism Development Centre under the Worcester Municipality.

His activities were closely tied to the central leadership in the township, and, in particular, he played an important part in implementing the M-Plan.

In 1985, Eric left with a group of eight young people, three from Zwele-themba, to travel across the country and cross at a border post in order to join the MK. They were arrested at the border. He and Zingisile, who was with him, believe that they had been betrayed by someone (whom they named) from the township and by a young man from Cape Town. The tor-ture they endured during the forced journey home at seven different sites and in the Worcester cells has marked the two men indelibly. The litany of the variety, intensity, and iteration of tortures Eric suffered at nine different towns during the journey back to and in Worcester was terrible to hear. It included bizarre actions, such as having his hair combed with an iron rake. He and the others were held for six months then released without ever hav-ing been brought before a magistrate. Neither he nor any member of the group (two of whom had escaped before the arrests occurred) was formally charged. They were released after six months. Eric bitterly regrets the loss of education and the lack of opportunities to learn new skills and improve his ability to advance in his career. After attending university in 1987 and 1988, he had to leave because of a lack of funds. He worked for the Worces-ter Municipality for many years, apart from a spell when he left to create a business. The brutality he endured has, he says, affected his temperament and his confidence; he has taken advantage of care from a number of sources, and he has had to draw on his strength of character. He had a solid presence in our group and was a reliable and wise leader.

We are informed both by what is marked on a map and by what is with-held from a map. There is, on this map, no one marked for having col-laborated on a minor level; nor are friends or kin who informed the police against them named; nor elders who resisted their activities; nor is anyone noted for weakness, whether lack of courage, timidity, or self-interest. It is an accounting that takes seriously only major forms of betrayal. The map does not record criminal or domestic violence or the pervasive violence of bureaucrats, farmers, or businessmen. In recalling their experiences, both the young and the adults made note of people who had been fair, generous, and kind to them. They included the names of farmers who had treated child laborers relatively well (a number of the men had worked on the farms during school holidays under bad conditions) or who had allowed activists on the run from the police to live among their workers, at significant risk to themselves. They noted those who contributed to the work of the Black

Sash, trade unions, and charitable groups. Other forms of the ordinary as represented, for example, by activities in schools, churches, offices of organizations, or on the soccer fields, have not been inscribed. They appear in stories told in subsequent chapters. It is possible that the ties that bind family and community were stronger here than in areas designated for blacks living in larger towns and cities, and, if that is true, it will have shaped relationships across the generations and among peers in particular ways that helped determine the character of the fight. It is a map of the way in which the young in a mode of resistance fought the local police who acted in defense of the status quo. As a document of a battlefront, the map represents the particularity of an asymmetrical clash that lasted a decade on the ground of the domestic arena.

Let it be remembered that race was at the center of oppression and the need for a struggle. However, the lines that divided groups were not always clearly cut during the fight. The government bureaucracy, including the army and police, employed people defined as white and nonwhite. There were divides within each group that had to do with a variety of differences, some more divisive than others. Extensive efforts were made by the government to divide and keep the groups separate and to nourish antagonisms within and between them, for example, in the 1970s between hostel residents and shack dwellers in Cape Town and between "Coloureds" and "Africans" in the matter of rights to employment and residence in the Cape Province. Like many aspects of life in South Africa, things were characterized by complexity. Persons officially designated as members of specific categories, spuriously declared to be based on scientific classifications of race, stood on both sides of the conflict. All this is not to deny that the majority of whites (beneficiaries of the system) stood on one side, backed by the apparatus of the state, and that the majority of Africans stood on the other, whether actively or passively. This observation may be obvious, but it is made because readers unfamiliar with the history of the country may be surprised to learn that the young activists in Zwelethemba (and elsewhere) were confronted by African members of the police, were tortured by Africans as well as by whites, and were informed on by people living in their community.

A Tensile System of Communication

It was vital to the planning, organizing, and direction of protests (and to the possibility of escaping and hiding from the police afterward) that a tensile system of communication should exist. A network was created based on intimate knowledge of the residents: each resident was pinpointed on an imaginary line that assigned his or her value between trust and distrust. Reassessment was frequently made. Sometimes their judgment was wrong, and when that happened, those in command admitted that they had been "caught napping."

As the mapmakers traced the elements of the action, they alluded to images conjured by certain yards or corners of buildings. Amos pointed to a place where a shot had felled him. Just prior to that, he had been alerted to the fact that a house was on fire, and he had arrived at the scene to discover what was happening. A crowd had set a house alight that belonged to someone whom they believed to be an informer. As the police Casspirs (armored personnel carriers) arrived, the crowd dispersed, but a woman screamed that there was a baby in the house. Amos ran in, brought the infant out, and handed him or her to the woman, by which time the police were close at hand, and they gave chase. He ran, leaping over fences, dashing across gardens, skirting barking dogs; then he ran into a house but saw a school friend who shouted a warning that it was a policeman's house. He ran out into the street and was turning a corner when a bullet hit his head. Blood spurted as he fell; young men quickly carried him into a house, then later to his home. In the evening, the police arrived searching for him. He was in the house next door, lying low, and they did not find him. The shot had ripped the flesh of his face near his left ear. There is still something in the wound, but it only bothers him if he bangs his head. He did not see a doctor, fearing that the police would be told that a wounded student had come for attention. (Amos and his induction into politics is described further in interlude 1.)

Other spots on the map were pointed out to me where "incidents" had occurred, sometimes instigated by the leaders to render the place ungovernable, at other times the result of unplanned youthful rebellion or eruptions among residents. They included the sites where school protests and boycotts were held; beer halls burnt down; and areas on the artery road that ran alongside the suburb where vehicles, usually vans carrying goods from local factories, were stoned or even hijacked—they would be looted, then sent to the "oven," a site for abandoned vehicles in Worcester. The leaders' attempts to direct or deflect action were often ignored or opposed. They did not have full control. They recognized passion aroused by anger and "dared not judge" all protests. They tried to use tact and skill in guiding crowds, and they developed a special language among themselves in the process. In the middle of the decade, the country seemed to the men to be on the verge of chaos, and they recognized that it could be dangerous to obstruct people's anger. This is not to exonerate them for participation in violence but to suggest that they tried to hold to the purpose, which was to instigate incidents that contributed to making the area ungovernable. That purpose was in itself inherently ungovernable.

On August 18, 1985, the United Women's Organisation held a peace protest against the excesses of the police who had, on August 16, shot Nkosana Nation Bahume on a street in Zwelethemba, and the young activists joined them (see Ross 2003, 141–144). The chair of the women's group addressed the police, demanding that they stop militarizing the area, end the curfew (which began each evening at 6:00 p.m.), and dismantle the roadblock at the entrance and exit to the suburb. The police were accused of implementing State of Emergency conditions when none had been declared (one had been declared on July 21, 1985, in thirty-six magisterial districts but not yet in Zwelethemba). It was during a period that fell between the first and the second States of Emergency. After the protest, police presence was pulled back for a while, and the youth ironically observed that they missed the targets for stone throwing that the police had presented. To hurl a stone and see it connect with a van was to vent anger and yield satisfaction, even if the effect was puny, some said.

Funerals became occasions for serious clashes between youth and police; it was said that each funeral marked the occasion for another (or others) to die. In an attempt to prevent funerals from becoming focal points for the display of support for liberation organizations and for stirring revolt, the state required mourners to obtain permits to hold funerals and imposed strict rules on the mourners: who might mourn; how the coffin should be carried and by whom; along what routes from home to church to cemetery, accompanied by how many; and who might gather after the burial. Not satisfied with the intrusion on private and communal grief, the police frequently caused chaos even when their orders were being obeyed. In anger and grief, the rules *were* disobeyed, and the young, in particular, responded to police interference. Vuyisile became embroiled in a clash with the police when he joined the protest against their actions at the funeral of Nkosana. He was chased by the police along the streets of the township. They shot at him as he leapt over fences and dashed across yards with people shouting, "Run, run, Vuyisile!" At a corner, people gathered to hinder the police, and they gave up the chase. They went to his home and questioned his family. He recounts other episodes of close shaves and scrapes with people who turned out later to have been spies. Shortly after his escape from the police, he was detained and held for three days. In August 1985, he left for Queenstown, where he remained for three years.

Vuyisile is the oldest of the fourteen men; he was born in 1960 in Zwele-themba, and he grew up with his father's brother in the Eastern Cape, where he began his political involvement. In 1980, he was imprisoned for a year. Thereafter, he returned to Zwelethemba, where he pursued his devotion to civic organizations by supporting UWO activities and helping to create COSAS in the region. He describes himself as an organization person, not an individual operator. He was involved with the establishment and running of numerous structures. As a chair of CAYCO he came under the direct surveillance of the police, and he was encouraged in August 1985 to leave Worcester. He went to Queenstown and continued his political involve-ment, in consequence of which he was arrested at the end of the following year and held in detention for three years. He says that the presence of Ad-vocate Dumisa Ntsebeza (who was later the head of the TRC's investigative unit) in the town helped to prevent the authorities from committing the worst of the abuses against him. Vuyisile described in detail his interrogators and the methods they used, including dangling him from a window high up in a building and threatening to drop him. On his release, he returned to Zwelethemba, where he was placed under restrictions that kept him in the township and forced him to walk to the police station in Worcester twice a day to report his presence, despite the existence of a police station in Zwele-themba. In 1982, he went to hospital for a checkup, fearing that he was go-ing to have a breakdown; in 1990, he was treated at the Trauma Centre for Victims of Violence and Torture in Cape Town.

A characteristic of the struggle was that there was very little institutional support on which the young could rely, either at the height of the conflict or during its aftermath. In general, schools, clinics, hospitals, doctors' surgeries, and public facilities such as libraries, police stations, and courts were sites of danger because the police and the wider population of Worcester reported anything that aroused their suspicions of "terrorist" behavior, although there were individuals who gave unstinting assistance when they could and organizations whose assistance was very important and greatly valued. Some people received extraordinary support from parents, kin, friends, and neighbors; others found themselves isolated, if only because their levels of pain or distress or guilt led them to erect barriers against help. Some visited *amaqhira* (indigenous healers), but none laid much stress on their interactions with them during that time.

Four of the local leaders participated in creating ZWEYO (Zwelethemba Youth Organisation), to take the struggle out of the high-school classrooms, where protest among the young began, to the wider community. It was a concerted attempt to include unemployed and working youth. One of the four was a schoolgirl, and she was recognized as a powerful leader in the community and is still regarded as having played an important role. She has since married and no longer lives in the Worcester area.

Arms were available among some of the activists in the country, but in Zwelethemba, as one of the men said, you had to be creative to get hold of any. Local leaders said that if any arms did pass through their area they would have done so via individuals in cells who would have known or handled only aspects of data or pieces of the weapons. The *tsotsis* (gangsters) had guns, and so did some businesspeople and drug lords; a few people obtained them in the "homelands," where the police and army were said to have been less vigilant in protecting their arsenals. Some activists managed to steal weapons from the police during riots, and there was infiltration of weapons from those in exile. Fire, gasoline, and stones were available and put to use. Violence was used on all sides. Nana Khohlokoana (who is introduced in chapter 4), taking the stand as an impartial judge, said that among the activists there were some who often resorted to violence and derived their sense of importance in society from it, at the same time claiming that its use was helping to rid the country of oppression. I remind the reader that thousands of the young joined the struggle between the 1976 and 1990 and that their behavior and actions varied widely.

There seemed to be four principles in accord with which the young leaders worked. The first was to operate in relation to the liberation movement, predominantly the ANC in Worcester and, from 1983, the UDF, as far as possible. They became members of a liberation organization and joined COSAS, ANCYL, ZWEYO, and other tributary groups. They acknowledged and paid obeisance to the leadership even when directives were sent in from those in exile instructing them to adopt new strategies and fresh tactics that they had already initiated. The second principle was to create alliances with the older generation, workers, women's organizations, unemployed youth, and others to secure their backing and allay some of their fears and doubts. The third was to carry the masses with them, for without that support the government could, they believed, easily quash any revolt. The fourth principle was to acknowledge that their main resource was self-consciousness and discipline and the monitoring and maintenance of relationships with one another (the next three chapters deal with these concerns, especially chapter 4). On the basis of these principles, they set about building leadership structures and taking action.

The bare patch of ground that is Zwelethemba was a scrap of the quilt. I am suggesting that the fight there was initiated and sustained against great odds, with but slight contact with national leaders and those in exile, with almost no resources, and with the knowledge that they would receive minimal support in the conflict as it unfolded day after day and year after year. It is not my intention to estimate the effectiveness of their actions in bringing about the demise of apartheid except inasmuch as they contributed to a youthful rebellion that, in turn, was part of broad liberation efforts within the country. Nor do I claim that the experiences described are representative of those among the young elsewhere in South Africa, but aspects of them certainly are. "We were," said the young men of Zwelethemba, "small fish in the ecosystem of the liberation movement."

Friendship

Friendship was vital for survival. It is, no doubt, true in any group involved in conflict. Facets of the fight at this particular time and place shaped its character. There was the camaraderie of plotting protests; firing up crowds; leading attacks against huge odds; glorying in the admiration of followers, especially girls; and gaining the respect, however grudging, from elders, despite that many were wary of the power the youths represented as a group. There was shared admiration for the talents, courage, and wit that were implied in invitations to join the leaders. And there was responsibility in watching out for one another, for covering risky ventures, for effacing one another's tracks, for paying attention to one another's weaknesses and irresponsible actions in order to limit possible damage.

Ties of friendship seem to have been placed under particular strain in four ways. The first was the manner in which it was put, again and again, to extreme tests by the pressures cleverly brought to bear by the security forces on loyalty as they tried to break confidences and turn comrades into betrayers. The second resulted from the fact that the conflict largely occurred on the streets and in their homes, so that their pain, cowardice, and fear before police retaliation was exposed in front of the community and their families. The third lay in the humiliation of incapacity and loss of control during or after spells of interrogation and torture, as they were, frequently, kept together in crowded cells or harmed in groups; besides, they held on to an ethic of never complaining about ill treatment and often did not seek medical care because of the danger of being reported to the police. And the fourth resulted from the difficulty of living as if in an overexposed negative: there was nowhere in which to hole up, retreat, lick wounds, and recoup energy, apart from the small houses that were usually full of kin and that were, themselves, exposed, standing on small plots lined along a grid on the unforgiving, hard earth.

An image comes to mind of one of the most fiery members of the group, Paulos, who, on return from each stint in the police cells, would be made by his mother to stand outside his house. She would bring soap, hot water, and fresh clothes from the house and have him strip naked, wash, and change before passing through the door. She supported his political activities yet insisted on cleansing him of the contamination of police brutality before resuming his place in the home. Paulos was exposed even in being cleansed of pollution.

The homestead where Paulos lived with his mother is marked on the map. She was Xhosa by birth, and his father was Sotho. They came to Zwelethemba in the early 1960s. Paulos was born on April 11, 1966. He has an older brother and a younger sister. His father deserted them when Paulos was three years old. He sometimes spells his name as Paulus, and he said that his name means "depression." He has too much fire in him for that appellation to be suitable.

Paulos is a wild card. Brave, forthright, active but impetuous. Sometimes, his colleagues said, he did foolish things. He would be called on to stir crowds and to lead protests. The police hated him, and he became a prime target, but he was wily and difficult to capture. He described seven occasions when his human rights were violated, one of which is given in chapter 3. Four of the violations were, he said, committed against his mother, when she was harassed for selling food outside the school; when she was jailed for three days for being in arrears on her rent; when she and his older brother fought the police when they entered the home to arrest him; and when the police searched the house looking for copies of banned pamphlets and when, on her denial that she knew where he was, they sprayed her face with tear gas. The tear gas affected her asthma, and she never recovered her health, Paulos said. She died in 1989. In a questionnaire that he filled in for me, he gave a moving tribute to his mother for her care, her help in his recovery from rage and hatred, for teaching him about human values and morals and how to face reality and the challenges it brought. The other three violations have to do with his spells of detention, during which he endured torture and gross ill treatment and, after his release, harassment that caused him to leave the area, abandoning his home and his job (see chapter 3). Once he was imprisoned with a man who later became one of Nelson Mandela's guards. The consequences of his experiences included the loss of education and physical damage. Paulos worked in a department of conservation for many years. He could speak five languages and acquired computer skills. He behaved impeccably toward me.

Trust was held by a fragile thread. There was little time for the glue of loyalty toward a unit and its members to be instilled, and there was no opportunity to experience the kind of techniques that organized groups use to bind recruits to "king and country" or cause and comrade. Nor was there much opportunity to learn to resist the precision and the wiliness of schooled security operators and interrogators. Not that loyalty or resistance was weak, just that responsibility was assumed early and preparation was scant. Friendships held across time and still do. Reliance on it in the 1980s was characterized by uncertainty—your claim not to have spoken a name but his claim that your friend revealed your name. A young man who participated in my 1992–1993 study and who was a highly trained MK operative told me that during his months of daily torture what distressed him most were the details of small intimacies that the torturers revealed to him as having been extracted from his colleagues under torture. In a discussion of the demands of friendship, T. M. Scanlon (1998, 160–168) formulates two questions: What kinds of priority does friendship demand, and to what extent are its demands themselves limited by some recognition of the demands of morality? He goes on to discuss the nature of friendship, its benefits, the loyalty it requires, and the feelings of loss and betrayal it can engender if one's friend is false or disloyal, and the feelings of guilt if one is disloyal oneself. He ties the case of friendship to that of morality and wrong. In particular, he examines the implications of our relations with others when charges of injustice or immorality are made. The discourse places in perspective the serious cast that conditions in the 1980s in Zwelethemba gave to friendship. (Further analysis of morality appears in chapter 4.)

It ought to be said that, unlike many kinds of battles, in leading the local struggle in Zwelethemba no single person acquired power. No one was the leader; the conditions militated against it. Power spiraled among a group of changing characters. Some spun away from the vortex, and others were drawn in, the latter having to learn without the benefit of much apprenticeship. A commonly held view is that the nature of youthful resistance is reactive and leaderless. Slavoj Žižek's recent book *Violence: Six Sideways Reflections* (2009) refutes with a close analysis of various cases the view as applied to any sustained action.

Covering the Ground

In summary, the tactics used and the ideals pursued in battle included the following: causing incidents to bring the forces of government out and, once having proved troublesome, evading the police and continuing to be active; gaining the support of other sectors, including women, unemployed youth, trade unionists, and community members, by providing them with information, using persuasion, and stirring emotions; acquiring and updating knowledge of people's attitudes and actions to secure lines of communication and mobility and, therefore, flight; establishing trust among colleagues

paralleled by wariness while attempting to maintain a balance between independence and dependence; pursuit of a knowledge of self to acknowledge
weakness and avoid pitfalls, to help rein in fear, and to behave in a manner
befitting a warrior to further the cause effectively; maintaining links with
liberation organization members elsewhere; and escaping capture and, if
caught, enduring the consequences with stoicism and in silence. Who could
hold to all of that?

The actions they took included stirring trouble and responding to measures taken by the authorities to keep tight control over the township by
gathering crowds, making speeches, breaking curfews, holding clandestine
meetings, attending funerals, tackling nodes of corruption (as they defined
them) within the community, attacking informers, and securing networks.

I used the map as a methodological tool to find out how a fight in a township was conducted. It is an item in the documentation of an asymmetrical
fight. It helps to detail the tactics used by the youth, tactics that, compared
to those used in major wars, may seem to have resembled the deployment
of fireworks rather than firearms. From where the youth stood, the following features characterized it: They conducted their operations in full cognizance that the area was under surveillance from a limitless "outside" over
a bounded stretch of earth, although there could be no foolproof cover-
age, nor could the boundary be sealed. The terrain on which they operated
formed part of a small, rural town in which a relatively wealthy and powerful section of the population had access to an intricate knowledge of the
conditions (particularly physical, financial, and institutional) under which
they, the youth and their kin, lived. Of course, just as there was knowledge
from the outside, so was there knowledge from the inside. The people of
Zwelethemba gained knowledge working in the centers of administration,
finance, commerce, and industry in a variety of institutions and in homes
in Worcester, yet it was hard for them to pierce the protective covering
that political, legal, social, and economic power can claim and secure. The
connections among residents of a small town and the satellite farming communities meant that "troublemakers" could be identified and often silenced.
One way was to ensure that they lost employment and were, thereafter, pre-
vented from obtaining jobs. For example, in the early 1960s, a trained and
experienced mechanic lost his job when he joined the protests against passes
and was unable to secure employment again.

The map is an extraordinary document, because it pinpoints the means used in everyday pursuits: how the community was monitored and what networks were established. Through the remembrance of events that occurred a dozen years in the past, memory was pressed into place. It is seldom that this kind of detail for this kind of conflict is mapped out in any form. It can be interpreted as a trajectory across time, as a series of movements, or as a log of relationships. The intricacy of detail in the recall was surprising. So too was the level of agreement among them of names, sites, actions, and incidents, and this recall was accompanied by a sober consideration of the ambitions, mood, perceptions, emotions, or motives that could be said to have determined behavior. The act of mapping was an act of political analysis. I watched as the blueprint of the township was crosshatched as the places of residence of twenty-five of the most wanted men and women in the suburb were marked—a small group that was gnawing at the ankles of the state, a group embedded among some thirty thousand (the rough estimate given by the municipal authorities of the number of residences at that time) or sixty thousand (the estimate made by the activists, who claimed that it was in the interests of the authorities to underestimate the numbers for whom services should be provided) people. The map is of interest too for the discussion it stimulated among the mapmakers and the recall of scenes in the drama. It was after 1985 that four of the men, Amos, Eric, Paulos, and Xolile, endured periods of extreme suffering while held in detention. Not one mention was made on either of the days we spent on the task of mapmaking about their terror and pain, some of which is described in the following chapters. Another reason that makes the map of special interest is that it demonstrates the unquestioned inclusion by senior male activists of the role that young women played as leaders. Their homes were plotted and their skill and courage celebrated not as exceptional but as equal to that of the men's.

In the 1980s, conditions in Zwelethemba could have been worse: wholesale slaughter, mass destruction. I am trying to estimate the heft of a continuing level of tension punctuated by terror. How to weigh the horror of an instant against the dragnet of the *longue durée*? It is the former on which the Commission focused and on which they based, in large part, their decision whether to declare someone a "victim" and, therefore, eligible for reparations. The latter has slipped through the truth net.

Induction into Politics

It is commonly held that young people were inducted into politics via the excitement and challenge of street protest against security force personnel, particularly the throwing of stones and running away from tear gas, *sjamboks*, and bullets, rubber or live. The view oversimplifies what was, for many, a carefully considered entry and one consequent on a variety of forces and relationships, not excluding the exuberance of *toyi-toyi*ing and taunting the police. There were, it appeared to me, more continuities across generations with regard to the handing on of political knowledge, exchange of opinions about strategy, and continuing support of various kinds than the literature or common opinion allows. Further, I came to understand that local-level engagement altered the political and social milieu and was not just a struggle toward change in the future. The brief descriptions of the manner in which three men were drawn as children into political activism lend support to these observations.

Amos Monde Khomba

Amos was born in Zwelethemba on November 26, 1961, the second of eight children, of whom five are girls. One son died as an infant, and the eldest son was killed when he was in his twenties in a disagreement on the streets of the township. The father of the family, Elijah Elliot Komba, was born in Tulbagh, and the mother was born in Cradock. In 1954, they settled in Zwelethemba. Amos attended the local primary school, and from the ages of nine to eleven he worked on a farm each summer and enjoyed it, although the labor was tough. The conditions were better on that farm than on most others in the district, he said.

Amos Khomba's first memories of politics are from the age of about nine. In that year, he said,

> When my father and his friends were at home, late at night, drinking tea and playing cards and talking about Africa and its leaders, and the [prison] sentences of "the men in prison" (no names [were mentioned]) and "the men on the Island." It had an attractive ring to it. I listened until I fell asleep. It was my first introduction to the question of [our] inferiority to whites and why. I began to question the way things are. Father claims to have been a member of a Transkei party, an ethnic party [concerned with] the rights of the oppressed. Not ANC, as far as I know.

In the last three years of primary school, Amos and a group of friends read newspapers with the encouragement of the principal. The friends competed in class for the top five or six positions. One day in 1975, when Amos was fourteen years old, the class was given a project to do for homework, and three of them decided that, as they were members of the public, they had the right to use the Worcester Public Library. Amos said that they had walked to the library in town to search for materials. He told the story of what happened next:

> We had never heard of a black who had been there except laborers. We were not stopped at the entrance. Nor were we [initially] noticed. After a few minutes, a person came and told us we were not allowed there. One of my friends said,
> "Why?"
> "Whites-only library."

"There is no notice. We would have known. It says it is a public library."

He was a big white guy. We talked to him. He asked us if we were schoolkids.

Then he forced us out with another man. We left and forgot about it.

The next day at school prayers, the principal asked, "Who has been to the Worcester Library yesterday?" We were afraid of being whipped: afraid to admit [that we had gone there]. We were all sent to our classes. The principal began [to make inquiries] in the senior classes. In our class, he asked again. No response. He called the six of my group to the principal's office. He said, "They must have been from your group." The three of us confessed. He asked, "Why didn't you know that you can't? I was telephoned and told that we can't go, that a black person is not a member of the public."

We questioned why (among ourselves), why he took the side of the whites. It ended there. It told us about the political system.

Their visit to the library was a huge act of resistance made "small" humorously.

Another incident that stirred Amos's political consciousness occurred at school a few years earlier. A junior secondary school had been promised to Zwelethemba but by 1978 nothing had been built, and the primary school had to cope with two secondary school classes and overcrowding. Some classes had eighty pupils and double sessions each day. The standard-six group protested, banging doors and breaking windows. The seniors who did not join in were accused of being *impimpi*. So much trouble was caused and so much anger was stirred in the community that within two weeks the building of a junior secondary school began.

The country was on fire in 1976, Amos said, but Zwelethemba was quiet until 1978, when the young began to protest and challenge the police. "The parents came out, remembering what had happened in 1960. They said you can't confront the whites as they have Casspirs, etc. They recalled beatings and imprisonment and were afraid for us. But we were in a better position to withstand [government retaliation]. We were daredevils: we didn't care about the experiences of the 1960s." He spent the last two years of his schooling at a high school in Gugulethu, a suburb (or "township") of Cape Town. Amos became friends with a scholar from Port Elizabeth who was a year younger but politically astute. Each day, after school, his friend went to the University of Cape Town to (he said) work in the library, but he would return with fresh political news. He paid for Amos to accompany him to Pietermaritzberg for the launch on September 27, 1979, of the Congress of South African Students (COSAS). Amos learned a lot from him. He said, "I liked him. In a way he politicized me. 'What is a launch?' I had to ask. I still don't understand why he was not an identifiable figure in the struggle in school. He knew more than the school political leaders."

Early in 1980, Amos was elected by the students to a committee to discuss with the school management their protest against a raise in tuition fees. The Governing Board turned them away, and a boycott of classes ensued. The protests were coordinated with those of three other schools. There was widespread disruption and confrontation with school authorities and the police. Amos said, "I was a bit active then and in the mood for happenings." By May, the school was closed, and Amos returned home, where the school protests had set in, too. He quickly became a leader in the political activities of the area, helping to establish and run political organizations and attract youth into participation. The police hounded him and caught and detained him frequently, yet they could not keep him from returning, each time he was released, to the fight.

Mrs. Khomba told me that three of her children had been deeply embroiled in politics, each one a powerful leader. Their trials and tribulations had caused her great stress, although she supported them and did her best to protect them. Amos was detained eight times almost every year of the 1980s. She kept a bag of his clean clothes ready. One of her daughters was seldom caught by the police because "she seemed to have a sixth sense as to when they were coming," Mrs. Khomba said. (See Ross 2000 for accounts of Amos's sister's activism.) However, she often had to search from prison to prison to find one or another of them. Once, two of them were in imprisoned in Worcester at the same time, so she visited Amos on Tuesdays and his sister on Thursdays. She told me many stories about them, and it was a pleasure to listen to her beautiful use of the English language. I shall recount just one of them. It was a Tuesday, and she, as the only person allowed to visit Amos, went to the jail.

I was told to sit. Amos came to me and asked me to wait for five minutes while he exercised. Ten minutes later I stood up because I heard a scream. I tried to look. A policeman closed a curtain. I heard Amos's voice and I asked the policeman what was happening. He said, "Your son is running mad." I went home and called the ANC lawyer and told him that they say Amos is mad. "When did it begin?" he asked. "I have just seen him. It was ten minutes before I left. At about 10:00 a.m."

By noon the lawyer had collected her, and they had arrived at the prison. She pointed to the policeman who had said Amos was mad. He apologized to the lawyer, saying that Amos had fought the policeman, who would not allow him to stop exercising so that he could see his mother. The UDF paid for the lawyer's visit. Mrs. Khomba became ill and thin under the strain. She says that her children did not tell her everything that was done to them in jail, as they thought she would not be able to handle it. Her children honor her for having stood beside them through hard times.

Action on the streets was just one item in a series, and certainly not the most important, that drew Amos into politics. Other factors included listening to his father and his friends, protesting at school against difficult conditions, becoming aware of youthful revolt in a city school, and attending to the guidance of a politically astute friend. I shall outline the experiences of two more of the young men who became politically engaged when they were at school.

Mawethu (Ex) Bikani

When Mawethu, who was born in 1969, was in a lower grade in junior school, senior school children burst into the classroom one morning, disrupted the teaching, and told the young children to join the struggle. The seniors were dismantling classroom doors, which were made of zinc and so noisy in the wind and rain that they hampered learning. They took the classroom doors to the police station and left them there as a symbol of their protest against the poor conditions and lack of basic supplies at the school. Mawethu says of the incident, "I was struck by what was happening. It was the beginning of my interest [in politics]." He adds, "I was never taught politics from anyone at home. I only heard it on the streets as a child. I became involved at school."

Mawethu's full involvement in school protests began when he was ten; it was an act of retribution against excessive punishment by teachers for low grades. On a test he received 2 5 out of 40 points, and the female teacher beat him on the palms of his hands with a stroke of a cane for every point lost. It was, he says, very painful. After that, his keen enthusiasm for school waned. He said,

> I began to go slowly, missing days. Then I realized I was punishing myself. I was involved with friends in soccer and we discussed the day's happenings. One boy said he was beaten forty-five lashes on his hands: I saw his hands; they were very bad. Another boy was out of school for the same problem; his parents moved him out. A discussion [between parents and teachers] was held, and beatings were said to be the policy of the school. The teachers came from our community. We saw ourselves as the victims. One of the teachers lived nearby. We saw her one night and beat her so she could not return to school next day.

The incident represents a complex moment in terms of gender. On being asked what he thought about using violence against a teacher as a response to violence experienced at school, Mawethu replied that he and his classmates had decided to make an example of one teacher to prevent the teachers from beating children. He offered another example of teacher discipline. Some pupils, including Mawethu, were beaten for their poor sketches. They were told to return to the classroom at 2:00 p.m., when school was over. They refused to do so, and each of them was given forty-five lashes on the palm of the hand. They cried. After a while, another teacher came and asked the children what was wrong and why they had been beaten. On being told, instead of commiserating, Mawethu said, "He, too, turned against me and beat me fifteen lashes. I was very angry. The teachers were never wrong. Each one acted [as if he was] president of the country. Parents stood behind their authority." He continued his account,

> Six of the school children targeted teachers. They began to act publicly, during the school lunch break. They would accuse a teacher verbally and when he or she retaliated angrily, they beat him or her. It had become hard to learn well, and it was not possible to ask questions and receive good replies: [the pupils had] become afraid to ask questions. They asked their parents to intervene, but the Parents' Management Committee fell under the authority of the principal and of the government, so they replied that they could not. The children determined to draw attention to the cruel punishments and canvassed each class to elect two pupils, one girl and one boy, to work with

them. They tried to avoid having ringleaders. There was no point in calling a teacher's meeting, and the principal, when told in a joking manner of their concerns, showed that he would not act. The group beat the principal and hauled him out of his office. The police arrived quickly, having been called by a teacher. Everyone ran from them. After a few days, the school returned to normal.

The revolt against punishment drew the attention of older school children to those who had led it, including Mawethu. Over the next five years, he was drawn into local leadership. He says, "I was not so involved [in political protest] but was taken as a leader. UDF was established, and we saw a chance to act. SANCO existed and we [those involved in 1982 and 1983] were called to set up CAYCO [Cape Youth Congress]. I was a child then and supported everything. I was not heard [in meetings], and I was not allowed to speak."

"The older ones," Mawethu said, "began to inspire me in politics around people's rights." Amos was one of them. Mawethu gave the following account of action at the senior school. The activists in school began to demand a Student Representative Council (SRC) to replace the prevailing prefect system, in which pupils were selected by school staff to represent the interests of the school children. The UDF called for students to establish branches of COSAS in their schools. Some pupils from Zwelethemba went to the COSAS Congress and returned with t-shirts inscribed with the slogan "Each one teach one." These shirts were much sought after. A steering committee was elected to establish a COSAS branch and a decision was taken to abolish the prefect system, as the two could not operate in tandem. There was a verbal struggle between the prefects and those calling for the establishment of elected representation. The mission of the latter group was to draw the attention of the student body to the important issues, like calling for accountability for expenditure on school events. During talks around the differences between supporters of the prefect system and those who wished to replace it with an SRC run by students, conflict sometimes arose, and school authorities and the police intervened. When that happened, some pupils were sent to warn parents living nearby to request that as soon as the meetings were disrupted by school authorities or the police, the parents should come out of their homes to witness what was happening. Songs were composed against the teachers using words that played on their names, and they were sung when clashes occurred. Mawethu observed that "the teachers were quiet. They were afraid to beat us as much as they had done before. The students at our school responded quickly to the call of the UDF to take on the struggle using the schools as a base. Parents accepted the SRC."

In 1985, the clash between the young and government security forces grew exponentially. A man from Cradock joined the teaching staff of the school in Zwelethemba. The government had expelled him from his teaching post in Cradock, where he had been a friend of the four men who, on June 24, 1985, went missing and whose brutally abused bodies were found soon afterward. It was widely believed that they had been killed by members of the security forces (the Commission established the truth of that belief). Their deaths triggered wide protest and deep mourning. Mawethu talked about the reaction at his school:

> We held a memorial service at school before the funeral. COSAS had good leadership who met with the teacher and asked him to talk about [the Cradock Four at the service]. The teacher was on the stage and he told all the students, "It is not planned, but I will tell you this although it is against the regulations of the school. I don't care." He told their history and that he had lived on the same street as Fort Calata. The students, everyone, were crying, they were angry. The teacher continued to talk as if he felt the pain. He cried. He gave the history of his involvement with Calata and of hearing about [their deaths]. Hate began in the students. The teacher was trying to convince the students to fight, it seemed. "Now act. It's enough. It's enough."
>
> Everyone was quiet. The police were in the streets and hippos [armored vehicles] were around. All were amazed, some afraid. They said, "What can we do? They won't allow us to go home." We said, "Open the gate and go free, go home for lunch." The police stopped them. We told them [the police] to be cool; the students were just off for lunch. A week later, members of the community, including some students, traveled to Cradock for the funeral service. That weekend was quiet in Zwelethemba. Only a few pupils arrived on Monday at school [to attend classes while others came] to meet one another. [A student] approached me and said,
>
> "We must do something. There is a call [for us to act]."
>
> "They are not back from Cradock."
>
> "We must act. We can't let the comrades be buried and do nothing as if we are happy."

"Go to the executive [of COSAS] and decide. Gather the views of the students. Ask why some have stayed away."

The principal supported the need to know the students' views on why some were staying away. A meeting was called. The chairperson [of COSAS], Desmond Yabo, addressed the meeting and views and views [were heard].

Police were patrolling the streets in their vans. Many pupils had stayed away in fear of the heavily armed police, yet they had done nothing wrong. The teacher who had addressed the school children had warned them that they stood to lose their leadership if they did not protest against the presence of police, who had arrived simply because they held a meeting. The school children marched to the police station and told the police that they did not want them in Zwelethemba, but if they remained they should stay in the police station, not on the streets. The police called for reinforcements, and two hundred extra men were sent in. They patrolled in vans and stood on every corner. Mawethu said,

> It was very, very painful for us. On the way back to school, near the school, they chased us. They said stones had been thrown at them. [They chased us] with batons and *sjamboks*. There were about six hundred students and parents. They fired teargas. I don't think stones were thrown. If thrown, they were not [by scholars]. Some of their tricks [to deliberately incite trouble].
>
> The students broke into the school to escape the police, clambering over the high fences, and many were hurt. At the school, "big guys" from the Cape Youth Congress [CAYCO] joined us and said, "Guys, lets act." At 6:00 p.m., a riot was begun outside the police station, and a beer hall was attacked and closed. The riot began with a song: "Botha, open the door. We are knocking."

That incident launched a period of dire conflict, death, and distress. Mawethu's account reveals the complex series of steps that he and others had taken before becoming fully involved in political activity. His awareness of oppression grew from watching older boys protest at school, from taking action against teachers' cruelty, from the encouragement of seniors to participate in local political organizations and to reject scholars' representation on institutional bodies answerable to school authorities. He participated in the response to the call by the UDF to make schools the center of activism, and he was roused by one teacher's account of the curtailment of his freedom and the death of his colleagues. Finally, police reaction to a peaceful protest triggered his full commitment to insurrection.

Isaac Lehlohonolo Tshabile

The third example of a young man's entry into politics fits more nearly into the picture many people hold of young people dancing and throwing stones to taunt the police. Isaac, born on July 15, 1972, tried to join a student protest in 1980, when he was eight years old. He was attracted by the *toyi-toyi* and was curious. He was chased away for being too young. He was warned that he could be tortured and made to reveal the other protesters' names or that he might be injured. He continued to be drawn toward protests, funerals, and even the burning of a house. A friend introduced Isaac to the issues that informed the political activism of the youth. He says, "I was caught up in the excitement." In 1985, aged thirteen, he joined the street committee in his area and went to Cradock for the funeral of the four men killed by security forces. He was involved in school organizations. His parents were opposed to his activities, especially when he and others patrolled the streets, joined people's courts, and threw gasoline bombs and stones at the police. He watched with interest as "criminals" joined in the activities for their ends. It was difficult, he said, to control them. He became a member of the South African Communist Party, COSAS, and WOYCO; he represented WOYCO in joint meetings in the region called by the UDF. In 1986, he joined a protest that attracted the attention of the police, who scattered the gathering. The police chased the participants, and Isaac ran from them and hid behind the counter of a local shop. The police found him and began to beat him. The shop owner tried to protect him, saying that he was her son. The police called her a liar, and in the midst of the argument Isaac escaped but was caught jumping the fence behind the shop. He was beaten, and a baton hit him in the mouth, knocking out his four top front teeth.

Isaac was arrested twice but released within a few hours each time because he was so young. In 1989, Isaac was active at the forefront of protest in Zwelethemba though there was, by then, much less conflict in the area. He did not finish high school in the 1980s, but in 1999 he rematriculated. After 1994, he joined the reintegrated SANDF but soon resigned. After that, he joined the Worcester Commando for a time, which was an extraordinary thing to do, as its members were local whites not known for their liberal ideas. When we met, he was a messenger in a bank, but he soon left their employ and had had no job for years. He spent one vacation from the bank shepherding, at my request, a number of children who had been mistreated as laborers by a local farmer back to their homes a thousand kilometers away. Isaac was part of a group that, after the first democratic elections of 1994, claimed rights as former fighters to council housing and took over newly built houses in Zwelethemba that had been assigned to families on the council waiting list. Some of his seniors in the group remonstrated with them. A young man of contradictions: full of anger yet polite and kind. He has continued to be active in local politics.

TWO

Untimely Suffering

Courage *is always original.*

— L U D W I G   W I T T G E N S T E I N

This chapter is in part a meditation on untimeliness, in that the young, some-times very young, suffered in the fight (Ellman 2005, xi). The events that caused it arrived too soon. Untimely, that is, if we are to grant that the kinds of pain and terror meted out by the security forces have greater effects on youth than on adults and on those who have had no training as fighters. But perhaps the tactics used—torture, solitary confinement, and humiliation— are always untimely. This chapter is about bearable and unbearable suffering experienced by the young who sought to make the country ungovernable and so invited state retaliation—and by the very young who were caught up in the conflict. The state struck out at the young in two ways, both of which contained structured and unpredictable elements. One required the careful garnering of knowledge about local leaders of the youth, on the basis of which they were targeted and sometimes killed but, more usually, hurt and terrorized. The other way was to sow uncertainty among the mass of youth by the commission of arbitrary brutal acts. In consequence, both those who chose to enter the arena of political activism and those who had not done so at all or had become involved only peripherally suffered, often in silence and in the absence of medical care. To bear suffering became less a question of innocence and more, for some, one of persistence through time and deliberate involvement and, for many, of simply being swept up in events. Such considerations raise questions about how the propensity to harm the young is unleashed when the forces of oppression are challenged and when existing institutional structures, including legal safeguards, are further undermined. They also raise questions about the limits of institutional inquiries once conflict has stopped.

The young in Zwelethemba who stood against the state had to withstand the corrosion of pain and fear in a particular concatenation of time and space, in which the everyday and the extraordinary were folded one into the other. They surfed the modes of time: public and private, personal and historical. The swell of the struggle took them from early adolescence into adulthood, across a span of up to ten or fifteen years. Crises came in waves, dumping them on the shores of pain and fear. The bodies of some were visibly marked by the loss of an eye or a limb, for example, as reminders down through time and as warnings to the public: others were held in cells until the marks on their bodies healed, to prevent their display in court or in doctors' surgeries. A few were led by the depravity of torturers into despair. (I am reminded here of a beautiful young woman in another small town who told me about the tortures visited on her, including having her breasts slammed in drawers, and about a policeman who took her from her cell, blindfolded her, and led her into a mortuary, where he uncovered her eyes, leaving her to stand alone beside the body of a man who had just committed suicide.) That kind of terrorizing was meant, supposedly, to cause the young who returned to the fray to live in anticipation of its repetition, and it entailed, on their part, a conscious attempt to guard against the intended effect. They lived every day in the awareness of the unpredictability of violence: they could be caught in the net that encircled small towns like Zwelethemba at any time, and even when they were caught and locked in cells the warders played with time—rattling keys, juggling meals, causing confusion by disguising day or night, leaving them in isolation for long stretches, or keeping them scurrying to and fro for interrogation at all hours. It was, they said, difficult to keep a purchase on time in solitary confinement.

We have seen that the stand against the regime was made in public and that the young activists had sometimes to withstand humiliation and harm in front of kin and neighbors. Even torture could occur in groups, so that the tortured's behavior could be witnessed by comrades. As members of the police force, kin and neighbors could be part of the team that meted out punishment, and the young were thus conscious of the knowledge that community members might have of how they had behaved *in extremis*.

In private, they tried to keep to the ethos among liberation fighters to neither speak nor complain about what they had endured. They were to avoid self-pity, not burden intimates with the knowledge, and not spread the word, knowing that terror was part of the government's propaganda. They had to live with the anxiety that they might have said too much under pressure. There was the threat of skepticism: such suffering for so small a contribution, the awareness that time lost was irretrievable, and the disruption in the unfolding of a life not yet come to maturity. Conscious efforts were made among the local leaders to balance an ethic of everyday conduct with an acknowledgment that even the smallest effort was a measurable contribution to the inevitable attainment of freedom. It took longer than they had anticipated in the 1980s and was, of course, contingent on forces, like the end of the Cold War, far beyond their battlefields.

In attempting to describe bearable and unbearable suffering, Bernard Williams emphasizes that "some suffering simply is unbearable. It can break people. This is true of physical pain, as is well known to torturers and to those who send agents into the risk of being tortured" (2006, 334). He asks what one can do with suffering if it has a meaning in terms of "bearing" it. He suggests that meaning may lie in there being behind suffering "a purpose that I acknowledge, or which has authority over me, or is, in some way, a purpose *for* me" (333). What it is for a purpose to fill this role, he adds, is a complex question.

Williams holds that there has to be an appropriate relation to a purpose that has authority for the sufferer. He does not wish to imply that "meaning" is an analgesic because "I cannot choose what will make sense to me" (334). He examines cases in which an external purpose has authority for the sufferer because it involves him or her in a project that expresses a purpose of the sufferer's own and one that makes sense to him or her in some larger context of life. A commitment to a political cause may work like this. "Suffering that is involved as a necessary means or constituent of such a project will make sense of the suffering, and that indeed can make it more bearable (always within the limits, that some suffering just is unbearable)" (335). Williams considers what is to be made of cases in which such a project does not succeed. He ends the discussion by suggesting that, in imagining someone who suffers for reasons bearable to him, we can ask what new sense it is that his life is now finding for itself (337).

I have drawn on these thoughts to lead into a description of suffering endured by the young of Zwelethemba. In the first section, I point to some of the ways in which my attention was drawn to pain, before discussing a testimony given by a slightly older man than the men in MAZE, one who was an important mentor to them, and three testimonies made in public by members of our group at the Commission's Human Rights Violation hearing (hereafter, HRV hearings) held from June 24 to 26, 1996, in Worcester. This is followed by an analysis of suffering experienced by very young people, as detailed in nine HRV hearings in the Western Cape, who were not deemed to be political activists by the Commissioners or described as such in the testimonies. The final section is a critical account of the method used by the Commission to document people's experiences of violence during the years under examination by the Commission. I return at the end of the chapter to the issue of bearable and unbearable suffering.

Talking About Suffering in One's Home Town

Subsequent to the killings of young, peaceful protesters on June 16, 1976, in Soweto, pain was inflicted on them (not, of course, only on the young) systematically, day after day, over many years, in a patterned way, to great excess, involving gratuitous cruelty, with intentional destruction and damage, on specific targets and on young blacks in particular, drawing on a stock of techniques that ranged from straight physical brutality to intimate intrusion into the orifices of the body and the intricacies of the mind. It was inflicted under orders from state rulers in cahoots with representatives of formal institutions in the land, including legal, medical, and educational institutions, and with the compliance of organizations and individuals at every level of society. Its receipt was experienced by the young in revolt and by those who were not. One concern in this chapter is that the infliction of pain is documented with difficulty, and another is that perpetrators of profound harm to the young have been held up to meager opprobrium and a minimum of accountability in South Africa.

The infliction of pain on the young was a weapon in the arsenal of the state security forces. It was used to hurt and terrorize. Its excess and particularity were only possible within a system of institutionalized racism. It unleashed cruelty on a massive scale. People's proclivity for cruelty exists everywhere, but certain conditions fertilize it, and reactions to it may call forth brutality in return. Institutionalized racism in South Africa was not confined to the exercise of power over only its main target: the ideology that framed it encompassed individuals and groups that challenged, threatened, or opposed its tenets, and they were often treated as badly.

I offer two precautions. The first is that there have always been people in South Africa who have worked against the infliction of pain. They were found in institutions, companies, churches, nongovernmental organizations, civic bodies, and among people of all ilk. Their actions were of great importance, and their records invaluable. The second is that there was a continuing resistance. The account that follows draws on those records and the documentation of the TRC. It is an account founded on experiences among the young in Zwelethemba and on data from the Boland, in particular, and the Western Cape more generally.

Pain was often part of the unfolding of the life of someone who resisted oppression under apartheid. It is often treated in the literature as having occurred during discrete events. The nature of the Commission's statement taking effectively yielded descriptions of pain as incidents and not as punctuation in the experience of time. In testimonies of suffering endured under apartheid and given in public, there were many references to silence: very often, neither the fact of pain having been inflicted nor descriptions of its effects had been revealed to anyone at the time. The other side of silence is the refusal to know: that refusal can be insidious, it can color and stain the response, and it instigates a continuing cover-up. Considering when and why pain is not spoken leads us to how, in the aftermath, ingredients like fear among those who caused it or were complicit in harming others make them seek to prevent its expression.

It is nonetheless hard to understand why hatred and violence toward the young can be so virulent and why fear is so entrenched that it holds sway when circumstances alter and evidence of past, unwarranted oppression is presented. While working in Zwelethemba, Fiona Ross and I used to take anthropology masters and honors students there to conduct small pieces of research. One of the students was troubled by the difficulty she had in balancing a new "truth" against the old one. She said, "the story is now an ANC story." She did not hear the stories of individuals but instead a group one (derived from the ANC), one already molded and asserted and therefore to be doubted. Her predicament points to a larger problem, that of hearing accounts of pain, especially those of the young, aside from the patterning of a tale held in common. It is also indicative of the problem of expressing and representing pain that I discuss below. Here, however, what requires analysis is the exponential expansion of harm with a willingness to hurt, and the failure of authorities to keep it in check when situations of conflict expand. The authorizing of the infliction of pain warps common conduct, and with the unraveling of everyday ethical mores, the young are not excused. Indeed, in South Africa, they were targeted (which is not to deny that some of the young participated in brutality).

The Young in Revolt

That young people (under the age of eighteen) should revolt in the face of imminent and continuing danger is surprising. Michel Foucault says that "in the end there is no explanation for the man who revolts. . . . [He is] outside history" (1999, 131). And, "One does not make the laws for the person who risks his life before power" (133). The young in Zwelethemba were aware of "the real limits of the power to resist" (Sebald 2003, 55; writing about Jean Amery). On entering the fight against the apartheid regime, they faced the full power of an armed state.

The description of suffering in the testimony that Amos Dyantyi gave on June 24, 1996, at the HRV hearing in Worcester is reproduced below. It is a horrifying account. Before giving it, I shall examine, in four steps, some of the reasons for and against publicizing accounts like his. First, I lay out some of the frequently heard arguments against the production and reproduction of descriptions of pain. This is followed by a few points drawn from a fictive account written by J. M. Coetzee in the guise of a lecture by Elizabeth Costello, in his book of the same title, on the matter and from an analysis of

Costello's reasoning (Coetzee 2003, 156–182). The third step offers coun-
terpoints from Elaine Scarry (1985) and some other writers; the fourth lists
my reasons for including accounts of pain here.

A variety of dangers are said to attend the description of suffering, including the incitement to voyeurism, sensationalism, the exposure of private
experiences, and the use of images that blunt the reception and inure the
public against the reality of suffering. Description is said to be unnecessary,
because the lineaments of pain are known and because the details may serve
specific political agendas not necessarily in the interests of those who are
affected. There ought, some say, to be the right not to look or hear.

Elizabeth Costello delivers a lecture in Amsterdam based on a book written by Paul West about the cruel and prolonged death of men who had failed
in their attempt to assassinate Hitler, and her thesis is "that writing itself,
as a form of moral adventurousness, has the potential to be dangerous" and
that "certain things are not good to read *or to write*" (Coetzee 2003, 162,
173). Her arguments can be analyzed in relation to the ethics of reading and
writing about torture, the making of rules to limit the articulation of private
pain, the justification for the repression of publicity, the boundaries between
thought and expression, whether censorship can have effects on the commission of harm, the conception of private pain and its communication, and
the contagion of evil through the product of the imagination.

Elaine Scarry (1985) is certain that pain must be described and publi-
cized. It should be said that she does not include in her reasoning questions
of description in journalism, marketing, or appeals to public emotion and
purse. She upholds the publication of pain on behalf of others who are, so
often, bereft of the resources of speech. She grants that "there are very great
impediments to expressing another's sentient distress" and "very great reasons why one might want to do so," but, if the attempt is made, the most
radically private experiences begin to enter the realm of public discourse
(6). She outlines four ways in which this happens: in the medical context of
diagnostic questionnaires and case histories, the publications of Amnesty
International, the transcripts of personal injury trials, and in poetry and
narratives. For her, "the assumption that the act of verbally expressing pain
is a necessary prelude to the collective task of diminishing pain" holds true
(9). And she applauds legal situations that require "that the impediments to
expressing pain be overcome" (10). She supports the entry of pain into "a

realm of shared discourse that is wider, more social, than that which char-
acterises the relatively intimate conversation of patient and physician" (9).
There are, she feels, political consequences of pain's inexpressibility. The
danger is either that pain remains inarticulate or, on expression, it silences
all else—nothing sustains its image in the world, and it is not seen in the
context of other events: "Its absolute claim for acknowledgement contrib-
utes to its being unacknowledged" (61).

Emmanuel Levinas lays stress "on the pain lightly called physical, for in
it engagement in existence is without any equivocation. . . . It is the very
irremissibility of being. The content of suffering merges with the impossibility of detaching oneself from suffering" (1989, 39–40). Its acuity lies in
the impossibility of fleeing it. For Levinas, the supreme ordeal of freedom is
not death but suffering. Pain is pure deficit (1998b, 55). About physical pain,
Alphonse Daudet says, "What's terrible is the gradual increase of sorrow, in
punishment," and "Pain finds its way everywhere, into my vision, my feeling, my sense of judgement; it's an infiltration" (2002, 44, 23). W. G. Sebald
suggests that we describe cruelty in the hope that the last chapter in the horror story under scrutiny will be written. Yet, he fears, our species is unable
to learn from its mistakes. He cautions against usurping the victim's cause
(2003, 148). South African society gave rise to a regime whose dominance
authorized systematic cruelty to the young to an unprecedented level.

I face, in writing about horror, a quandary: the desire, on the one hand,
to confirm that pain is irreducible and, on the other hand, to confront the
abiding question as to the purpose of representing cruelty. Nevertheless, I
write here of others' pain and justify doing so in the following ways. I describe pain to record the extremes of state retaliation against the young; to
clarify the nature of conflict (that embroils children and youth, as war always
does) that occurs within a country involving the state and other groups;
to add to the consideration of what rules of constraint may aid the young
in situations of vulnerability; to pay attention to the consequences for the
young of the suffering endured, and to notice that their interests are not
foregrounded as they could be, should be, if prevention is the aim—if, as
Costello phrases it, the "wanton . . . obscene energy" of the hangman who
exceeds his commission is to be limited (Coetzee 2003, 177). Of any government we need to ask: Under whose commission is pain inflicted on the
young? What marks the excess? Who draws the line that exceeds? What

is the source of that energy? Who grants impunity and lustration? There needs to be a consistent examination of the ways in which the infliction of harm is systematized, masked, implemented, and excused.

Nana, whose profile is given in chapter 4, rejected the commonly held notion that the experience of pain was part of the induction into being recognized as a committed activist and its implication that pain was expected. He said:

> We tried to avoid pain and fought against the people who were inflicting pain. We never wanted pain [and] that is why we never put ourselves in the line of danger [except in the interests of a liberation organization's interests]. That is why there is so much secrecy in the struggle—we wanted to protect our loved ones from the pain apartheid has inflicted on them. The pain that cuts deep down, deep down into your bone marrow, it is so painful that it makes your heart sore: this is the pain you feel as a victim. Apartheid dropped a label on you, and you had to live with this striking pain that was inflicted on you. Apartheid was a pain that was so painful it made you prick your bravado and go into denial. Sometimes we could strategize so that when we were caught the court trial would be turned into a political seminar for people to hear about. There were dangers; people were hurt beyond any words. Less than a kilometer from where we are now [I was interviewing Nana in the University of Cape Town residence in which he was living at the time] is Valkenberg [a hospital for the mentally ill], and this is where one of the combatants of the MK is after being tortured. He is permanently disturbed. He was labeled "the president's patient." Such a person is incapacitated and cannot testify on how badly he is hurt. Such people are examples of how brutal apartheid was. Apartheid has brutally obstructed the record permanently in a case like this. [He] is a living example of the brutality of apartheid, and no amount of healing can give [him] his youth.

Testifying About Suffering

The TRC provided the time and space for South Africans to give accounts of their experiences under apartheid. Commissioners repeatedly claimed that to talk about suffering was to begin to heal. The hearings were held in a variety of venues, including city halls, community centers, school assembly rooms, and meeting rooms. There was a pattern to the use of space at the hearings. Two tables covered with white cloth were set, often on a stage, at an angle to each other and to the audience. At a long table, seats were placed for the Commissioners and, at a shorter one, seats for the witnesses, kin, or friends accompanying them and the counsellors provided by the Commission. A booth was set to one side of the stage for the translators. Vases of flowers, pots of greenery, the new South African flag, and TRC banners decorated the scene. When Archbishop Desmond Tutu presided, he dressed in the purple robes of office. Red tape divided the space from the audience. Care was taken to ensure that the testifiers were briefed and guided throughout the process of preparation, hearing, and aftermath. Great lengths were taken to provide instantaneous translation in as many of the eleven official languages as possible. The task of translation was difficult and demanding, and the toll of having to tell stories of rage, pain, and loss was great. Few trained translators were available between some languages, for example between Xhosa and English. I give, below, the testimonies as they were translated and printed by the Commission's staff, and I have edited them, on the basis of the notes I took while listening to the testimonies, only where the meaning was markedly obscure.

The Boland Hearing was held from June 24 to 26, 1996, at Sohnge College in Worcester. The deputy chair of the Commission, Alex Boraine, presided, and three Commissioners and a Committee member assisted him.

AMOS DYANTYI

Amos Dyantyi (in the TRC testimony his surname is spelled Dyanty), a resident of Zwelethemba and a former councilor of the community's Civic Association, gave testimony on the first day about the suffering he had endured as a political activist. I had interviewed him in 1993 as part of an earlier study of young activists, and at that time he had spoken very little about himself and more about his desire to support the young who had been drawn into leadership, as he and his colleagues were being cleared from the terrain. In the 1980s, he had spent many hours with the recruits (some of whom I worked with on this study), and they later recalled that sometimes as they sat with him his body would begin to shudder from head to toe, as if the tools the torturers had used on him were again being switched on. They would wait quietly until he was still, then resume the conversation. In the figure of Amos they had dire warning of what the fate of an activist *might* be.

Commissioner Wendy Orr led the team as they listened to the story that Amos had to tell. (Elsewhere, I have removed the names of people given as the perpetrators of harm by testifiers, but, in testimonies from those I knew in Zwelethemba, I have left them in the text.) I have left intact the orthographic style adopted by the authors of this report and resort to my own when I insert my own notes.

Amos Dyanty [*sic*]
Public Testimony
When the policeman came to arrest me they arrived around five in the early hours of the morning—they came with three vans and one hippo. The leader of this police force was Lieutenant Van Loggerenberg—I believe he was the entrusted one. They took me and they roam around the location with me at the back of the van. They took one of my comrades and they took us to the detective's office. When we arrived there, they took us inside the offices, what they did they separated us but he was not that much far from me—that's Boyiseli—they handcuffed me with the table, they took Boyiseli away.

Van Loggerenberg was the organizer of this whole thing, saying they must take away Boyiseli, they went as from five till six o'clock in the morning, when they came back I was tired of sitting. They came back with Boyisely [*sic*] again, they didn't cover my head at that moment when they arrived with Boyiseli—I saw it was Van Loggerenberg who was taking the leading role. They took Boyiseli to me, what they did then, which they were sure of what they were doing to people.

He [Boyiseli] was wearing a tracksuit now, he was wetted his tracksuit, there was another load at the back, that I couldn't identify and they said can you see, I said yes. I asked Boyiseli what happened—he said as from today, I am under the comradeship I've got nothing to do with that, I am leaving you alone. They said I must leave . . . they. . . . I disregarded this and it was my first experience. I was not afraid, I just felt that I have just to see and experience for myself, I couldn't just take what happened to someone else and think that it would be the same with me.

I was handcuffed, and they put one a—lighted on my head, Loggerenberg said to me—two cars should be filled with Security Officers and then I was taken to one of the vans. I was still handcuffed, they pulled me because I was blindfolded and they said I was—they put me at the back seat, then somebody pinned me down and I could feel that someone had his foot on my neck and also on my waist. I didn't realize that I was being taken to my place. I felt that I could see what was going to happen to me.

The car was at very high speed, and you could feel that it was travelling a long distance. Later on I realized that there was something terrible which was going to happen to me, but I felt that I would see what was going to happen at the time. As I was—I was lying on the car, you could feel that the road corrugated, and you would also feel that it was bumping over bushes, the way in which they were in a hurry, you could feel that they were really rushing for something terrible.

And then they took me away, they pulled me and they pulled me with my belt, dragged me because I couldn't walk—covered my face, you must remember that, so I couldn't go on my own. They also took the handcuffs and then under the head you could feel that there was something heavy which was on my head. And Loggerenberg said to me, somebody should put my—my handcuffs, the handcuffs which are on my hand, and put my knees inside through the arms and then said somebody should pull me apart. What he did, he put his foot at my buttocks and then he said it was enough.

He said Amos it's Zwelethemba you are a member of the Civic Organization, then I agreed. He said you are the people—you are making havoc in the location, I told him he cannot say anything that he doesn't know, because he doesn't stay there. I knew that the Civic was the most prominent organization in our area, we were bust because we knew that the ANC was banned and wanted to perform duties as we knew that the ANC was working underground and then the Civic Association was using the platform because they knew that they were able to speak as they were speaking about civic matters.

Matshoba, Harry Sibeko and Ivan Kholo and Abel Ligilili were also the members of the Civic and were united. And everybody had confidence in us. Van Loggerenberg stated that he knows what was going on in the location and he knew about our involvement and that was going to be put to end and he stated that it is you and me inside here and the first thing that he stated was that I know what was taking place at your place, we know what was going on, we know the people who always attend meetings at your place, so you are going to tell us the truth.

The first thing that he did was to take a cube, when you try and push it, as it was put on—over my face, it was difficult to remove it. Then at the end you it was difficult for me to breath[e], he took electric wire I do not know whether he poured water over those but he . . .

Convulsions. You could feel the shock waves in my body. This was happening on my fingers, on my toes—a person who has never experienced that doesn't know anything, it is just beyond description. Especially if it is done by someone who is not considerate as if he is a hardened criminal, a merciless person.

Then Loggerenberg—you could imagine what type of person I was dealing with—after shocking me, he removed the cube from my face and I was screaming. When I was calling my father . . .

During the Truth Commission Hearings you always see that the people [who have hurt others] are requested to come forward and present their cases and confess but they never do.

So other things that I did, I was crying in pain, because the pain that I was experiencing was excruciating, I was praying in my language which is Xhosa and he took—he removed those electric wires from my neck and then they turned me on the other side, he opened my trousers and the back, and then they took these electric wires, put them through my anus and they inserted them deeply.

This continued for quite a long time—it was those wires at the buttocks [and] on the neck and this torturing was taking place simultaneously. I would like the Truth Commission and the people who are listening here to just sit down and imagine what was taking place.

After they have removed those wires, I cried extremely, I tried to hold my breath so that I can endure the pain that I was experiencing at the time, I was praying so hard, but they didn't listen to me, they just said they have no time to play, I must just confess and state [what] is taking place there and inform them about it. He said he was going to show me.

The most crucial part of the testimony is missing from the printout that I was given by the Commission. In my notes, I recorded Amos as saying: "Von Loggerenberg said, 'You know that machine used in building—a jackhammer to drill concrete? This one had sharp iron points.' They took off my trousers and they inserted the jackhammer into my anus. (He stops and drinks water.) Sorry. I apologize for the expression of my emotion. He switched on this [the machine and placed a] plastic tube over my face. I was screaming but I could not be heard. It seemed as if my intestines were coming out. I felt as though I was being disemboweled."

Mr. Chairperson and the listeners here, the audience, I would like to thank you for the support that you've given today. If you can think what happened during the apartheid regime, those repressive laws are beyond description. The people were so evil you could liken them to Satan himself.

What they saw to me was that they could see that now I was weak, my body was giving way. They were shocked to see that I was severely injured. Loggerenberg put his hand on my stomach and then he said "Let's take him quickly to the doctor" and said "Amos you are still alive?" I couldn't answer him. He repeated it again and said "Amos you are still alive?" I couldn't answer him. And then they took me and then he put—he was hugging me and he put me on his lap, he was—he had his hand over my stomach and then they were driving off quickly to the hospital.

They said to me—I was ordered to—they took me down and threw me on the floor, thereafter many police came in. The first one took a bucket of water and threw it over me, I could feel that I was wet, I couldn't speak but I could hear what was being said, I could feel what was happening. They were alternating among themselves trying to revive me, the others were trying to carry me along. The other[s] were trying to open and stretch my fingers, apparently I had spasms. What I could hear them saying was "Let's call the doctor." The doctor came when he arrived the first thing that he did he put his hand on my forehead—I didn't understand that my tongue was hanging outside, thereafter I could hear a sound like whap, whap, in my tongue. And then he said they must all go out, he said I want to be alone with the patient . . . [except for] only one security branch officer.

The only thing that I could think of at the time is that I was about to die, but I was conscious all the time—physically I was dead as far as I was concerned. You could understand that when you are [indistinct] in the sun or you are sitting around the fire you can feel the feeling when the fire is too hot now, the pain that I was experiencing was beyond that pain that I just presented to you. I could realize that they were not yet finished with me.

[Dr. ORR]

"Why did he send them out?"

[Mr. DYANTY]

The reasons I am asking them to go out, I can't hear—hear—what the doctors, what they were trying to say to me, because I was almost losing conscious[ness]. The doctor try his best to talk to me, it was Dr. . . . , the reason I call you alone, this is not a mortuary, if this case could be investigated, we'll find a solution and a reason for all this that he [they] did, I advise you to take this person straight to the hospital. On your way to the hospital, you must take a mug or cup with porridge, you must apply porridge on to his mouth through his nostrils, I for one now I am going to give him two injections.

This part of the testimony is particularly confusing. Amos cannot move at all, but he can hear, and he listens to what the doctor advises the senior security force officer who has stayed in the room with Amos to do. The doctor tells the officer that they are not in a mortuary, and, therefore, questions will be asked if Amos dies, in which case they need to provide a cause for his death. He suggests that they stuff porridge into his mouth and nose, making it appear that he has suffocated while trying to eat. Amos's reply to Dr. Orr reads in my notes as follows: "Dr. . . . said this is not a mortuary. If you take the person to hospital we shall investigate these dirty deeds. Take a mug of porridge and apply it in his mouth and nostrils. I will give him two injections."

Dr ORR:

I just want to make sure that I understand exactly what was going on here. The police thought you were dying or nearly dead. And they called the doctor and the doctor said you must make it look as if he has suffocated on this porridge in his mouth or nose, so that it looks as if that's the cause of death, is that correct?

Mr DYANTY:

Yes it was like that, their first mistake was that they thought I was dead, that's why they were making all this tricks and take all this decisions; they were sure that I was dead. Because the situation I was in, it was as if I was dead. Even this attempt that [they] were doing—it was only God who was on my side and I survived through his will. But it—today it's not a nice experience, everyone is trying to run away from death, but even through this injections, I couldn't accept them—out of his statement because I didn't want to die. [I did not want to receive the injections after what the doctor had said because I did not want to die.]

Know[ing] the work of the security officers' deeds, I want[ed] to utter and say no I don't want to die, but as I said before, I was just out of the world, I couldn't understand what was happening; although I was conscious I was unable to speak and express myself, so they took me and put me to the van again and then I bumped my head along the wall of the van then they took me back to the cells. I do not remember whether I was taken to hospital or where I was taken to, I don't even know whether I was injected, but I lost consciousness. So the following day, I was in the basement, but I was still in [a] cell. During the night I woke up, I was very cold, I was just naked and I was still having these contractions. When I woke up from the cell, there was somebody who was in the cell, I thought that I would be able to speak and explain what happened to me so that somebody can investigate what was happening. So when I woke up I thought I was going to be able to speak but I couldn't speak anymore.

In the morning I was taken again by Van Loggerenberg [and his] team and then [somebody] asked, "Where are you taking this person to?"—they responded by saying they would take me to the doctor. I was taken to Dr. . . . surgery and then he examined me. I was bleeding and especially on the wrist where I was handcuffed. I could realize that there were some people around me and my comrades were informed about what was happening about me. Lizo and others and Harry Sibeko and Ligilili were informed so they make contact with the lawyers, Zurina Abduraman and David Standton at [indistinct] David Standton. Those were the lawyers who assisted me and then they came to the police station and visited me there. The police [denied that I was] there . . . the lawyers said they will never rest until they find me.

[At last the lawyers were able to see me.] They asked me the questions and I couldn't [communicate very well initially but later I was able to] respond to the lawyers [when] I [was] ultimately taken back to see them. I couldn't understand and communicate very well with them. They requested that . . . there should be a court hearing otherwise they stated that they would like me to be released. I was afraid that if I was taken home in the condition in which I was, my family would be very shocked, so I was trying to protect my family and refused that I should be taken to my family in the same condition in which I was.

Amos was charged in court with having kept in his home two AK47s. They were not brought forward as exhibits. He was acquitted and released on bail under restrictions that required that he report to and sign in at the local police station three times a day. He was harassed by the police. There was a Supreme Court hearing in Cape Town, and this time he and twenty-eight others were charged with arson. He was acquitted. In 1986, he was detained again under the State of Emergency law and was released in 1987, when he was very ill. He had been detained with Trevor Manuel (the minister of finance from 1994 to 2009) and others, and he says that Trevor Manuel and he were hospitalized and that three others died in a car accident. Amos had been poisoned, as perhaps they all had been. Amos was ill and kept in bed for a long time: he was sent to the hospital. He had an operation on his neck, and in Groote Schuur Hospital he was given tests that included a head scan, radiotherapy, and a bone marrow transplant. He had a stomach operation and was discharged when still unwell. He asked to be dropped at Cowley House in Cape Town rather than the station and was seen to be so ill that he was escorted home by, among others, Dullah Omar and Winnie Mandela. Amos paid tribute to the healing care of Dr. Leslie London and his family.

Commissioner Orr later telephoned Dr. . . . , who denied the accusation and said he did not have the time to attend the hearing. Some of his patients attested, by telephone, to his good services as a doctor. The doctor was not subpoenaed to appear. This was announced at the hearing on one of the following days.

Amos died as a result of his torture a year after having appeared at the hearing.

Among the young to whom Amos had given guidance and who took over the local leadership are three men with whom I worked and who told their stories in public at the same hearing. First I shall draw from the account given by Zandisile, then Xolile, and finally Ntando.

ZANDISILE NTSOMI

Zandisile gave testimony on the first day of the hearing; his case number is CT/00320, and the violation was labeled "Shot in leg by police leg amputated." Wendy Orr assisted him. A portion of the account is given below. The whole testimony can be read on the TRC website.

> DR ORR:
>   And now you going to tell us your own story. It was around the same time 1985 in Zwelethemba, a time of State of Emergency, curfews—the township being blockaded and intense police activity.
>   Can you tell us about the events which happened to you starting on that evening 12th October 1985?
> MR NTSOMI:
>   I will start by saying what—I would start by stating on what happened on the 12th or I'll start the day before I was shot.
>   There was a funeral in the location. It was one of the comrades who was shot and dead, his name was Thomas Segolo. So it was his funeral and it was on Friday. The situation in the location was not stable. There was a tense

situation I would explain it that way. The youth was not stable either. More especially in the youth although it involved the whole community. And then on Saturday there were protests among the location because as it was that tension people were not that much happy—there were many things that happened as Mamma Bahume has stated before. Some of the youth were shot dead and some were shot and injured.

So on the 12th of October I was also shot—the year was 1985—it was a tar road where I was. After the policemen shot me I was in someone else's yard, I was visiting my friend called Zimphiwe—he was staying there.

After that incident they beat me up, they were kicking me, insulting and assaulting us. They dragged me, pulling me out of this yard taking me into the police van. What I can state that not at that moment I was taken to hospital—I was bleeding heavily—I can't even mention how the way I was bleeding. They couldn't even take the opportunity to take me to hospital, they were taking rounds around the location. Sometimes they decided to stop their van chatting to each other, having that negotiations that I couldn't understand and take their exact meaning of what they were trying to say.

They used to use the torches to light me. At times they used to point their guns at me, so I don't know what was behind all this motion. I knew—the only thing I knew that they were the perpetrators, the culprits. They can do anything because they've already shot me.

At a long last I thought they were bored—tired that's my thinking they decided to [do] something because at first I couldn't understand why they did not take me to hospital. They took me to Eben Donges Hospital. I arrived at the hospital and they put me on a stretcher. As I was laying there on that stretcher I was under police guard. They asked me to wait there for an ambulance. They told me that I would stay there for a long while because the ambulance were not around—hopefully they were busy in the location taking some others who were also shot.

At a long run an ambulance came—I asked for some water from the one of the guards—police guards and this police guard told me he is not allowed to give me water. He was told not to give me anything. After a while or after some time as the ambulance came it took me to Tygerberg Hospital. It was around about in the morning or it was still midnight around ten. Around about 6 o'clock I was taken to Tygerberg Hospital. When we arrived there I was admitted.

I woke up in the morning and a doctor woke me up—the time was around about 6. I had a watch I believe so, it was still on my wrist. I noticed

that the time was 6 o'clock in the morning. I was awoken by the doctor and
he told me that I was badly injured and he told me that they would try their
best as doctors. They will try and examine me up to their utmost best.

They were going to take me to the X-ray first and they did as they
say—as they said. I was taken back to the ward again. After a while—it was
just a short period this doctor came back again and he told me that guy you
are badly injured. And we have noticed that there is nothing we can do about
you. The only thing we can do to you is to amputate your leg. So that thing
must be done as soon as possible. Can you see the time now and I said yes,
and he told me that around 10 this morning your leg must be amputated. So
the operation must be through already or else if we can wait up until ten—
there is a possibility that you won't live, you can die. Or else if you can take
a risk and tell ourselves that we would try our best and examine your leg and
do all our best we can do to your leg, it will affect the whole body of yours
and you will get sick.

I had no other option and I was forced and bound to accept the doctors['
perception. I said if it's the way you are telling me it's okay with me, I have
no problem—can you please bring me the forms—I will fill in the forms.
I filled them and after that I told them that before you can do anything can
they do me a favour and phone my family at home because I find out that my
parents are not aware of what's going on.

I gave the doctor the phone number, my neighbour[']s phone number and
I told him to try and phone my parents and he did so. So my parents was the
time they only get the message that I was in Tygerberg Hospital. They were
not aware all this time. They even—they came as soon as they could. They
were not allowed to talk to me—they said they were not allowed so it was
that situation—because it was time for me to go to the theatre. They were
told to come later.

The operation was done to me—my leg was amputated and it was okay—
that was Sunday the day was the 13th October 1985. I stayed there the
whole—the whole day on Sunday under a drip. And then on Monday, it was
about lunch time at the hospital they brought me some food. My face was
swollen because the policemen had beaten me, had kicked me, so that was the
result of their assault and the way they dragged me from where I was lying in
that yard. It was very painful so it was—my swollen was resulted from that.

I tried to walk slowly—I am sorry I tried to eat because I was very hungry
I couldn't eat for the past two days. This policemen forced me to eat because
after you finish I am taking you—I can't remember whether I asked him
whether—I asked him a question about where are we going to because I

knew that I am going to the police cells. And I had no option so I can't even remember that I asked him a question.

I try—I forced myself to eat. After I finished my meal a nurse came along and brought me a wheelchair, took me from the bed to the wheelchair— they brought two packets of pills, put them in my pocket. By that time I was wearing—I would say it was a night gown—a hospital night gown and then on top I had some—I had the other thing on top like a gown. There was nothing I had underneath, I had no shoes on, no clothes on. I had no idea what happened to my clothes but when I came into Worcester I heard that they had taken my clothes home.

They drove me out of the hospital—I was on the wheel chair, put me in the police van—I was operated yesterday, remind you. [Dr Orr asks questions of clarification ending with the following question.]

DR ORR:

How do you feel about that doctor?

MR NTSOMI:

To me that situation is very unacceptable—I really can't describe and explain it, it was very painful—seemingly those days the system—the whole system of the country was corrupt—upside down. Because I don't think a qualified medical doctor could discharge a person from the situation I was [in] knowing that that person is being taken back to the police cells.

What I was thinking of I thought that I would stay there for about six months, I had no idea what happened to a person who has been amputated. I thought I was going to stay there, get proper medication and examination as someone who had an operation. That's what I thought I was going to get.

I am very painful and heartbroken because I just can't expressed [*sic*] my feelings of the situation that I was in that time. Because I would say—I would say maybe I am inhuman because I don't think that was not a professional doctor. I think the professional doctor is the most person [*sic*] who could care for a patient and he is the one who must care for you even from the police torture and all those things. But that one discharged me.

I went to Parow Police Station in Cape Town, that's where I realised that I will wait for policemen from Worcester. I sat on a bench in the charge office. I sat there for along time—there were people coming in and out and I was taken from there. I was not given crutches to walk. As I was taken from the wheelchair two people gave me support, [to] take me into the van— police van. [The need for support as I walked showed that it] was not the right time for me to be discharged from the hospital.

I was taken to the police cells telling me that I was waiting for the police from Worcester to take me back to Worcester. I waited there for a long time. They arrived there around about five. They opened the cell and they woke me up because I was already asleep. They told me that they are taking me and they said I must prepare myself we are on a journey. There were two Coloured policemen—they supported me, taking me to the police van.

This police van—there were two drivers who were wearing the camouflaged uniform. They drove it as fast as they could. The speed was very high—I can't even explain or describe—they were in such a hurry that they were driving at a very high speed.

I was sitting on this—at the back of the van on those small benches that's where I was seated—with pains and in that terrible situation and with my leg that was amputated was so swollen—I couldn't stand even the pain. As they were driving recklessly I was seated on the left side of the van.

I couldn't tolerate the way they were driving because my leg was painful and the situation—I couldn't stand because there was also a wind that was blowing inside the van. I could not bear the pain and I told myself—I tried to wave my hand to the police station and they stopped the van. We were—we were just [at] Paarl—it was just a minute we passed Paarl and they stopped the van. They get off, they came to me—they asked me what was my problem.

I tried to plead with them and tell them my situation at the back of this car. I tried to explain the pain I am having and the way they are driving— can't they assist or help because I saw there was a space there were only two of them in front a third person could fit in there. So I asked them can't they do me that favour. They looked at each other, they nodded their heads, I think they had a little bit of humanity because they couldn't resist and they take me into the front seat.

They were supporting me to the front seat of the van. As I was—as I was seated there I was—I felt much comfortable and I had to thank them a lot because I was relieved of the situation I was in at the back of the van, I thanked them a lot time and again and they drove off.

We arrived in Worcester. As we were in the charge office that—the one here in Worcester, I think they even called those who were inexperienced to come and see this fool that was here because there were a lot of policemen by the time we arrived here, even those that were not on duty, they came in.

I was—they could—they had the guts to say anything that they can. They told that this were the fruits of what you are doing in the location. The way you try to put the situation in the location—so they were saying things which one could not accept as a human being—terrible things that I couldn't even listen at because they were very terrible.

I still remember one of the policeman saying to me you mustn't worry— your leg will grow again. It was funny to me because I have never seen a leg growing again, seemingly he was very happy of what happened to me. He kept on saying that thing time and again. I accepted it at that moment although it was unacceptable because I can still remember they said it and it's still in my consciousness.

Zandisile cried as he told his story. He was kept in Worcester jail and then released on bail. He appeared in the Worcester Magistrate's Court on three charges relating to public violence. He was acquitted. His lawyers laid a claim on his behalf against the state. They lost. They appealed. The appeal was dismissed. In 1996, the state sent a letter by registered mail stating that he owed the state R450,000 for the costs of the appeals that had been lost, adding that the money was liable to be garnisheed. In his testimony, Zandisile appealed to the Commission to query and cancel those costs.

There is in the text mention of his political activism—that he was a member of the Zwelethemba Youth Organisation (ZWEYO) and that he continued to be active and to be harassed and beaten by the police even after the release of Nelson Mandela and during negotiations for a new state dispensation. Zandisile testified to poor treatment at Worcester Hospital and the costs he still owes for his artificial leg. He named the policeman who shot him and expressed his sadness at no longer being able to play soccer. He said, "I am not the same person whom I used to be—or I know myself to be."

NTANDO MRUBATA

Pringle Ntando Mrubata was paralyzed as a result of being shot in June 1986 by vigilantes in Ashton, a small town not far from Worcester. Ntando lived in Zwelethemba but had gone to stay with a cousin in Zolani, a township at the edge of Ashton, where the police were working with vigilantes against activists who were aligned with the antiapartheid movement. The vigilantes patrolled the area at night and instituted a curfew and a roadblock at the entrance to the township. After a funeral in the suburb, there was conflict between a man named as a vigilante and a young man said to be a comrade. In the ensuing struggle, Ntando and his friends heard a cry and went to investigate. The cry came from inside a van. As they approached, guns were fired to chase them away. Ntando took refuge in a house and emerged when he judged it safe. Unfortunately, when he came out of the house vigilantes saw him and, Ntando said, they called out, "Here is the dog we've been looking for." A shot was fired. Ntando said, "Then I knelt down and I realized that I was unable to crawl." He was taken to the hospital. He lost consciousness, and when he regained it he saw that he was under police guard. (He told me how distressed he had been to find that even though he was paralyzed, he was handcuffed to the hospital bed.) It seems that after he had been shot, the comrades questioned the vigilantes and began to burn their houses until the police arrived. The bullet had passed through his lower back and injured the spine. The next day, he was told that there were two things that might happen to him. "The doctor said, 'I might die or if I could live I would be a cabbage.'" He returned to Zwelethemba but could no longer stand, and he had bedsores from being unable to move. He said, "I was informed that I could die due to these bedsores." (And he indeed did, on February 10, 1999.) Both of his legs had to be amputated; he was paralyzed from the waist down.

Ntando was born on January 1, 1969. He never knew his father, and when he was about eight years old his mother left Zwelethemba to work in Queenstown. She never returned, although she maintained contact with him. Her sister and her sister's husband cared for Ntando and his younger brother; the latter died in 1985 in a car accident. His kin cared well for the boys, but the strain of attending to Ntando once he had been paralyzed took its toll. Ntando lived in a shack in the backyard that provided inadequate shelter, and he had to use an outside toilet ill adapted to his condition. He needed a modern wheelchair that would allow him to travel in ordinary vehicles. He suffered greatly from bedsores, and from February 1992 to February 1995, he was hospitalized. In 1997, the bones of his buttocks could be felt through his sores, and an operation was required, without which, his doctor told me, he would die. I was told that the waiting list was too long to save him. I was unable to raise the large amount that an operation in the private sector would have cost. He received only an interim-amount sum of money (UIR) before his death. Ntando was always bright and friendly, and he was a faithful participant in our meetings. His comrades organized a large funeral for him and honored him for his contribution to the struggle.

XOLILE DYABOOI

Also on the first day of the Boland Hearings, Xolile Daybooi (his profile is given in chapter 3) gave his testimony to the Commission. His was case number CT/00232, and the violation he was recounting was labeled "Torture/Detention." The full testimony can be found on the TRC website. Below I give a summary of the first section of his testimony, and the rest is given in his words; he spoke in English. Xolile was sworn in by Dr. Wendy Orr, and he was assisted by Advocate Denzil Potgieter.

In 1987, five young activists decided to leave South Africa to join the fight in exile. There was, Xolile said, a witch-hunt being conducted by the police in order to capture them and, under the State of Emergency legislation, it was difficult to continue to be politically active. Edward's twin, Edwin, was a member of the exile group. They traveled by car for two days to Bophuthatswana, a homeland that shares a border with Botswana, where they were arrested by soldiers and policemen. They were held in Mmabatho Prison and beaten. Then they were moved to Zeerust, where Xolile and a comrade were handcuffed together, blindfolded, and placed in the middle of a road. Xolile's companion realized where they were when motorists honked their horns, and he managed to pull Xolile off the road. The policemen took them into a building and up three floors. They were pushed down three flights of stairs, still handcuffed to each other and blindfolded. The handcuffs were removed, and they were beaten. In the evening they were taken, still blindfolded, out of the building, toward the police station; en route, a white officer who spoke fluent Tswana held a gun to Xolile's head and told him in Afrikaans to run. Xolile recognized a common trick (to make a captive run, then shoot him in the back, so that it would seem as if he had tried to escape), so he stood still. In the police station, the two men were placed in separate cells. Xolile's account continues:

> We were taken time and again to these offices, they were beating us up there,
> my face got swollen, I had scratches—whole of—the whole of my body
> and then the following week they take us from those cells—we were given
> to the South African Government. I can't remember the day that we were

taken there—they were—they put us into a Kombi, we were chain[ed]—
tying our hands—hands and feet were tied with chains [linking us together]
from the first comrade up till the last one. When we about to approach the
Bridgetown near Mafikeng, we were taken off this Kombi.

There was one I could identify known as Lucas . . . from Worcester. They
called me aside—they asked if—is Xolile Dyabooi, I am Xolile Dyabooi,
I said yes that's me. And then they let me into the van, they drove off. We
arrived here the following day around about three in the afternoon. We were
taken to the Sanlam Buildings here in Worcester, we were photographed
there and we were told that you are being detained under the provision of
Section 29 [of the Internal Security Act]: it was the law.

I was taken to the Strand police station; some of my comrades were taken
to different police stations. Days after that we were tortured by the police—
severely. By this time each and every morning they use[d] to take me to
one of the rooms in Macassar, or Stellenbosch, I think they were the police
rooms. They use[d] to bind me—bind my feet to . . . the table, they seated
me so that I can't even move an inch. They took a bag known as [indistinct]
it was like the post bags and they . . . put it on me, I just couldn't defend
myself because I was bound feet and hands.

As they were beating me this—this bag drags—thereafter I would be
very dizzy, they would take me—when they were about to knock off at four
and they would take me back to the cells. A few days later [while I was in a
cell], they would give me food, but at times I would just throw the food down
the drain, or down the toilet. We were always [suspicious that the food was
poisoned].

Time went by until we served [in] detention for six months—I think I am
mistaken—I was ill whilst I was still in detention and they took me to Hottentots Holland Hospital at Somerset-West. I was swollen and I had lumps
and swollen glands, I was given treatment, but I don't think that was effective
enough.

And the leader of the investigation team was Lucas van Loggerenberg and
. . . and a few others, there were so many of them, but he was the leader. And
he was also the one who was giving orders for my beatings. After six months
Lucas came—he told me that the Section 29 Detention Order has expired
and I was supposed to appear in court. We were going to hear what we were
accused of. A few days later we were taken to court and we were charged and
convicted as terrorists.

We were sentenced and it was said we were sentenced for contempt of
court. As we were detained under Section 29 we were also put into solitary

confinement for all these months, I didn't even see anybody, nobody visited me, I was taken to Brandvlei maximum security . . . there was a certain Major who gave orders that I should go and be detained in a *donkergat* [a "dark hole," i.e., a cell] that is where I spent my sentence [in] solitary confinement.

So I got indemnity in 1990 when the President [Nelson Mandela] of the country was released. I thank you.

Xolile said there was a call among the liberation organizations and their supporters for unity at that time and that there was a need for people like him to lead by displaying fortitude when directly faced by the crushing power of the government, for example, at the trial in which they were defendants. Assurance had to be given to the people, and they had to see that the government could not win by turning people through torture into witnesses against the activists. The courtroom was used as a place to reaffirm their stand and to call for continued efforts against injustice. Xolile had an extra six months added to his sentence for his contempt of court in singing and calling out to those assembled.

The full testimony and the three other testimonies discussed above concern the pain inflicted on the bodies of committed activists. The testifiers are among the few committed activists who appeared before the Commission's hearings on human rights violations. In the next section, the findings of a survey of harm done by security force members to the young whose stories were given at a selection of hearings in the Western Cape are reported, and some incidents relating to the perpetration of violence against children under the age of sixteen are recounted. These children were not known to have been activists, did not claim to be activists, were not said to have been activists by their kin, and were not addressed as activists in the hearings. The descriptions are presented in order to describe the context in which the young were hounded and the brutality with which the security force members sought to control the activities and movements of the young.

Senses

While listening to the testimonies given before the Human Rights Committee of the TRC, I was struck by the frequency with which people's sense organs were the targets of those who inflicted pain. On reading my notes and the published testimonies, I find that again and again the organs of sight, hearing, touch, taste, and smell were harmed. The five senses are part, perhaps, of a folk metaphysics, but that there should have been deliberate attacks on them may tell us something about the intentions and techniques of the people who defended the entrenched system of oppression. The attacks comprise a grammar of control. They were used to communicate terror, to humiliate, and to cause damage. One must remember that most cruel acts by security force members occurred before the recipients had been formally charged and subsequently brought to court. In other words, those they hurt were, under the law, innocent. Many incidents of brutality happened in places not formally designated for interrogations—in temporary buildings, on farms, at shooting ranges, on beaches, in the mountains, beside rivers, in offices belonging to an insurance company, and in apartments clandestinely hired for the purpose. Many of those hurt were let go without having been charged or imprisoned, so no record of their detention or treatment was kept. There was almost no redress: often the head of police in a small town to whom one might have complained was the person who had led the attack. There was both "ordinary complicity" and "ordinary heroism" (Nieman 2002, 276).

I shall take a few examples of attacks on three of the senses from testimonies given in the Western Cape. We need to know what was done to the young, in what ways, in what places, by whom, and for what purposes, if we are to begin to know the nature of organized brutality. Due acknowledgement of what was endured calls for an analysis of what was done. The Commission has compiled an invaluable collection of testimonies that deserve closer scrutiny from many angles. Their archive is, however, not easily accessible—only statements given in public are available, and they comprise only 10 percent of the total. It should be borne in mind that many of the testimonies that were given about or by people who were hurt when they were young contain no evidence that suggests they were engaged in sustained political revolt. The Commissioners did not often ask for details of political alignment and activism: it can, therefore, only be surmised from the details given in testimonies. The details suggest that many of the very young, aged between nine and thirteen, were not involved in political activities and were not engaged in such acts when they were harmed.

Very few of the accounts heard in public were given by leaders of the youth. Many of those whose accounts were heard represent the experiences of young people who had been targeted because they were young and black and, therefore, seen to be potential, if not actual, activists. The nature of the hearings may have precluded evidence of political awareness and activity because gross human rights violations were made the focus in order to facilitate decisions as to whether the one harmed could be declared a victim and, thus, deserving of reparations. The TRC database was designed to record violations rather than the character of a given youth's revolt. In many of the incidents that were described during the hearings, other young people were harmed besides the one who gave the testimony, but they did not come forward to describe their experiences. It is difficult to see the harm inflicted as anything but gratuitous: its excess, its iteration, its infantile crudeness, and its cowardice require explication, if only of the conditions under which such evil is let loose. What form of social reordering can answer the indictments of such cruelty to children?

Surveillance and arbitrary interference by those in authority clouded everyday life. The young experienced frequent intrusion into their affairs and were expected to answer any questions put to them by police and their accomplices. William Golding (1959, 65–66) describes a child's sense of the impossible predicament in which questioning places him or her:

> I knew I should be interrogated with terrible adult patience. I knew I should never grow up to be as tall and majestic, knew that he [the interrogator] had never been a child, knew we were different creations each in our appointed and changeless place. I knew that the questions would be right and pointless and unanswerable because asked out of the wrong world. They would be righteous and kingly and impossible from behind the high wall. Intuitively I knew this, that the questions would be like trying to lift water in a sieve or catch a shadow by the hand: and this intuition is one of the utter sorrows of childhood.

Golding's character was not caught in a predicament as terrifying as that in which many of the young in South Africa were placed when authority figures terrorized them while their parents and other adults who held them in their care were unable to protect them. I am thinking particularly about those who were under sixteen when they were maltreated, and the following accounts relate the experiences of very young people.

There was no clear divide along lines of race in the climate of fear that surrounded the lives of many. Security force personnel were black, white, or "coloured" in the Western Cape, and while only some of them were cruel, all fell beneath a hierarchy of control and often had to act as directed or risk losing their jobs. Or worse. Some school principals and teachers protected students as well as they could, some encouraged them in their revolt, and some collaborated with the police in identifying activists. There were almost no zones of safety for the young: neither home nor class nor church nor clinic. Not that people acted passively: many children were hidden, many policemen were misinformed as to their paths of flight, and many people diverted attention onto themselves to save others. One testimony describes how a woman and her sons fought the police when trying to protect a family member.

AN ANALYSIS OF HARM

An analysis of the stories told in 1996 and 1997 in public at thirteen of the Commission's Human Rights Violation Committee hearings in the Western Cape shows that ninety-six out of 234 of those who gave testimony (or about whom it was given) of human rights violations were, at the time of abuse, under the age of thirty. Of these, a third identified themselves (or were identified by those who spoke on their behalves) as committed political activists. Some of the remaining two-thirds participated in mass actions, but most were not active or were said not to have been involved in political activities. Ten of the ninety-six testifiers were girls or young women.

A careful analysis of the descriptions of harm done to the young in eighty-eight testimonies, drawn from nine of the hearings, reveals that half resulted in death, two in disappearance, twenty in serious injury (many from shootings), and nineteen in torture. Another three young people were abused and then placed in detention, but no further details of their treatment were given. Damage of that order suggests either a state out of control or one at war against its own people, specifically the young. If the data do not accurately reflect the nature of abuse, then the Commissioners' claim that public statements were chosen to represent the range of violations is wrong.

My focus in this section is on the children identified as not having been political activists, because the violence meted out to them can easily be seen to have been gratuitous, whereas the defense used in the past by the servants of the apartheid regime was that the children involved in political actions were terrorists and therefore deserved any harm that was inflicted on them. Their experiences represent those of thousands of children. I draw only on the accounts of those who were under eighteen years old when they suffered harm.

In framing an account of pain endured, I catalogue the harm done to the organs of sense. The catalogue is unpleasant, and I give but brief descriptions as examples of what happened. I can only wonder how the harm changed the young people's perceptions of the qualities of the real world and how it affected their lives. In the brief descriptions, I draw on Jonathan Ree's marvelous book, *I See a Voice: A Philosophical History of Language, Deafness, and the Senses*. He reminds his readers that we do not really perceive the world through our five separate senses but with our bodies as a whole (1999, 11). Ree explores "the obvious assumption (shared by philosophers and children, poets, scientists and inventors) that all our perceptions can be traced back to several supply-routes, namely the five senses, each conceived as a separate conduit giving access to different qualities of the real world" (8).

The body was the first target. It was beaten with flat hands, fists, boots, truncheons, whips, iron bars, fortified hoses, and a range of other objects. Beating accompanied, it would seem, every interaction between authority and suspect: it punctuated torture sessions and frequently formed part of everyday experience for those held in police station cells or prisons. There are very few cases in which it was alleged by the security forces that the suspect was armed, and I am not drawing on any of those here. The person being beaten was often handcuffed and in leg irons and in a confined space with two, three, or more security force members present. Or he or she was simply dominated by the size, strength, authority, and arms of the officer or officers. I have used pseudonyms for the young in the testimonies because I did not work with them or with those who testified on their behalves and because the subjects of the accounts are young and may not, later, care to have had accounts of their treatment offered to a wider public. It is for that reason that I have also given pseudonyms to those named as having hurt them.

TOUCH

Touch entails an intimate relation to the world and is connected to the primacy of doing over contemplation, a particular kind of doing that reveals the vulnerability of the self to the world. For Levinas, touch is a metaphor for the impingement of the world as a whole upon subjectivity (quoted in Jay 1994, 557–558). It is the vulnerability of touch that is exploited in its violation. Ree, writing about his childhood, says, "And touch seemed to me the central kind of sensation, as well as the most reliable and realistic" (1999, 18).

Onele testified at a TRC hearing about his treatment by the police. Twenty young people were arrested by officers with guns during the State of Emergency in 1986. He was fourteen years old at the time. He was hit on the back of his head with a handgun and fell unconscious. After having been held in the police station for three weeks, he was taken alone to an office and asked if he knew his father. He denied knowing him because his father was an activist, and he feared that he could be made to reveal details about his father's actions if their kinship was known. He said:

> I denied all these things and they beat me up, klapped me, they kicked me
> and I denied all the time they forced me—there was a drawer—they put my
> penis and my testicles into a drawer, it was the first time I . . . of my private
> parts. I went unconscious; I woke . . . [in] the cell.

He and several others were kept naked in a cell for a month. At the same hearing, two others, one of whom was fifteen years old at the time of the incident, spoke of having been tortured in the same manner. They were accused of having been involved in public violence. At the time that the evidence was given, the police officers involved were still living in the area.

SMELL

People's sense of smell was deliberately assailed in prison. Toilet buckets were kept in the cell, infrequently cleaned, and not always properly washed. Inadequate provision was made for washing the body or clothes. One young boy was not allowed to wash his clothes, bloodied from his having been beaten, for three months. Vusi spoke at a HRV hearing about an incident that happened when he was fifteen years old and in standard six at school. Police interrupted a discussion between parents, teachers, and school children at the school. The police insisted that the meeting be moved to the town hall, and transportation was organized for the move. There was not enough room in the vehicles provided, so some school children walked. While walking, they passed a man whom they identified as being from the

"Special Branch" (a security force officer) who was holding a *sjambok* (a rubber whip). He forced the twelve boys at gunpoint into a clinic, where they were told to wait until a van came to transport them to the police station. While waiting, they were taunted about a sticker one of them had, bearing a picture of Matthew Goniwe, who was one of four leading activists who had been brutally murdered—it was widely believed he had been killed by security force members, but this was only established after 1994. The officer asked, "Is this Matthew Goniwe? How is he related to you?" The young boy replied, "He is my brother," and the officer asked, "Where is he?" The boy replied, "He is dead." It was brave of him to claim brotherhood with the activist and to admit that he knew he was dead.

There were many police at the station. The boys were accused of having set the clinic on fire. A policeman said, "We are going to put these children straight because they don't listen." They were terrorized and beaten from 11:00 a.m. to 4:00 p.m. At one point, a black policeman called John stood at the cell door drinking guava juice. Vusi was called forward and told: "Here is Ali-Ali standing here." John was a boxer and well known in the area—the reference was to Mohammed Ali. John poured juice over Vusi's head, and then he and another policeman took him to the toilet. John hit him with his fist, he fell, and the other man kicked him. Vusi told the Commissioners that "John said, 'I think we are slow, let's take this person and make this person drink water from this toilet tub.' And then he held me by the waist saying that I was stubborn and they forced me into the tub—toilet tub. And I suffocated and he forced me and I tried—they kicked me and he force me down saying that I was going to stop being stubborn." They took him to dirty water outside the cell, beat him, and again tipped him head first into the water. Eventually one said, "Let's forgive him." Vusi: "Then they said, 'Let's take him to show to the other people.' And the cell was full of water, they asked me to sit down and they said they were not through with him—they were—with me they were coming back."

At the end of the day, they were threatened then released and forced to run back to their home area, and, as they ran, they were followed by a police van. The slowest runner was beaten. As they approached home, they encountered a group of people who were setting out in search of them.

Vusi named the three policemen involved in beating them, and when the Commissioner leading the testimony asked if he had laid any charges against them, he replied that there was no point in laying charges with those who had assaulted someone, especially as they were friends with the local doctors, and if one complained one would not be treated. Vusi no longer hears well and still fears the policemen. John, at the time of the hearing, was still in the local police service. Vusi's request from the Commission was for money to obtain a driver's license, as he was unemployed and wanted to seek employment as a driver.

HEARING

Being forced to hear one's involuntary screams of pain; others' cries; shocking, crude abuse of one's mother; shots whizzing past the ears as one stands blindfolded, fooled into thinking one is hearing people being executed in the bush; hearing a generator starting up, knowing its purpose is to deliver electrical shocks to one's body, sometimes to one's ears; hearing dogs bark and being told that they would be set on one's private parts; listening for the jangling of keys with the knowledge that one is to be collected for another torture session; hearing disinformation being fielded to one and not always knowing if it was a lie—a father's death? a friend's betrayal? a lover's rape? There are experiences that testify to each. And more.

In testimony after testimony before the Commission, people, especially young men, said that their hearing had been impaired. Blows with fists and instruments: not once but again and again, often day after day. Many cite their inability to hear and their feelings of dizziness as reasons for having dropped out of school and for being unemployed. One example came from Cebo's testimony at a hearing. A security force officer known as "Twice" arrested him at his home at midnight, addressing him as "Mandela's child." He was handed over to the police in Kimberley, where a white officer asked, "'Who are you?'" Cebo replied:

> "I am Cebo." And he slapped me on my ear and he said: "If I speak Afrikaans with you, you don't have to speak English with me." He wanted me to speak Afrikaans with him . . . and he told me that he had heard from Twice that I'm a clever boy [from a small town] and that I've been sent to [a larger town] so that he can work with [i.e., on] me. They assaulted me with fists, they kicked me and I fell to the ground. They didn't ask me anything, they didn't tell me what do they—what did they want. He said to me, "Right Cebo, tell me what

do you do [in your town]?" I said to him, "There is nothing more that I will tell you. I am a scholar." They left me. They went to Bongani. I was sitting there on the bench, whilst sitting I heard from the other room Bongani crying and I realised that they were assaulting him.

Cebo was kept in prison for three months. After his release, he was harassed and threatened and had to leave home for Johannesburg. He is deaf in one ear.

The chapter so far has taken accounts of the suffering from the Commission's hearings. The narratives represent one form of documenting the experiences of the young living under conditions of conflict. The last section of the chapter examines the means used by the Commission to record the recent past as it concerns people they categorized as victims. Ninety percent of the data on which the Commission relied in determining whether to grant reparations to victims was garnered from the two forms that those who sought to tell their stories were asked to complete. The *Report* affirms that findings were made on the basis of the statements, corroborating evidence, and the balance of probabilities, and it admits that corroborating evidence "proved one of the greatest challenges faced by the Commission . . . [it] was an extremely difficult and time-consuming task" (1: 142–143). There were two objectives in collecting the data: to make defensible findings and to hold to "a moral and therapeutic process." In the text, it is written that "sometimes the effort to satisfy one objective made it more difficult to attain the other" (1:144). Statement takers were vital in the collection of data (see 1:396–398 on their training and the problems faced).

Forms

The Commission's database on human rights violations was founded on two forms that applicants completed. The main reason for documenting violations was the desire to record the truth about what had happened in the recent past and thereby facilitate the setting aside of that past to clear the way for the task of nation building. In particular, the Commission aimed at initiating the process of making adequate and fair reparation and rehabilitation to those victims of past violations; of acknowledging the pain, anguish, and loss they had suffered; and maintaining that an important element of justice is restoration, restitution, and reparation. Victims were declared as such on the basis of an application made only through a "Designated Reparation Statement Taker" (DRST, hereafter statement takers) or an organization contracted for the purpose. On the basis of the application, which consisted initially of a form and supporting documentation, where available, persons were declared to be "victims" if they had experienced harm in the form of physical or mental injury, emotional suffering, pecuniary loss, and/or substantial impairment of human rights. Statement takers were remunerated.

The Commission firmly stated that respondents would not be asked questions that could stir painful memories and result in distress unless they were accompanied by trained statement takers. The initial plan was to require that only one form needed to be completed by each person who sought to have his or her story told. Toward the end of the collection process, another form was added. The initial form was distributed, and over twenty-one thousand statements were gathered, on the basis of which some nineteen thousand persons were awarded "victim" status. Each was required to fill in a second form on the basis of which reparations would be granted. The figures in the *Report* are derived from the data thus acquired.

What follows is a critique of the method of documentation. In offering it, my intentions are to wonder how to improve methods of recording young people's suffering and to contribute to the analysis of the process, so that it may be improved on when and as this model of a truth commission is replicated.

While working in Zwelethemba, I was drawn into investigating pain despite having had no intention of doing so. My earlier study of ex–political prisoners had given me more descriptions of pain than I thought I needed for my purposes. Besides, the Commission was documenting violations, and I did not wish to intrude. My interest was in young activists' induction, action, techniques of survival, political consciousness, and so on. However, I was drawn in by members of the community and by the fourteen young men in the study. I helped people fill in the forms at their request or at the request of the local statement taker. I learned a great deal in doing so and ought to have known that the question of pain could not be ignored.

Most of the first forms that I helped others fill out were accounts of young people's activism and the pain they endured in consequence. Xolile Dyabooi had appeared at the Worcester HRV hearing, and he placed pressure on his former comrades to give statements, as they had made sacrifices and deserved reparations. He brought me into the process, and, with the permission of a Commissioner, I filled in forms with twenty young former activists, including eight from our group. Four others in the group had already filled in the form (three of whom had given public statements), and two did not wish to apply.

There was one rather remarkable scene. Fourteen young people and I were gathered on a Saturday morning in Amos Khomba's house to fill in the initial TRC application form. Each person had been an activist in the 1980s in Zwelethemba, some as leaders. Some could not write at all or not well enough to complete the forms, and two were unable to frame stories coherent enough for Xolile and I to be able to assist them. There was a cheerful atmosphere, and gradually people called across the room to one another, asking for details of maltreatment, even torture, that they had experienced together or in adjoining cells. There was humor and teasing in the exchanges and surprisingly graphic descriptions of experiences. It was the only time that I heard a discussion of pain outside our group, and the first time among men and women.

It was a very difficult task to move from one to another, asking for details of their suffering in order to frame them concisely into a few sentences, to fit into the allocated spaces on the forms. By the early afternoon, I was troubled by my appointed role as the scribe of pain. We had shared cool drinks and lunch, and the television had become the center of everyone's attention, as an Africa Cup soccer match between the South African and Egyptian teams was being broadcast. Most people had completed their forms, but a few still required assistance. I sat with one of the young men, writing about an incident of torture before summarizing it to slot onto the page. His eyes were glued to the television set. He had described his arrest with a group of comrades by the police and their maltreatment at the police station. From there, they were shackled together, forced into a van, and driven to the banks of the Breede River. They were chased and thrown into the river, still shackled together, and *sjambokked*. As he was describing the scene, he leapt to his feet, shouting along with the others in glee over the scoring of a goal by the national team.

"Yebo! Hayi! Yo yo yo!" He sat down again, eyes glued to the box. I said, "And then?" "They took us out of the river, removed the shackles and led us, one by one, over a small hill where a generator had been switched on. We could see nothing, but we could hear the person scream as electrical shocks ran through his wet body." Another goal. Again he stood to shout and whistle. He sat down, and I said, "And then?" So we progressed. South Africa won.

To indicate the extent of physical and psychological suffering that people in the room had endured, I shall tell of another incident involving Amos, in whose house we met that day. One often blunders in the field, and this is an account of a blunder that I committed. Fiona Ross and I had organized a three-day workshop for the women with whom she was working and the men with whom I was working. The twenty-four men and women had fought beside one another in Zwelethemba in the 1980s. We went to a guest farm not far from Zwelethemba, a very beautiful and rather exclusive place nestled in a vineyard against the Hottentots Holland Mountains. The owner was a retired senior executive of an insurance society, and he did his best to hide his surprise at the composition of our group and to be courteous to us all. There were many funny scenes. He elaborately taught some of the men how to play billiards: they listened politely then beat him soundly at the game. On the first evening, he welcomed us with a long speech on the new South Africa, in response to which Isaac asked, "Tell me, sir, what do you know about poverty?" I nudged Eric with my elbow and whispered, "Save the situation." Eric stepped forward and gave a model response, incorporating a mild rebuke to Isaac and a gracious acceptance of the host's welcome.

On the third day, we were deep in discussion about the effects of terror when two young people arrived to lead a session on the psychological healing of trauma. They had come at my invitation. The men had recently expressed the need for support in handling the effects of their trauma, some of which, they suspected, were leading them to abuse others, and they had requested that I invite the administrators of a Cape Town center to send a psychologist to conduct a session with the former activists, so that they could better understand what means of healing were on offer and what they entailed.

The center sent two young people. They joined us and began their session. They soon set the first task. They said: "Tell us about an incident in which you or someone close to you was hurt." After a moment, three of the men stood up and left the room. I followed and joined them as they leaned against the lintel of a large fireplace. They were upset. I apologized. Amos said that, on being asked the question, what immediately came to mind was a scene in which he was being tortured while a tape was playing of his sister screaming while she was being tortured. He cried and left the room. On his return, we held each other.

I returned to the session and made some interjections, as I found the process unsuited to our needs. The psychologists were angry with me and felt that I had set them up. Later I apologized. The blunder was mine.

On May 6, 1998, Archbishop Desmond Tutu, chairperson of the Commission, published a statement on the posting of notices to the first seven hundred people who had been officially declared victims, informing them that they were eligible to apply for reparation. The notices were sent out with reparation application forms. It had been two years since the first statements had been taken. In the interim, over twenty-one thousand statements had been collated, and the accounts of violation individually corroborated. Over 90 percent of those who had testified had been declared victims. Tutu's statement invited recipients to apply for interim reparations that he described as one-off payments, normally a maximum of R2,000 (www.truth .org.za, March 31, 1998).

My attention was first drawn to the existence of the form when later that month Ntando asked me to help him fill it in. The week before, Ntando had said to me, "This is my twelfth anniversary." Stupidly, I had said, "What do you mean? You are not married." He replied, "Since I first sat in this wheelchair." Twelve years since a policeman had shot and paralyzed him. Ntando had filled out some sections of the form. I read what he had written as he watched me. I was distressed to see how little of the pain he had suffered, the poverty and lack of care he had endured, and the loss in terms of education and employment that had resulted from his paralysis he had been able to record in the small spaces allocated on the form (at the end of the form there was a statement saying that extra pages could be used if required, but I never came across anyone who chose that course). Having told his story in public, it did not matter in terms of his access to reparations that his completion of the second form did not give the full story.

Others asked me to help them to fill out the forms, and so did the statement taker assigned by the Commission to assist people in Zwelethemba. I filled in twenty in the community; each one took two to three hours to complete. It was a deeply distressing task because of the nature of the form (which is critiqued below) and because many of those whom I helped were not well known to me. And since it was important, as we then believed, to describe the violations endured accurately and comprehensively in order to secure the appropriate amount of reparation, I had to request details of suffering without having established relationships of trust and empathy. Most of the people whom I assisted could not read or write in English, or not well enough to handle a complex form. I wrote to the Commissioners and spoke to Archbishop Tutu to voice my distress at the pain the process was causing. It represented, I thought, the micromechanics of control in its harshest form. Some of the grounds for my objection follow.

The Commission had made much of its sensitivity in assuring the public that no one would be asked to remember his or her pain without being accompanied by a trained statement taker. Imagine having gone through the process of recall in order to submit the initial application and then, a year later, receiving in the mail an eleven-page document, written only in English, that, once more, requested full details of the trauma or loss experienced. Imagine sitting alone and confronting questions like this one:

"Did Gross Human Rights Violations hurt your feelings?"

I wanted to know why the details of trauma and people's feelings about it were being asked for again and why a new set of forms had been sent out with the requirement that they be filled in and returned within fifteen days, when statement takers had not been marshaled to accompany and assist them. Many respondents were reluctant to seek help for a number of reasons, including the desire for privacy, the fear of recounting moments of humiliation before another, and the wish to defend against envy, should reparations follow. There were nine pages on the form to be completed, yet even the single-page-long national census form had caused problems. It was written only in English, and the responses were required in English—there are eleven official languages in South Africa. On the last page of the form was a note to the effect that one could write requesting that a form in another language be sent, yet the instructions were to return the form within fifteen days. The time limit meant that, for example, a woman could not wait for a husband's return from his place of work on a farm or in a city. It was written in an absurdly complex style: for example, the respondent, oneself, was referred to as "deponent/applicant"; references were made to "spouse(s)"; one was told to initial every page—nobody in Zwelethemba or in the department of African languages at the University of Cape Town could give me a Xhosa translation of the word "initial." There was an instruction to have the completed form signed by a commissioner of oaths, and the only ones available in Zwelethemba were the police, and it was possible that the very person who had tortured one or shot one's son would be on duty in the police station. There was no instruction to sign the form in front of the commissioner of oaths, so that the attempt at meeting a legal requirement was half-hearted. I spent hours with respondents waiting in weekend queues at the police station and instructing the police about initialing each page.

The depiction given on the form of "a relative and/or a dependent of a victim" was impossible to apply to the complex nature of people's kinship and other ties. The layout of the form was very hard to negotiate. Many questions lacked clarity. One, for example, asked: "After the violation, were you wrongly accused and/or given a criminal record? If yes, please give details." What is an applicant to make of the term "wrongly accused"? Yes, I was wrongly accused of fighting apartheid? No, I was not wrongly accused of trying to cross the border into Botswana to join the MK? Many detainees, especially young ones, were not told whether they had been formally charged or whether the charge constituted a formal record. None of us in Zwelethemba was given access to police records in order to check them. Besides, records throughout the nation had been shredded. The form did not elaborate on the reasons as to why a respondent might wish to have his or her name expunged from the criminal record, and thus responses to the question "Would you like to have your name cleared?" could not be made in the light of possible legal repercussions. Few knew that a criminal record could hinder certain job applications or requests for visas to visit certain countries.

The question supposes that there had been only one violation and one consequence in terms of formal charge and/or criminal record. Many activists were detained again and again. Statements made under torture were inadmissible, but many testimonies given before the court about torture were dismissed. It would take careful legal argument to contend that many criminal records were, therefore, false. It is hard to see exactly what the intention behind the question was—to clear people's criminal records on the basis of these statements? What difference did either the nature of the accusation or the criminal record make to reparations? If it was simply a matter of collating data, then it was ill conceived. Respondents were asked to attach supporting documents to their forms. Documents are kept safe with difficulty in areas like Zwelethemba, and they are precious. To make a bureaucratic call for them was cruel. The form did not say that authorized copies would be acceptable. Nor was a promise of their return made. The request stirred anxiety about not being able to substantiate statements.

There were other questions on the form that elicited complex responses, ones impossible to simplify and reduce to a few phrases. I said to a woman whose son had been shot and killed by the police, "I am sorry to put this to you, but there is a question on the form that asks how your feelings were hurt and your emotions affected." She let out an excruciating wail and cried. Another woman whose son had been shot and killed responded to the same question by looking up at a dovecote that had belonged to him and saying, "Every morning I look at his doves, and my pain is the same as on the day he died." An older man told me about his involvement in burning pass books in the 1960s and how the police had taken him, tied him to a tree, and beaten him with a pole until he urinated blood. They ensured that he was dismissed from his work, and he never secured full-time employment again, despite being a skilled mechanic. He said, "I used to be so proud. Since then I have never held up my head in dignity."

Just three months after Amos Dyantyi died as a result of the torture he had endured, I assisted his widow and relatives with the form, and I was so distressed by further details they revealed about his experiences and their own that I failed to express my sorrow and shame to them.

Two of the Commissioners discussed my reactions with me. Their responses were different. When asked why the Commission had found it necessary to rekindle past suffering in this way, when the data had already been gathered, one replied: "It has been inadequately gathered, that is why. The form had to be compiled as a legally Promulgated Form; therefore, in large part, its character. The process has been driven by the Finance Department, who are terrified of fraud." The other Commissioner admitted that the initial application form had provided the Commission "with very little to go by in terms of descriptions of the impact of violations," and "evidence, proof" was required for the database. Statement takers had, it was said, "undermined questions of impact"; therefore, they had to be asked again. I was invited to send in a fax about my concerns. I did so and received a reply from the chairperson of the Reparations and Rehabilitation Committee.

I called a lawyer working for the Commission and said that, as I understood it, in international law, once a state declares a person a "victim" of gross human rights violations, then reparation is owed, if so promulgated, *despite* what the "victim" feels about the violation; therefore, why is the form required, especially as presently designed? The reply was: "You are absolutely correct. It's just for our data as well and to get it into our records. It is not to do with the legality." I asked, "Please explain to me the purpose of a legally promulgated form." The lawyer answered, "I have to go to a meeting. The head of the division will call you." I received no call.

Archbishop Tutu told me that the form was a *fait accompli*.

Assurances were given that money had been raised for field workers who would help respondents when future batches were posted.

Mechanisms of Control

Michel Foucault put forward methodological precautions in regard to his investigation of war and the analysis of political power (2003b, 25–34). They relate to the examination of mechanisms of control at the extremities of power, at the point where it becomes capillary; at the constitution of multiple bodies as subjects; at the relaying of power in the face of which individuals are never inert or consenting; at the manner in which control comes into play at the lowest levels, through local agents, and is then invested or annexed into the general and economic levels; and, finally, at the actual instruments that form and accumulate knowledge. I suggest that the infliction of pain on children and youth was used as a mechanism of control in the closely surveilled urban areas set aside as locations in which the disenfranchised people of the rural towns and the capital city of the Western and Northern Cape had to live. In Worcester, the power to punish was embodied in local, regional institutions: in the police cells and prisons and through the intricate web of security forces, whose personnel traveled through the veins and arteries from capillary to heart, conducting torture sessions, recruiting informers, and sharing information about political activists' connections and international techniques for the infliction of pain and the spreading of terror. Accounts of suffering implicated some employees in the offices of magistrates, social workers, hospitals, and factories, as well as some doctors, farmers, and business leaders. Those in control anticipated little effective counteraction or reprimand. Which is not to say that there was neither active nor passive objection to brutal domination from people at every level and in almost every institution, just that the immunity guaranteed by the body of the state was strong.

The apartheid regime concentrated with clear intent on constituting subjects preferably in line with, or alternatively in obedience to, its ideology. Punishment of those who stepped out of line was, in Zwelethemba, meted out with brutality both cleverly targeted and randomly applied. Infinitesimal mechanisms of resistance were evident in actions like those of Amos Khomba and his friends, who sought to claim the right to read books in the Worcester Public Library. Their headmaster's scolding at their presumption helped to crush that moment of resistance but not the revolt that they soon joined (see interlude 1).

It is hard to square the granting of amnesty against the details of cruelty consciously, systematically, repetitively, widely, unmercifully directed by government servants toward the young. This chapter has detailed some of the consequences that those who refused to submit to power (even as children) suffered at the hands of those who consented to the exercise of power in the attempt to control any revolt. The attacks on the senses are an aspect of that dynamic. It seems to be a technique widely used in recent wars (see Lutz 2001, 227).

Most of the young with whom I talked spoke about their pain with "laconic understatement." Indeed, few found words to describe their pain, yet much was expressed in gesture, look, and hesitation. There was a gradual acknowledgment of pain's effect over time. Some regret and anger was voiced, though surprisingly little: there was anger about the lack of skill training or employment opportunities as recompense for opportunities lost and some distress at false claims to histories of activism made by younger, better educated people. There was a wry recognition that heroism's shelf life is short. Pain was not a central trope; nor were its effects absent. We know that it is terrible enough in itself to call for the unremitting denunciation of injustice (Sebald 2003, 157). At the hands of the police, the young were taught fear—

its "sheer dread" (Daudet 2002, 9). Pain invaded their being and, for many, it increased as it was inflicted hour after hour, day after day, detention after detention, and its sorrow grew as damage done undermined thought and action, with limbs lost, hearing diminished, sight gone, concentration shattered. Indemnity should not be granted to those who hurt the young as it was to the men who poisoned and murdered Simphiwe Mthimkulu. Against the young who violate others, the course of law should be followed.

Many therapies hold that talking heals, and the Commission affirmed that view; Commissioners often told testifiers that, having spoken, healing would begin. But recapitulation of terrible pain can take one to the "borders of what language can convey" (Sebald 2003, 153). Peter Handke writes about the nameless, "speechless moments of terror" (2002, 33–34). Perhaps Walter Benjamin is right: "Language shows clearly that memory is not an instrument for exploring the past but its theatre" (1979, 314). Perhaps the Commissioners knew that. For Talal Asad, "Pain . . . is, literally, a scandal" (1997, 290). Its results can be social death. Which brings me to the final question about what the analysis of pain can contribute. Four things, perhaps. It can encourage cognizance of the way in which new wars devastate the ground of all being in targeting civilians, including children. It can provide warrants for the fact of harm's effects without requiring a theory to predict and explain those effects. It can confirm commitment to the maintenance of "unbreakable law and unbridgeable right" (Foucault 1999, 134). Finally, it can make experience capable of public decipherment (Sebald 2003, 4).

Propensity to Harm

Much has been written about the seeming ease with which people perpetrate harm when the order in accord with which they usually live breaks down. Sigmund Freud suggests, among a slew of reasons, that a government, in defending against challenges that threaten the state, can turn to illegality, make use of the violence in law, implement censorship, enforce secrecy, demand extremes of obedience and sacrifice from its citizens, and permit itself any injustice, including lies and treachery. In consequence, a community "ceases to accuse," so abolishing the suppression of evil desires, and people can then "commit deeds of cruelty, cunning, treachery and barbarism" in excess (2005, 173–174). Apart from threats to the state of peace (conceivable only in theory) that originate from other states and between communities, he identifies a threat that lies within a community, for it incorporates unequally powerful elements from the outset—men and women, parents and children—as well as those subjected for one reason or another by the dominant (224).

Hannah Arendt describes the collapse of order under Hitler in Germany that led to an "almost universal breakdown of personal judgement" (2003, 24). She lays emphasis on the cruelty of bureaucracy, the complete reversal of legality, the criminality embraced, the utter consistency and care with which the regime built itself, the early commission of atrocities to spread fear and terror, all done within the frame of a legal order. Of concern here is that she identifies the failure of many to stand against the new regime as having been attributable, in part, to the absence of clearly stated (rather than implicit) categories and general rules for moral behavior: the human mind is unwilling to face realities that contradict totally its framework of reference (25, 37). She raises two questions to do with personal responsibility under dictatorship: In what ways did those who refused to consent differ from those who did? And what made those who participated in the new regime's reversal of legality do so? (43).

Her answer to the first question is that those who refused to participate in terrible acts did so because they would not then be able to live with themselves; that is, they judged by themselves, they thought. The answer to her second question is that such people saw themselves as having acted in obedience to their superiors and the laws of the land. She declares this argument to be fallacious, as obedience does not equate to consent, and governments rest on consent. To refuse to obey is to withdraw tacit consent to the constitution, and, she suggests, if enough people do so, it can be an effective weapon. She declares that "there is no such thing as obedience in political and moral matters"—it is rather a matter of giving or withholding support (44–48).

The situation in South Africa was different, but thousands of the young who were on the cusp of adulthood refused to consent to be governed under apartheid rules. It took courage, and the costs were high.

In retaliating against youth in revolt, the state used pain as its main mechanism for ensuring control within the borders of South Africa. The young were targeted both with microscopic intent and indiscriminate reach. The mechanics intruded in the everyday and transported the ordinary into the extraordinary. The question of evil inevitably arises. Susan Nieman analyzes how evil has been approached in modern thought and finds it is understood to have no intrinsic property (2002, 9) and no hierarchy of quantity or cruelty (255). We can, she says, give no adequate account of it or general formula for it. Modern evil has shattered our trust in nature, theodicies, and our ability to make sense of evil. It has uncovered the paucity of our theoretical resources for approaching evil (300). In Nieman's opinion, Hannah Arendt believed that evil can be comprehended though not explained, and it could be overcome if we acknowledge that it begins in trivial and insidious steps. It overwhelms us in ways that are minute (301). If that is true, then causing pain to the young ought to raise the red flag.

Heroism and sacrifice were barely mentioned during the recall of the past by the men in MAZE, except in relation to national leaders. Their talk hinged more on the labor involved in continuing to protest despite the realization of their own and their comrades' frailty before the forces arrayed against them. They placed their trust in what they knew of, or believed about, the mass movement and the combined power of national and international organizations. Some of the work involved self-care, despite the constraints of silence and the lack of medical attention, and close observation of their colleagues for signs of disintegration. None came through unscathed: some forged strong subjectivities; others seem to have retreated behind the lines they drew around themselves. During the time of conflict there was not much scope for forgetfulness. Living was a deliberate business that demanded constant monitoring of their own and others' moods and patterns of behavior. They relied on many people for their safety and nurturance, yet they had to be wary and keep their antennae tuned to rumor, especially for items of disinformation. The concern of kin and lovers had to be kept at a distance. Advantage was taken of the admiration of young women and later remembered with both pleasure and shame. Some forged close links to older women leaders, which mothers frequently resented, because they suspected that the women recklessly encouraged their sons to enter dangerous arenas. A few of the women who stood thus accused reported to me that they had seen themselves as having offered protection and succor to the young.

In the aftermath, the men increasingly sought information about psychological support as they attempted to come to terms with the effects that, they suspected, past suffering was having on their lives, particularly on their relationships. Long-term consequences of harm done were apparent, I thought, in the expressions and gestures of some of them, and most of them came to analyze aspects of their behavior in the light of what they had endured. None had received sustained care except for physical ailments. Which is not to say that the consequences were necessarily disabling. Ntando's paralysis was deeply disabling, and Zandisele's loss of a leg changed his life but did not undermine it. There were no overt signs of maladjustment in our group meetings or in their behavior toward and cooperation with me. Many of them identified poverty and the absence of training and job opportunities as among their most pressing problems. Some of them were relatively successful (though not to the satisfaction of each one of them) in securing jobs, while two of them obtained university degrees (see the epilogue).

In response to the question raised at the beginning of the chapter, with regard to the limits of institutional inquiries about the harm done to the young, I shall put down the following thoughts. The experiences of youth in conflict are not acknowledged in detail and formally entered into the archive because it is not in the interests of those in authority to do so. It is easier to conform to commonly held views than to document with detail the lives of those who have no platform from which to speak with authority.

As I understand it, young leaders of the youth (though not all, not everyone) in Zwelethemba entered the conflict for carefully considered reasons. They fought in full cognizance of the possible consequences and in the hope of seeing change in the near future. They endured suffering over time and saw it fold the extraordinary into the ordinary. Some of the suffering was bearable, some unbearable. They formulated and tried to hold to a series of tactics (with regard to the aims of the liberation organizations but with scant direction from them) that included a set of rules tied to an ethic of behavior and an attempt to obtain self-mastery in relation to the endurance of pain.

I come, again and again, up against the response to my understanding that says: but the youth (somewhere else, Soweto, say) did not behave like that—they were unruly, destructive, had no moral compunction, undermined others' attempts to conduct orderly lives, and contributed little to the demise of apartheid. Someone else turns my spade.

THREE

Turning and Being Turned

Turning and turning in the widening gyre

— WILLIAM BUTLER YEATS

The trope (from the Greek *tropos*, "turn") in this chapter is of turning, doubling, in an encapsulated place where moves spiral around one another: a turning away, against; a doubling of pain; a ring of mountains hemming in the valley, the prison cells, the proscribed network of friends; the local fight. Betrayal shoots through the stories. It is enacted. It brushes, clears, maneuvers, undermines action. It surprises, being neither neat nor easily categorized. The chapter is about betrayal as an indicator of the nature of the context within which a stand was made. It is about protest under close surveillance against powerful odds, with minimal resources and dire consequences. It depicts the everyday nature of the lives of youth in revolt against the government, from the base of a small rural town. The chapter touches on a specific aspect of a state's tactics in controlling revolt; on the character of youths' resistance, their resources, the obstacles they faced, their experiences, and the consequences. The story of twins is told to reflect on issues of self-governance that entailed the holding of relationships under conditions of deep crisis, when choice, blame, guilt, forgiveness, revenge, and fidelity were matters of daily concern. Their story is supplemented by incidents of betrayal experienced by others in the group and a glance at a summary of betrayal in the TRC's *Report* (2:555–582). The young, in accord with the aims of the liberation organizations, determined to cause the apartheid regime's demise. A great obstacle to the success of their endeavors, apart from the power of the state and the reach of its order, was betrayal—the treachery of another.

Scanlon writes about the importance of conditions in determining how we live in relation to one another (1998, 263). He emphasizes the need for a society to offer its members "the possibility of a satisfactory life within the law," consisting of the provision of education, the dissemination of information about the law, and the maintenance of social and economic conditions (264). He testifies "to the value people set on the belief that their lives and institutions are justifiable to others. Of course one could say that what people care about . . . is that their institutions be just and their lives not be morally corrupt" (163). He makes the claim "that what is particularly moving about charges of injustice and immorality is their implication for our relations with others, our sense of justifiability to or estrangement from them" (163). Under apartheid, the people of Zwelethemba were fully aware of the injustice and immorality of the systems of control imposed on them. In their charges of injustice there is the sense of a failed accountability to those pressing the charge. A sense, too, that society or something equivalent owes them an account of why these things happen. In the sense of Scanlon's "estrangement," there seemed to be a feeling that the world they lived in placed them in at least two moral universes.

Nana describes conditions in Worcester as the root of the rebellion:

In essence, our experiences of poverty in the townships militarized us. . . . We were ready to receive radical ideas about society. [The literature on apartheid had already described it] as an inhuman system, a heresy biblically. It was seen as a crime against humanity. It was seen as a Frankenstein, as [Archbishop Desmond] Tutu used to say. It was seen as a plague. It was seen like a cancer, a disease in society that had to be taken out. So, therefore, it was easy for us to act upon it. If apartheid is this thing that is not human, that is obstructing human beings from enjoying full human life, [then] this thing has got to be eliminated.

The young men in MAZE impressed me with their cognizance of the complexity of moral choices that their political engagement made them face. I cannot say who among them maintained full regard for the other: perhaps nobody did. I shall examine here the pervasiveness of forces that undermined loyalty and trust; the realization of the likelihood of betrayal; and the glue that nevertheless held many relationships and obligations fast.

Friendship, Trust, and Uneasy Relationships

I have described in chapter 2 the nature of the revolt in Zwelethemba given its geographic isolation and exposure to close surveillance by the security forces. As I see it, the young who had leadership at the local level thrust upon them drew on a combination of trust in others and self-reliance. In their need for protection and for the assistance of others, like all resistance fighters, they formulated terms to guide the conduct of relationships and an ethic of political behavior. Given the conditions in which they lived in Zwelethemba, there was little else on which they could depend. Both political action and safety called for the establishment of sets of relationships, based on political commitment, among peers (initially at school), within families, across the layers of local and national political leadership, among neighbors, and between the generations of old and new activists. While their revolt pitched activist youth into conflict with their elders to some extent, there was also a careful passing on of political attitudes, understandings, and commitment from generation to generation (see Ross and Reynolds 1999). Generational divisions and antagonisms existed alongside close interaction, deep care, and active support.

Each layer of leadership inducted candidates from among younger cohorts. From 1980 on, one layer after another was wiped off the scene—killed, imprisoned, maimed, chased into banishment or underground or into exile—and their juniors were pushed into the limelight or, rather, under the scrutiny of the security agents' gaze. Sometimes their apprenticeship was brief.

The young were stirred by the same fervor to eliminate apartheid as their elders had been, but, according to Nana, the 1980s were different:

> The generation of the 1980s was similar to that of 1976 but, in terms of the context in which they conducted themselves, 1976 caught the regime off

guard. In 1980 we faced a regime, the apartheid regime, that was fully prepared to face us. So they mobilized the white people to fight against us. Some young people were conscripted into the army and sent into the townships. The troops came to settle in the townships in order to quell the uprising, so now the townships were battlegrounds. . . . We were the ones who had to bear the brunt of all that repression . . . and there was an increase of military activity on the part of the liberation movement. . . . So the young people had to take it on themselves to liberate the country because our parents had really seen it all before. In 1960, in 1976, they saw how the apartheid repressive machinery [worked], and it [was] quite brutal. We were naïve and, luckily, because we were naïve, we were more prepared to take greater risks than others. And also we were carefree because most of us had never had any family responsibility like having children and so forth. So we were rather like free radicals.

Xolile describes the young leaders as *opstokers* (those who stir up trouble), yet, in the process, they discovered themselves. They were, he said, called in to solve a wide variety of problems as if they had the wisdom of elders. They learned from their failures and successes, changing their patterns of behavior in the process. According to Xolile, most were too young to analyze the process and, on that basis, make decisions about how to act. There was an old guard in Zwelethemba from whom they learned, but the most effective leadership at that time was drawn from among the youth. Xolile says, "We learned to survive collectively." Nana's description of being young and politically active is evocative, funny, ironic, and searing:

Our lifestyles were hectic because some of us had to make many sacrifices really; for example, I was a sports person. I still love soccer even though I no longer play it. I used to play soccer. One had to make a sacrifice to stop playing soccer and involve oneself in the struggle, and therefore I was lost to soccer. We made a lot of sacrifices like losing ourselves, like our youth. You're living that thing of having a carefree youthfulness, playing, and attending school and so forth. And also being a child again. You lost it in the heat of the struggle. You see, because you're now meddling in national affairs in the adult world. And your experiences in the struggle transformed your consciousness. You were no longer [going] to be a child again: even if you went back home, your parents would notice a change in you. You [would be more] mature than the rest of your brothers and sisters who were not involved in the struggle. We became rebellious even [in front of] our parents.

And it was difficult for our parents to control us because now our eyes had been opened, and we had bigger responsibilities, and we were daredev-

ils. We were the ones who were fearless in treading the ground where our
parents were afraid to tread. So now we [were] on a higher pedestal than our
own parents. If they admonish you for doing something [you taunt them] as
cowards. . . . . Meanwhile your parents, out of concern, are trying to show
you [that you must] be careful in your actions because they know the risks of
involving themselves in the struggle. . . . There was no middle ground. There
was no ground for bystanders. . . . And everyone—you [were] either with us
or against us. So you had to join us. Our parents had to join us, or else we
would label them lackeys of the system. And the consequences . . . were too
harsh.

And sometimes we had to be very protective. When you get involved as
an activist in struggle, you have to be extra careful. Trust no one. No one.
Including your own parents. Even your friend. You [were] the best person
to keep the secrets about yourself and your involvement in the struggle. . . .
We feared the enemy, but, at the same time, we challenged the enemy. We
realized that the enemy was shrewd and cunning. It could use the enormous
resources it had at its disposal to convert those who were amongst you to be
on the side of the enemy and to give information [about] you.

So in order to stop that from happening, you dare not tell your parents,
nor your brothers and sisters because you did not want them to inform on
you when you are in trouble, because the police will obviously go for your
family in search of information about you. If they [family members] did not
know your whereabouts, your activities in the struggle, they [would] not have
anything to say to the police. It will be better for the revolution than to be
betrayed by your own family. It was one way of protecting them.

But it was also a contradiction in terms. You expected them to protect
you, but at the same time you did not trust them enough to give them information about yourself, thinking that you are protecting them. It was a very
uneasy relationship. The struggle created an uneasy relationship between
those youth who were involved in it and their parents. The gap widened.
It lessened and closed if your parent was or [became] involved . . . and then
you [could] confide in that person. But if your parents were not involved in
the struggle it was difficult. So you [would] rather trust another person who
was involved . . . than your own parent, even though your mother [would]
tell you that, "I'm the one who will never betray you." You see. So it was a
difficult kind of situation.

In Zwelethemba, as in many other places to which Africans were confined, the strain between moral demands and personal relations was great—

the strings were taut, and they could snap. Under the circumstances, dependence on friends was tempered by the possibility of betrayal. Sociability posed risks in such a context where the stakes of loyalty were very high and stark; harsh action could be taken against someone who was close to an activist, whatever her or his political position or level of information was. For example, the "fact" of being a member of an activist's family exposed a mother to certain experiences, regardless of what she "knew." The opposite of trust was suspicion, and when passions ran very high, sometimes summary justice was dispensed. Sometimes people were punished for failing to support the fight against the government (refusing to boycott shops or continuing to drink at *shebeens* [beer halls]) or for actively promoting the interests of the regime (performing duties as appointed town councilors or working as paid informers). Harm done by activists to others in their communities has been written about and was aired in the Commission's hearings. Three people were "necklaced" in Zwelethemba (see chapter 2).

Here, though, I want to consider the nature of friendship under difficult conditions.

The young developed strong bonds as they entered politics, usually having been drawn in by classmates or slightly older boys at school. When leadership roles were assumed, the bonds were solidified, and trust was assumed to inform all interactions. Part of friendship was the nurturance of one another's talents and skills in, for example, learning how to deflect passions that quickly spread among crowds. Many activists thought that in the second half of the 1980s the country was on the verge of chaos and that their role was to hold a line of clear action and intention within the community. They knew that it could be dangerous to prevent people in crowds from venting anger, so they learned to use songs and humor to capture attention and to divert anger, and they would call for certain speakers known for their abilities to hold a crowd. The task in many crowd situations was to direct or deflect anger rather than to lead, and in order to achieve that, quick responses and firm support for one another were essential.

As a young leader, one had, I was told, to try to maintain a clear level of consciousness in order to be able to guide the struggle on an everyday basis. One had to face the fear of failure and of envying those who seemed to be more popular or more successful in balancing the demands of politics and school. Revolution was not an escape but an enhancement of possibilities, and, therefore, it required personal philosophical development to survive. The demands were difficult to meet. Signs of fatigue could quickly lead to failure. Idealism had to be matched with realism, pragmatism with ideology. The establishment of close links with others based on trust was a practical necessity. Familiarity with one another's weaknesses and strengths was accompanied by an intricate knowledge of the community.

There was opposition to leadership by the young from many angles. That, plus the concerted efforts of the security forces to break loyalty, undermine leadership, and craft complex nets of information collection (into which people were drawn or coerced as informers) ensured that trust was placed in few and, even then, cautiously. One of the men in our group is said by many others to have betrayed another member. Neither the one named as a betrayer nor the one said to have been betrayed talked about it. Indeed, eight of the fourteen are said to have been betrayed. I shall examine both what betrayal means under such conditions and young people's attitudes toward it.

In the interests of friendship and self-preservation, vigilance had to be maintained over one another's safety. When a colleague was thought to be in extreme danger, measures to protect, warn, and advise him or her were taken. Paulos was fanatically hated by the police, and vigilance on his behalf had to be shared. Some were told to go underground when the situation became too hot. Living within the law and acting against the law threw up paradoxical situations: for example, Edwin Rasmeni and his twin, Edward, were sent into hiding in Cape Town, but they had to return to Worcester to attend a court case relating to a previous charge and were arrested on a new charge when they appeared in court (their story is told below). Some of the leaders had, as one of the men politely phrased it, "social problems," by which I think he meant certain notions of grandiosity coupled with sexual indulgence and the consumption of beer in excess, which endangered them all.

A picture emerges of the young trying to sustain trust sufficient enough for the work of revolt. They had to live within the law while acting outside it. They had to balance their commitments to those among whom they lived in the ordinary ways of the everyday, knowing that it was through these others that the state attacked the resistance.

The security forces in Worcester were backed by a large state infrastructure of police, defense, and investigative machinery; vast resources; a legal armature; and a panoply of clandestine support systems. They had a wide network of informers at international, national, and local levels, and they had infiltrated the top of the resistance organizations. They had the cooperation of people who lived in the same communities as did the young protesters, people who were directly in their employ, for example, police officers, or those who were somehow obliged to the official bureaucracy, as were, for example, employees of the municipality: some of them were labeled collaborators by the youth. Temporary policemen, called *kitskonstabels*, were deployed after a brief and rudimentary training. They and sometimes other groups were transported from one region to another to mete out punishment to local troublemakers and to tamp down local protest. In the Boland, where most Africans spoke Xhosa, Zulu speakers were brought in, and their harsh methods of dealing with protesters stirred deep anger. People arrayed on the side of "law and order" (as defined by the government) used a variety of techniques to obtain information from and to warn and terrify activists and their followers, family members, friends, neighbors, teachers, and mentors. It was all a matter of turning the screw.

Security force members attempted to defuse local protest by gathering information, frightening people enough to keep them from becoming involved, and breaking or silencing activists. Their rationale was clear—to protect a democratically elected, white, Christian government. The local police were hampered by five factors. It was not possible to kill all the young people who were protesting against their predicament, as there were rather too many of them, and, I was told, the official policy was not to have to dispose of bodies. Nor was it possible to imprison, torture, or turn all of them, if only because, as the leaders were undermined or sentenced, others took their places. Besides, there were legal niceties to obey, including the requirement that charges should be laid after someone had been held in custody for a certain time, preventing the indefinite detention of people without a legal hearing at which evidence had to be produced to sentence and incarcerate detainees formally (in practice, many ruses were used to keep people in detention and to falsify evidence). The need to obtain evidence presumably exaggerated the importance placed on catching people with banned literature in their possession or with lists of members in banned organizations or minutes of their meetings. It was an odd game that both sides seemed destined to play: the search for records and the compulsion to compile them. A game of war. The search was for proof, and the compulsion had to do with the nature of the revolt, which depended on mass support and individual commitment, necessitating some of the paraphernalia of organization that bolstered identification, proved membership, and symbolized resistance. The players chased information and sought written evidence, even though they knew how deficient or ephemeral it probably was. (There is, perhaps, an irony in the effort and expense that officials of the apartheid regime expended in shredding thousands of documents before they were ousted.) The last of the five factors that hampered the local police was the existence of double agents, although the term seems too formal to apply to those who had access to information within the structures of local government, including the forces of law and order in Worcester who might have passed it on to local leaders. A few African members of the police who lived in Zwelethemba gave information to the young activists, even tipping them off about planned searches or raids. The activists named three whom they described as "good policemen." Some prison wardens came to admire their charges, carried messages for them, and brought them newspapers and parcels from home. Finally, there were those who watched and listened and passed information about the police to activists but who were paid no regard by the police, perhaps because they assumed that those subservient to them (cleaners, builders, gardeners, messengers) neither saw nor heard nor talked.

I want to emphasize the local character of the conflict between the youth and the police. Both had their tentacles into and drew support from a sphere beyond their territory, but the fight was corralled in the circle of mountains that cossets the beautiful, fertile valley of the Breede River. The police and their colleagues had access to detailed information about the residents and could ensure that they were cautioned or punished at school or that they lost their jobs. The jailers and the jailed, like the torturers and the tortured, came to know each other only too well; they carried an awareness of the other that could impinge on their emotions as their paths crossed in the small town. The only time I ever heard Nana express deep enmity toward anyone was against a man who tortured many of the young in Worcester, including him.

If, under torture, someone gave another's name to the police, in all likelihood the police already knew who was doing what at the various levels of organization and protest. Their most pressing search was for information about the few whom they suspected of belonging to secret cells of the liberation forces and who may have had access to details about arms stores and resistance operations. In the search, many people were hurt and terrified despite not knowing anything. Others were shamed and humiliated after having given information that they feared had led to activists being harmed, whereas they actually had, perhaps, revealed little or nothing new. Information was understood in certain ways, deployed in certain ways, withheld in certain ways, and it was on all of this that betrayal hinged. There were intricate flows of information and misinformation between activists and security forces, with diverse members of the community, and even kin, caught in the middle—and betrayal played a complex part in this overwritten text of local information. Families were jeopardized by activists as much as the latter were made vulnerable by family.

The local police had no easy task. The young learned, if they did not already, to hate them. Nana drew on revolutionary ideology in describing the propaganda that was sometimes used to recruit new members for the cause:

> And also it was the question of developing enough hatred for the system to want to change it. In the process of developing that hatred—because the system was manned (I don't know which word to use, because I have to be gender sensitive)—but the people who were servicing the apartheid administration, the police, the bureaucrats, really, had to be identified as people who were part of the problem. And we were seeing ourselves as part of the solution. And, therefore, in the process of building up a solid mass which can be dependable to make sure that the revolution succeeds, you had to have your own kind of propaganda, you see. So a discourse of revolution or some kind of way to . . . to . . . to build hegemony for the revolution project. So, in that sense, the energy had to be depersonified. When you saw the National Party you didn't see human beings. You saw people who were not worthy to be human, really. So you had to use words like "enemy." Enemy—when you see an enemy, you don't necessarily think twice before you act upon the enemy. So you have to produce a kind of discourse that will justify any kind of brutal action that you can take against the enemy. In military psychology you . . . you are taught to devalue a human being . . . that person is seen as an enemy, that is as not fully human, that is a problem, or that is an obstruction to the progress of humanity . . . in that sense you realize that if only this person can be eliminated, or if only this thing called an enemy can be eliminated, [then] freedom can be available, can be accessed in abundance. It is in that context that young people found it rather easy to [take up] arms.

Here Nana was talking about the Gugulethu Seven and therefore about people trained at a more sophisticated level than almost all the young of Zwelethemba. The irony was that the Gugulethu Seven were trained and armed by an *askari* (defined below) planted by the security forces as part of a trap being hatched to kill them and then claim that they were terrorists.

The situation of protesters in Zwelethemba (and in similar areas on the edges of small towns) was difficult in particular ways. They lived on a bare patch of land over which there was tight surveillance, and, given the restrictions of poverty and their relative isolation, they were rendered vulnerable. The senior leaders of their organizations were not at hand, and the borders, which offered escape into exile, were very far away. The young activists and leaders were aware that they might break under pressure and lose their sense of identity and self-worth.

The scene I have set is one of the exposure of the young to forces far greater than themselves, in which they depended for protection on the trust, loyalty, and care of family, friends, and neighbors. When a shelter shattered or their activities forced them to seek other protective cover, they were as vulnerable as hermit crabs scuttling across the sands in search of another shell in which to squat. In these circumstances, the replacement of trust, loyalty, and care with distrust, disloyalty, and carelessness (to be anticipated in the ordinary run of things) could have dire consequences, and betrayal took on particular connotations.

Four definitions of the verb are given in the *Concise Oxford Dictionary of Current English* (*COD*): "Betray v. tr. 1. place (a person, one's country, etc.) in the hands or power of an enemy. 2. be disloyal to (another person, a person's trust, etc.). 3. reveal voluntarily or treacherously; be evidence of (his shaking hands betrayed his fear). 4. lead astray or into error (. . . from Latin *tradere* 'hand over')" (*COD* 1995, 122). The possibility and likelihood of betraying or being betrayed in the above ways and in other ways was for many part of everyday life. Four other words aligned to a betrayer, stalked their days: collaborator (one who works jointly or cooperates traitorously with an enemy); *impimpi*, or informer (a person who informs against another); sellout (one who abandons principles, honorable aims, etc., for personal gain, or one who betrays); *askari* (one who has changed sides as a result of yielding to the efforts of the enemy to turn him or her into a traitor, usually after prolonged physical and psychological torture). According to the *COD* (1995, 73) *askari* is, or was, an East African soldier or police officer (in Arabic, *askari* means soldier). The word "spy" was seldom used in Zwelethemba: its meaning was subsumed under informer, *askari*, or double agent. Betrayal was not a simple, single idea: it was kin to deception, collusion, compromise, complicity, infiltration, and so on. It could occur at many levels, from the betrayal of one's parents, by inviting the violence of the security forces into one's home as a consequence of one's activism, to turning state witness against one's comrades. The horrified imagination of the country was caught by the revelations of a man who had become an *askari* working for the clandestine security force unit that operated from Vlakplaas. My purpose is to focus attention on the everyday character of turning and being turned and of the consequent pain and loss that lasts, for many, every day, for the rest of their lives.

It is not entirely clear what counted as betrayal. Suspicion stuck to certain people. A close watch was kept for signs of turning, including behavior among peers, new spending patterns, or fresh patterns of behavior and movements. Betrayal under duress could be followed by threats of exposure, possibly spread by rumor; therefore the behavior of those released from detention was monitored. There were two aspects that attached to betrayal: one had to do with those who gave information and may, thereafter, have endured guilt, shame, humiliation; the other aspect was those affected by the revelations, who might as a result have endured imprisonment, torture, or other forms of suffering. Among the former, punishment may have followed, including rejection, a house burned down, or even necklacing; among the latter, those informed on may have already been identified, caught, exposed, or even "confessed."

A Shadow of Pain

I have a sad tale to tell. It is a story of boys breaking into adulthood. Of sharing and intimacy; of doubling the pain. It is a story of betrayal. The tale from Zwelethemba concerns Xolile and the twins Edwin and Edward. The story was told to me by Xolile and Edwin.

Xolile (Maqoma) Dyabooi, born on October 12, 1965, was the fifth of seven children. His father came from the Transkei to Worcester in the

1950s. He had passed standard eight and had earned a junior certificate that, at the time, could have been expected to secure him better employment than selling fruit in exchange for bottles. Xolile's mother had a few years of education; she knitted jerseys to earn money. As a young boy, Xolile labored one summer on a fruit farm, but the work conditions made him so cross that he left after a fortnight. In 1983, one parent died, and in 1984 the other one died, leaving the family in dire poverty and Xolile bereft of support through terrible times; he refers to himself as an orphan.

I came to know Xolile well, as we often traveled together between Cape Town and Worcester. He has a warm, open, laughing manner and is a kind man with a dignified bearing. He very seldom speaks ill of anyone and is articulate about the ethical grounds relating to politics in accord with which he tries to behave and with regard to which he estimates the worth of others' actions, at least in reflecting on the fight to end apartheid. In talking of his past, he glosses over the details of his suffering. His childhood was spent in Zwelethemba, where he attended the local schools and, as a teenager, played for the neighborhood's soccer team until his political activities forced him to stop.

However, he had perfected the art of dissembling and disappearance. Try finding Xolile at an appointed spot, or watch in bewilderment as he dissolves into the smoky dusk of the streets of Zwelethemba. Try nailing him to a detailed narration of his own history, try keeping to a course already mapped.

The death in 1977 of Steve Biko, in police custody, stirred Xolile's political consciousness; he was then twelve years old. He read the newspapers his father bought and followed the issue around the establishment of advisory boards in the community. He became politically involved at school and, having passed standard eight, dropped out in 1985, during the tumult of the conflict. His elder brother was detained for a few days in 1980 in relation to the protest at the primary school. Xolile was soon involved with student politics and youth organizations. By 1985, he was wanted by the police for stirring uprisings at the high school, and he began to sleep in a different place every night.

He became one of the most prominent local leaders and much sought after by the police. A younger brother became embroiled in the struggle, too, and Xolile believes that he was caught and tortured having been mistaken for Xolile; he feels guilty as a result. His brother is now fine, he says, and has secure employment in a national service. Xolile was detained twice and once imprisoned for two weeks in 1984, in Victor Verster Prison in Paarl. He had been detained for public disorder, beaten, and harshly treated—then released without being charged.

By 1986, Xolile was in danger, and he was told to go into hiding. He decided to leave for exile, and he traveled to the border region of Lesotho, then walked across the border high in the eastern mountains, arriving in an isolated district. From there he was unable to make contact with the ANC, so he made inquiries at a police station. He told the policemen that he had left South Africa to join the ANC in exile. They listened, then left him alone for a while; one policeman slipped back into the room to warn him that the local police chief was about to arrest him and hand him over to the South African police. He said, "Quick, leave now." Xolile did. He walked across the mountains back into South Africa and then to his family home in the Transkei. In telling the story, he laughs at his predicament. His trousers had become so torn that they hung about his legs like a skirt. Near the village where his relatives live, a man in a truck stopped to give him a lift but was angry when he discovered that Xolile was a man. After some time, Xolile returned to Zwelethemba. In 1986, he again left home for exile, this time in a group that included Edward.

Edwin and Edward Rasmeni were fraternal twins. They were born of Xhosa parents—their father was a boilermaker, their mother a cleaner in a hotel. Their home was a nurturing one, and the boys had been taught to respect the authority of elders, including their parents, senior kinsmen, and teachers. Edwin is a fine-looking man of serious and gentle demeanor.

At the age of sixteen, the twins were drawn by older school leaders into protest against state oppression. Early one morning in October 1985, they were netted in a police sweep of troublemakers in the suburb. The police entered the twins' home to arrest them, intruding with their customary brutality and disrespect, and dragged them off to the Worcester Charge Offices. Already the boys were carrying the guilt of having exposed their parents and siblings to a police invasion of their house and the accompanying gratuitous violence. At the Charge Office, they were led, one by one, into a room and ordered to tell the truth about their involvement in the burning down of a house in Zwelethemba. Each twin said that he had had nothing to do with

it. Each was a schoolboy, and neither was a leading political activist. Edwin
recalls what followed:

> We were both put in a cell. We were in the cell for three days. On the fourth
> day they took me to a car: Mr. ***, Mr. ***, and three or four others. They
> placed a hood over my head. I lost the way. They probably took me to Nek-
> kies [a spot beside the Breede River just outside Worcester]. We arrived.
> They asked me my name. I told them. I was told to sit on the ground. I
> was told to tell the truth and, if I did so, they would release me. I was asked
> who burnt the house and the man. I denied knowledge of it. They put steel
> behind my knees and handcuffed my arms beneath it. They placed nails on
> my neck, ankles, and hips for electric shocks and a tube over my head to cut
> my breathing. They shocked me. There was terrible pain. For about one and
> a half hours they shocked me and questioned me continuously. I pretended
> to faint. They left me. They tried to revive me. They took me to a car, they
> carried me as I was too weak. I was taken back to the cell. My brother asked
> me what it was about. They took him immediately. They did the same to
> him. They brought him back to me. It was terrible to see. We were left in the
> cells, and on Monday we appeared in the Magistrate's Court charged with
> murder and arson, with public violence. There were about thirty of us. We
> were charged and held until December. We were bailed out by our mother,
> both of us.

It is difficult to imagine the horror of their experience, especially as one
of their torturers was a kinsman (he is discussed below). Having been tortured, the first twin was thrown, unable to walk, back into the cell where his
brother waited—knowing that he sees you at your most vulnerable, to witness his horror at your state and to feel his fear at his own imminent torture;
you knowing as you die into the pain of your body and your bewilderment
exactly what is going to be done to him; he is returned in the utter humiliation of pain's excess to join you on the cold cement floor of the cell, where
you are both left to recover sufficiently until the marks of torture are not
visible to others. Then the release: to tell no one what has been done to you
but knowing that the other, one's brother, knows the hell to which one can
be sent. Neither was able to return to school. Edwin said, "Our lives had
been turned upside down."

They continued to protest and were drawn closer to the leaders. In 1987,
they were warned that their lives were in danger, so they left for Cape Town,
where it was more difficult for the police to track them. The trial that re-

sulted from the arrest in 1985 was spread over two and a half years, and when they were forced to return to Worcester to attend a court session, the police arrested them. This time they were charged with having stoned someone's house. Again they were badly treated and held in prison for six weeks. The UDF paid their bail and for a lawyer to represent them in the first and second cases. They were acquitted on both charges.

On release, the brothers decided that they were easy targets in Zwele-themba, and their political activities were, therefore, severely curtailed; they resolved to leave for exile and continue their fight under the direct command of the Umkhonto we Sizwe. Two groups laid their plans for the journey to the Botswana border and, in October 1986, Edward left with the first group. Very few people knew of their plans, and they took care to change them as they drove north, but nevertheless they were arrested at the border post. During interrogation, it became clear that the interrogators had known of their every move. The activists knew who had sold them out. A bare-bones summary of the treatment meted out to them as they were hauled back down the length of South Africa was given in testimony by Xolile, at the Worcester TRC hearings.

Members of the group were held in various prisons in the Boland for six months. Legally, state prosecutors were obliged to procure evidence of the detainees' intentions to join a guerrilla army in a foreign state in order to sentence them. It was provided by persuading Edward and the driver to turn state witness at the trial—the character of the persuasion (torture) was illegal, but the complaints were set aside by the court. Those who were nailed by the evidence of the state witnesses never held it against them, although the evidence helped to condemn them to sentences of as many as seven years in prison. Xolile said about them, "We were not angry with them. We understood their conditions and the types of torture; even the torture was bad for us. We can feel the torture." He said about Edward, "He was young. They tortured him beyond endurance. He cannot be blamed. We saw at the trial that he had been driven mad." He added, "He was my neighbor: we grew up together like a family. . . . I know his person. He was very militant and he wanted . . . to fight back. After his first case [of torture and imprisonment] he was too terrified of the conditions [that would accompany] another sentence. He didn't think properly. He was determined to fight although he knew he couldn't stand the pain again. He was still too young."

About the driver, he said, "He had not been politically inducted. He is blameless." Xolile said that the driver, a man older than themselves, was an ordinary man, not an activist, and therefore had been neither politicized nor prepared for the treatment he had to endure. Xolile was sentenced on the charge of terrorism to five years and six months imprisonment, of which he spent nearly three years in solitary confinement in Brandvlei Maximum Security Prison, near Worcester. Six months of the sentence was for contempt of court, for making statements in support of the ANC and for shouting slogans during the court proceedings:

> During the trial [after months in solitary confinement and severe torture every day] I felt that [the courtroom] is the only place where we can continue our struggle; we had no option. But that was the reason why we made so many slogans, and we tried to convince the people during the proceedings that this is a political trial; they must continue with the struggle, and we will return sometime. So the people supported us [when] they saw that we had high spirits. And we tried to convey messages [so] that people must not lose hope and must try and organize and establish firm organizations.

The young men against whom Edward gave evidence said that when he was brought into court they saw that he had been driven mad. One of his co-accused said that when he was brought to court he "was acting like someone who was not well mentally." On his release after the trial, Edward went home, but he behaved strangely. When his twin tried to reach out to him, Edward grew angry and turned from him. They had been very close and had made a pact to care for and protect each other. It is possible that Edward kept his pact with his brother and gave evidence against his comrades, in part because his interrogators had threatened to harm or kill his twin unless he became a state witness. (Many people gave evidence to the Commission of similar threats to kin during torture sessions.) Edwin learned that Edward had tried to kill himself several times in his prison cell. There was less than a year between his release from prison and his death. On December 12, 1988, Edward either jumped off or was thrown from a moving bus. Young men from the area, not his comrades in action, had accused him of being an *impimpi*, a sellout, as they were traveling together.

Edwin said that after his brother's death he was filled with anger, a sense of isolation, depression, and the pain of the rejection that Edward had experienced on release from prison. "I feel constant sadness at the loss of my twin brother. I feel I will see him one day." He speaks of his hatred of the torturers and his initial desire to avenge the treatment of Edward. Desire for revenge dissipated with time, but he would like to see his twin's name on a monument to those who died while fighting to end apartheid and to have a tombstone placed on his grave. Edwin's own experience of torture left him with back pain, dizziness, and difficulty in concentrating. He was unable to continue far with his education, although he later returned to complete two years of school. For seven years he worked as a forklift driver at a local factory but was retrenched in 1999. It became very hard for him to maintain the small house he had bought. He has a wife and young children.

There are three kinds of betrayal in the story. One of a kinsman harming his nephews; another of betrayal from a comrade in arms who revealed the group's plans for going into exile, making it easy for the security forces to capture them at the border; and one of a young man in prison turning from a warrior against the state into a state witness. It is a story of pain and blame and guilt and shame. It is, too, a story of love and loyalty between two brothers and of forgiveness by those immediately harmed by the betrayal. Revenge may have been taken by young men who were followers, not leaders, in the struggle in Zwelethemba, when they threw Edward from the bus or caused him, in anguish, to throw himself out.

Edwin told me the story ten years after his brother's death. I had worked with him and his colleagues for two years, but we had not discussed the details of his pain. Nor had Edwin made a statement to the TRC, and the opportunity to do so had been foreclosed. However, Xolile (against whom Edward had testified in court) was insistent that his colleagues make statements and so qualify for reparations that he saw as only just, given all that they had sacrificed. I sought permission from the Commission to take statements and set about doing so. I sat one Saturday morning with Edwin and three others filling in the forms on the basis of which the Commission's staff would decide whether the testifier would be declared a "victim" and granted reparations. It was cold, so we took our chairs from the small room that a trade union in Zwelethemba had loaned to us and sat outside in the spring sunshine to continue our work. One of the questions in a section having to do with gross human rights violations (GHRV) in the Commission's form asks, "Where and when did you last see the perpetrator(s)?" Edwin replied, "One a few years ago, he is still in Worcester. And the other is watching us." A man stood fifty yards away watching us intently. He was the kinsman who had tortured Edwin and Edward. Edwin will not speak to him. Another young man in the group sitting with me said that he, too, had been tortured by the one watching us.

The tale ends here with Xolile's account of his experience in prison and in the aftermath. The story of his journey to Botswana is told in chapter 2. From October 1986 to December 1990, Xolile was in police custody in a police station cell, then in a high-security prison. He spent up to three years in solitary confinement. In the first four months (he refers at different times to this spell of detention as having lasted for two, four, or six months) he was tortured every day of the working week, almost all day. The torture he endured, he said, included "the usual—suffocation, false execution, the helicopter, and so on." During that time, he lived in a state of terror. His parents had died and, prior to the court case, no one in the family knew where he was. His brother tried to find him in the police stations and through lawyers, but he could not. Xolile kept going by doing exercises and playing draughts with pebbles on the floor. He read the Bible so much that he "earned exemption from Hell." Xolile was sentenced to five and a half years of imprisonment (of which he served two years and eight months); he was sent to a maximum-security prison in the region where he gradually made friends with a few wardens, who smuggled out some messages to his colleagues and brought him the occasional piece of fruit or a newspaper. He heard of the national hunger strike among prisoners to protest against their conditions and demand release under the new terms following negotiation toward a change in South African politics, and he joined them in solidarity. He ate nothing for twenty-five to twenty-eight days and demanded access to education, better food, and a mattress instead of a mat. A lawyer persuaded him to stop the fast, promising that he would negotiate on his behalf. Conditions improved, and he was allowed to raise his fist in salute and say "Viva" when meeting other prisoners or visitors.

On release, Xolile felt disoriented. He was frustrated at being so far behind his friends in education. He enrolled in a school in Cape Town and completed the last two years of his schooling. From 1993 to 1996, he was lost. He was unable to study, although he had enrolled at UNISA, a distance-learning university, and wandered among friends, spending most of the time in a shack with his co-accused. He was so frustrated that he drank and contemplated suicide: "I was just lost." He received help from the

Trauma Centre for Victims of Violence and Torture at Cowley House, but it was not enough to really help. At the end of 1995, Xolile returned to Zwelethemba to look for a job. Miriam Moleleki (a resident of Zwelethemba who succored many of the young during the time of conflict) helped him, and so did the TRC process. He felt that his failure to secure employment, garner material goods, or find a respectable place in the community made people turn away from him. "I felt that I was neglected by the people around. . . . People just saw you then they saw you as nothing and walked past you." This perception soon passed: it is one common among fighters who return home. He did not feel that he was making progress; he still felt very weak. The rapidity of the process of negotiation bewildered him, and he felt excluded. All he could do was read big documents. He was no longer in touch with ANC leaders: "I was just doing my thing. . . . Conditions were harsh on the ground. Some of us were disillusioned. We had expected handouts; all I achieved was to be left in one of the history books. I did contribute. I see a difference in the community."

Years later, in the mid-1990s, he sat on a Peace Forum with two of his white torturers (whom he named). "They said nothing to me; I just greeted them. I felt blind. Dissatisfied. They shouldn't still be in the police force. It is distressing that they are given power. There should be a court case, and I would hope that they would get prison sentences." There was no lustration set in place in South Africa.

Paulos Mnyuka

Another member of our group, Paulos, told the four of us gathered outside to fill in the TRC forms that he had been betrayed by a kinsman. In August 1985, he and a fellow scholar had been harassed and pursued by police for three months, during a time of great unrest. They had been at the forefront in stirring trouble, and many young people had been detained. Some of their parents were angry with the two of them, because they had led their children in the protests and, while they were in the police cells, Paulos and his comrade remained free. In response to these accusations, the two handed themselves in at the police station. They were photographed, and Paulos said his given name and his surname the wrong way around, and, therefore, he says, the police did not realize who he was. That night, they and fifty others were thrown into a dark cell with no windows, where they stayed for two days. They were interrogated. Paulos continued,

> On the second day we were all about to be sent home and were being loaded into a police van and a special branch man noticed me being put in, too, and whispered to his colleagues, "That is the most wanted man." [The man who pointed him out was a relative.] My friend and I were off-loaded. In the afternoon we were taken to separate rooms. About seven or eight [security force men] were in the room. [The officer in charge] *** sat [listening to] the radio—there was a radio recording of a bomb blast in Pretoria. He said, "Hear?" He gave me a chair; they began to tie me with ropes—feet and arms—and black bands over my eyes and mouth. I was beaten, mostly by ***. I couldn't see the person in front of me, [but] could recognize his [the kinsman's] voice. Others beat me, too. *** beat me. And ***. All were white except a black, *** ***; he is my [relative]. I cannot speak to him. He still lives in Zwelethemba.
>
> They took the pantyhose from my mouth and said there would be a big problem if I told no truth. I said, "I know nothing." I was shown a list of student leaders with the signature of an informer. I was written [down] as the chair—I was the chair of the SRC and COSAS at the time. About seven names were written on the list. All were in the cell already.

They again covered his mouth and eyes and gave him electric shocks. They continued to interrogate and shock Paulos, and they increased the voltage until he was thrown to the floor and against the tables. He lost consciousness and regained it in the cell. The next day he was interrogated and beaten. *** and *** punched him until his tongue split and he could not eat for several days. He and his friend were put in a cell together; both were in terrible pain. Paulos said, "We couldn't talk to each other. We just cried if we looked at each other." Over a week later, they appeared in court charged with public violence and were denied bail. They were accused of having set on fire the Municipal Office Building in Zwelethemba. They were held in Worcester Prison with hardened criminals for two months. There were members of two gangs, and one set accused them of causing unnecessary trouble to the government and determined to place them under their authority in prison. They gave them female names. Fortunately, they were able to play one gang against the other largely through bribes of food parcels brought to them by their families. Another kinsman sought his release and was able to secure it after paying bail of R500.

Paulos had been betrayed by a kinsman and a colleague (the informer who gave his name to the police). After his release from prison, the police harassed him, attempting to make him become an informer. Later in 1985, they visited his home and searched for incriminating documents. Paulos was not at home, but they sprayed teargas into his mother's face when she said he was not sleeping at home and that she did not know where he was. They called her a liar and a bitch. From then on she was never well. She was asthmatic, and the teargas affected her health and her eyes. She died in 1989.

In 1987, Paulos was unable to study full time for lack of money and because of police interference. He found employment cleaning and running messages for an institution in Worcester. The police pursued him there. One of the men who had tortured him and another officer visited him. Paulos said,

> They spoke to me. "Paulos, we have no problems with you but understand that you are a leader. Cooperate with us." They showed me money in a briefcase. They took out cigarettes. I said, "I don't smoke." It was not true. And Bells [whiskey] and Klipdrift [brandy]. "I don't drink this. Only wine and not at work." They said they knew of Mother's suffering and they could make our lives luxurious: they could obtain a driver's license for me by eleven o'clock; an account at a furniture store; a bank account. *** said if I didn't cooperate I would be arrested. He gave me a telephone number, several, and a codename. I said, "I will see what to do." They left. I went to Comrade . . . and told him I must get out of town. He said I must report to a lawyer. We called one. Serious harassment followed. I was even expelled from my job for being a communist. I was not. I had to leave the township in late August 1987 for Cape Town.

In 1999, three of the white men who tortured Paulos were still in the police or security forces in the town. His kinsman has retired.

I shall touch briefly on other acts of betrayal that caused great pain, loss, and distress to members of the group with whom I worked closely. Eight of the fourteen were betrayed in one way or another. Three were betrayed to the police while attempting to leave South Africa to join Umkhonto we Sizwe in exile, and the consequences for each included great brutality and imprisonment (the experiences of two of them have been detailed here). Two were betrayed by kinsmen, another by a close friend, a third by a comrade, and yet another learned from his sister that the police had beaten her into agreeing to betray him: their trust in each other was damaged. Some of their stories are told elsewhere, for, as we have discovered, betrayal was wound into many aspects of the lives of political activists.

Betrayal was not, of course, particular to Worcester. It was pervasive in the land as a fear if not a fact. It became a major issue of contention in communities, and it caused widespread distress in the camps of the liberation forces in exile.

A Fine Mesh

A fine mesh of betrayal was insinuated, instigated by the security forces among friends and families and in communities. The regime's actions, tactics, and politics wreaked devastation and decay on some social institutions and relationships. The spread of mistrust helped to break or fracture social ties, to strain bonds and obligations, and to disturb structures of care, all of which played a crucial part in the undoing of some people's lives—for how can such wounds be easily healed? Betrayal is ambiguous in the way it operated in Zwelethemba: it was not clearly cut; it could not be known in advance (was the information one was about to give going to lead to a new police action?) or even in the moment. Sometimes, perhaps, its ramifications could be known only in retrospect, as they became clearer—the nature of the information given or extracted, its newness or value and the way it was actually used; the trauma of those broken, humiliated, shamed; the unfolding of multiple events into time, through and beyond the end of the regime. What kind of economy of power was this? Betrayal seems to have operated as a weapon aimed at inflicting wounds on the will to resist, damaging the conviction and strength of the resistance and belief in its capacity. That is why the security forces worked on those who had little to reveal.

What is remarkable is that once the fight to secure democratic representation ended, so few people took revenge on those they believed to have been informers and to have caused immeasurable pain and fearful consequences. The Commission states in its *Report* that by the end of the 1980s paranoia existed regarding informers (2:581). The word "paranoia" suggests levels of anxiety and suspicion beyond reasons well grounded in fact: almost a misperception (*para*, "beyond"; *noia*, "perception").

A particular ethical stance was required by those fighting for democracy under the conditions outlined above: one that asked what can be done, taking into account the question of frailty and given a set of circumstances in which there was an expectation that something could be done within impossible parameters. It called on the capacity of the spirit, a capacity that encompassed not holding one accountable for not being accountable (breaking under torture yet obliged to let others know as soon as possible). Accountability becomes absurd at some moment in turning and being turned. In this chapter, I have tried to depict the murky edges of betrayal, its infiltration into the everyday, its pervasiveness, its ties to lies and cynicism, and how it was wielded to destroy lives and integrity. Elaine Scarry in her fine book, *The Body in Pain* (1985), does not fully capture its veiled complexity and iteration through time. She emphasizes the relationship between torturer and tortured, but for the men of Zwelethemba, there were seldom fewer than four security force personnel present, and various officers participated in the physical exercise of torture. Thus the intimacy between torturer and tortured that Scarry discusses so well was not established. Other forms of intimacy between kin, for example, formed. Turning and being turned was part of the architecture of unmaking.

One question, to which I have no answer, is: what made it possible for the men to speak to me as they did? When is it possible to talk to the reception? Did the TRC offer that, satisfactorily? Did I? In terms of ethnography, when does engagement stop? The young placed themselves in the movement of history, and it remains to be seen how history records it. Ralph Waldo Emerson said, "I am ashamed to see what a shallow village tale our so-called History is. . . . What does Rome know of rat and lizard?" (quoted in Cavell 2005, 258).

Coming to know what I know was difficult for me and for those with whom I established relationships. I know only a little about the difficulties some had in holding onto a secure sense of self after such experiences. Jacques Derrida, discussing the trouble of the archive, includes "the trouble of secrets, of plots, of clandestineness, of half-private, half-public conjurations, always at the unstable limit between public and private, between the family, the society, and the State, between the family and an intimacy even more private than the family, between oneself and oneself" (1996, 90). I know about some of their failures and assume that few have untarnished images of themselves. By this I mean, in Stanley Cavell's words, that we have come to understand "the dependence of the human self on society for its definition, but at the same time its transcendence of that definition, its infinite insecurity in maintaining its existence" (1988, 174). He talks of his having been taken aback that the human requires a "doubling back ceaselessly upon itself, and that the re-encounters with ourselves . . . hide themselves in their familiarity; as if we are surprised by the incessance of childhood" (1979, xiii). For so the young seemed to me to have been: dependent on family and peers and community for a definition of themselves, yet they reached beyond that definition and had to face the infinite insecurity of maintaining its existence before powerful antagonistic forces, including concerted efforts to crush identity and instigate betrayal.

Many people have lived beside those whom they know betrayed them, and they continue to live beside them. The issue of betrayal is the obverse of the issue of trust. Each of the young men depended on trust to achieve anything at all and to stay as safe as possible, but each lived with the consciousness that trust could easily be compromised—compromised by extreme suffering (emotional, physical, and psychological) and carefully wrought patterns of disinformation.

It is possible that "living beside" (despite betrayal) tells us something other than or more than the lack of revenge. Perhaps in this context of multiple structures of loyalty, obedience, and respect, there were disjunctions, conjunctions, and coincidences that stretched its meanings. Some structures (the apartheid state) were fought, and others (kinship, filial, and communal loyalty) glued or shredded responses. Despite the fact that many kinds of trust could be and were betrayed, a certain clarity in resistance held. In the tumult and chaos of conflict, state oppression, and social disorder, selves were constructed and reconstructed. The fashioning of identity and the reorganization of social forms, albeit embattled and weakened, occurred in the face of repression and terror, and morals were reworked, examined, and deployed even as attempts were made, or so it seemed, to bring about social dissolution.

Nana Charity Khohlokoane

Amos Monde Khomba

Eric Ndoyisile Tshandu

Xolile Dyabooi

Paulos Mnyuka

Zandisile Leonard Ntsomi

Mawethu Bikani

Vuyisile Malangeni

Zingisile Yabo

Edwin Mnyamana Rasmeni

Isaac Lehlohonolo Tshabile

Sonwabo Sitsili

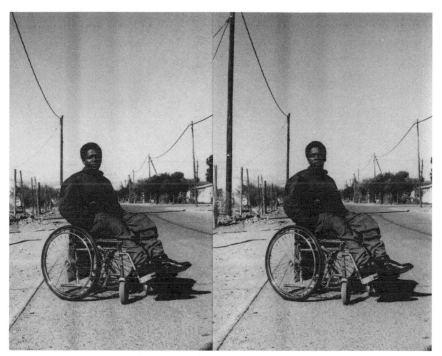

Ntando Pringle Mrubata

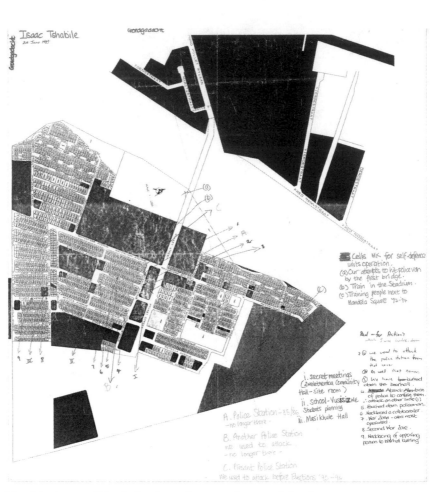

Municipal map of Zwelethemba with annotations made by the men

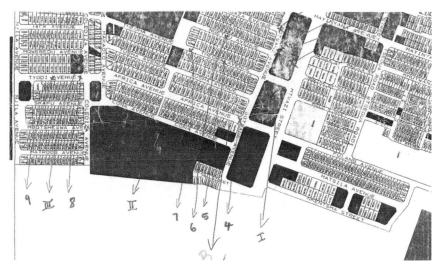

Detail of annotation

Worcester

Three Men and Loss

Three men, all born within three years of one another, are widely respected among the comrades in Zwelethemba for their contribution to the fight. They are Nelson Sonwabo (Sox) Sitsili, Zingisile Anthony (Z) Yabo, and Nation Andile Maart. Each suffered severely as a consequence of their activities, and each saw his life as having been seriously hampered in its fulfilment because of what he had been through. Each came from a family of activists: the mother of Sox was imprisoned for her actions, a brother of Zingisile died, and the parents of Nation were both activists—his father was imprisoned in 1960 for a year then banished to a homeland for a year. The early curtailment of their education, the loss of employment as a result of activism and frequent arrests, the absence of opportunities to obtain training in skills, and the harsh treatment meted out to them seemed to have combined in undermining their abilities to restructure their lives to their own satisfaction in the town in which they had made a stand. Their loss is representative of the loss experienced by many people in the country after the fight had ended.

A Gentle Man

Sox was born in 1963 in Zwelethemba. His mother was a committed leader in politics in the 1960s, and when he was a young boy, she was jailed for three months. She drew her son into political activism. His father was a trade unionist. Sox spent some years living with a kinsman of his father in Queenstown, where, as a schoolboy, he began his involvement in politics. He completed standard nine and in 1978 returned to Worcester, though not to school. He obtained a job in a factory and, after some time, became a shop steward; he also became immersed in the politics of the youth in the township. His colleagues spoke of his devotion to the cause and his contribution to leadership in the early 1980s. One of them said that he had "shared the trenches with renowned leaders" of the antiapartheid movement. At one point he was the national publicity secretary of a large union.

Sox died on February 18, 2007. He was very thin in the years that I knew him, and he suffered from chronic tuberculosis. He was always a kind and gentle man, and, toward the end of our interaction, he could no longer sustain a conversation about his past. It seemed to me that he had been deeply harmed by maltreatment at the hands of the security forces. He faithfully attended our meetings but seldom said much.

Trying Not to Remember

Zingisile was born on October 18, 1966, of Xhosa parents in Zwelethemba. He was the last born of nine children. Members of his family were activists, and his parents were fully aware of his political engagement. An older brother went into exile, and on his return he was killed by a policeman in an incident the nature of which remains unclear. During the 1980s, the family was targeted for awful harassment. Zingisile was in the top layer of leadership among the youth, and he contributed to the establishment of a number of local structures. Having completed standard eight, he left school because of his involvement in the struggle.

Toward the end of 1985, he left in the company of others, including Eric, from the area to go into exile and continue the fight from there. The group was arrested and detained at a border post, and it seemed to them that they had been betrayed by a member of the group, a man not known by them. They were hauled back to Worcester and were severely tortured en route and on arrival: he was held in captivity for six months. He did not see a doctor on his release.

Zingisile admits having been full of rage against white people for their treatment of him. His torture included repeated near suffocation and false executions, and the hearing in both his ears was affected by the beatings he received. He found solitary confinement difficult to bear. He says that he used to be a gentle and patient man, but the pain and terror made it hard to hold down a job after his release, especially because he found it difficult to take orders from white people and because he always intervenes when he thinks that another person is being unfairly treated. "I was so full of hatred that I tried not to remember them, as I feared I would take revenge," he declared. Of all the men in MAZE, he most clearly admitted to having experienced psychological suffering expressed as rage and despair. He wanted to learn to control his rage, as he disliked his new aggressive persona, and he said that he needed therapy to help him to change. He resented his lack of education and his inability to advance in his work, yet, despite failing for a long time to sustain gainful employment, he continued to participate in community projects.

Zingisile was the one who questioned me about myself most persistently and who asked me the most questions about the world. After some time he was able, he said, to drop his longing for revenge, although he found it hard when thinking about a policeman who had tortured him and was still, in the 1990s, in the local police force.

When I met Zingisile in 2001, he was unemployed but was a volunteer for the ANC on recruitment and HIV and AIDS instruction. He said he no longer wished to take revenge on anyone. He seemed warmer and more talkative than before.

After we had completed our project, in 2002 I invited the men in MAZE to join me at a restaurant in Worcester. First we gathered in Zwelethemba, and Zingisile said quite forcefully that his wife and children were hungry, and therefore how could he eat? He was speaking on behalf of the unemployed, he said. He looked ill, and he was very thin. He had been diagnosed as having anemia, he told me. I said that I understood his position and that he need not dine with us, but if he did I would add the cost of the meal to give to his family. He accepted money from me but did not join us.

A Harsh Toll

On June 4, 1962, Nation was born to a large family (he had four brothers and four sisters) in Zwelethemba. His parents were activists, and he says of his father, "He was a powerful figure, he influenced me." At the age of twelve, Nation began to take a close interest in political activities; he left school early and completed only standard three. At eighteen, he was employed in a textile factory. His active involvement in the youth movement began in the early 1980s. In October 1985, he was arrested with twenty-eight others, including Amos Dyantyi and Amos Khomba, and was held for six months awaiting trial, then released on bail. The trial of seven of those who had been detained was only heard in court four years later; they were acquitted. While awaiting trial, Nation was tortured, and he said that he never regained the feeling of physical well-being. Initially, he experienced a lot of anger and despair as a result of the harm done to him as well as poverty and loss of employment. He often questioned me firmly but politely as to what I could achieve out of my research that would help them. His sadness was palpable. His wife left him, and he lost his home and his job. His parents and his friends stood beside him. He saw no doctor or healer, and no ritual was held for him after his incarceration. Nation was a member of the ANC, and he was involved with COSAS, ZWEYO, and the UDF. His friends affirm his contribution to the struggle.

FOUR

Imfobe: The Reach for Moral Principles

If there were ethical flowers one would surely be yours.

—ADRIENNE RICH

Walter Benjamin said that the image of history lies "even in its inconspicuous features of existence, in history's rejects" (1979, 35). Inasmuch as history leaves out of account the experiences of children and youth in conflicts, it cancels their contribution to social and political change and fails to acknowledge their courage and effort. It also underestimates at best—or denies, at worst—the morality the young had to hold to and the consciousness that required under harsh circumstances. Descriptions that gloss over the efforts by many of the local leaders of the young to act in accord with moral principles may result in an underestimation of the nature of their contribution. I suggest in this chapter that in order to lead the fight and sustain their commitment and interdependence, they had to hold to moral tenets and attain certain levels of consciousness that continuing action required. (The matter is explored in relation to an earlier study I completed in 1991 and 1992 with a different set of young leaders in the conflict; see Reynolds 1995a, 1995b, 1998, 2000.) I follow Benjamin's image of history, seeking to locate young people's moral development in the context of everyday life. The specific nature of the urban guerrilla warfare they were engaged in, as outlined in chapter 2, presented particular challenges. The best defenses lay in the quality of relationships and in intellectual and physical agility. Local leadership was passed to the young, and some handled it well: the accompanying power with good sense and the subsequent punishment by forces of the state with fortitude. Working around the Xhosa concept *imfobe*, variously translated as morality, virtue, goodness, and grace, I examine the critical self-consciousness to which they subjected their experiences and decisions, and I offer a record of some of their actions and thoughts. I contend that they had to acquire self-knowledge and to act, however imperfectly, in accord with a code of ethics, however shakily manufactured, in order to survive and to direct local operations, however impromptu and small in scale and effect. I am attempting to draw out some facets of the reach for self-knowledge and the formulation of ethics, or at least to suggest an aspect of what we might need to know if we are to understand the experiences of children and youth who become embroiled in conflict. I do not mean to suggest that young leaders were innocent.

There was little systematic training in ideology by liberation groups in small towns or even in many of the urban dormitory suburbs. The young of Zwelethemba rebelled against and contributed to social order and moral judgment. They examined, with microscopic skepticism, formal rules and obligations, especially those imposed by the oppressive regime and by the force of a patriarchy out of kilter with current possibilities.

I write out of my admiration for the men and their goodness toward me. Over four years, from 1996 to 2000, we came to know one another well: our relationship is based on trust, despite our having failed each other on a number of occasions. My safety in Zwelethemba was in their hands, and I held their trust in the vulnerability of their intimacy. There is a risk in writing about morality. Danger lies in the traps of sentiment, romance, exaggeration; in writing in ignorance of faults, errors, harm done, or in ignorance of the extent of damage incurred to self, especially over time; and of having heard tales of the past given with hindsight and in accord with current biases or as shaped by me only in the knowledge of the afterward. I do not know everything about them. If we could describe how their moralities were formed; in accord with whose ideas of the good; in relation to what sets of restrictions; in the anticipation of what limits of stoicism and courage under torture they were shaped; with regard to what monitoring, disciplinary action, checks and balances—we could contribute to the process of understanding the development of ethics. The chapter begins that process by documenting young people's self-understanding, drawing especially on the experiences and reflections of one young man, Nana, and a definition of moral behavior given by Xolile.

I am conscious of the difficulty (impossibility?) of furnishing sufficient evidence to support this exploration of the development among some of the young activists of a moral self. A refutation of the claims I make could sound rather like this: "The majority of young political activists made very little, if any, contribution to change; they made little systematic, concerted effort to work toward a better dispensation. Most were immoral, and no admirable degree of consciousness was necessary for the manner in which they conducted themselves. They were part of a large, well-funded terrorist network, and they were intent on disrupting well-intentioned, efficient forces of law and order. They were not leaders but rabble rousers. They displayed little fortitude under pressure." It is the kind of implacable refutation that was often expressed in the past and can still be heard now. Conditions in Zwelethemba held young protesters in greater check than did conditions in other areas of the country. The men and I are aware that ideology imbibed from conscientization by the members of liberation organizations echoes through the words of the men as laid out below.

In the attempt to approach the virtue evinced in the young men's thinking and actions, I call to my aid the writing of Herman Melville in *Moby-Dick* (1992, 124–127). He talks about "that astounding dignity (in man) which has no robed investiture," and he continues,

> If, then, to meanest mariners, and renegades and castaways, I shall hereafter ascribe high qualities, though dark; weave round them tragic graces; if even the most mournful, perchance the most abased, among them all, shall at times lift himself to the exalted mounts; if I shall touch that workman's arm with some ethereal light; if I shall spread a rainbow over his disastrous set of sun; then against all moral critics bear me out in it.

Once I asked Xolile if he could give me a Xhosa word that describes how one holds to one's moral fiber through difficult times and how one acts in accord with values despite the pain of the world. I had had in mind something like "grace," but the weight of Christianity lies too heavily on the word. Something more akin to Emmanuel Levinas's "small goodness" was a closer fit (1998a, 230). Xolile offered the word *imfobe*, which he defined as "goodness of heart to the extreme." I shall use the words *imfobe*, morality, virtue, and grace somewhat interchangeably, but my aim is to describe goodness of heart as expressed in the everyday, as consciously sought, and as acknowledged by members of the community as being in existence among these young people. Nana wondered if I was searching for meanings resonant in what he called that "mostly abused term *ubuntu*," for which, he added, there is no comparable word in English. He explained:

> NK: It is the ability to understand, to sympathize, to empathize, and to rise above yourself and to recognize the goodness in the other person despite knowing that the other person is doing you wrong. But you understand that this person is a creature of God, like you, like yourself. In you, you have this thing, both positive and negative. It is conditions, really, it is life conditions, our everyday conditions that shape how we relate to really intense situations. If today your happiness and sadness is contextual and it is relative to survival, you relate to something in order to be happy. It does not exist in a vacuum.
>
> PR: So it is about relationships, in part?
>
> NK: It's about a relationship between two people—it's a relationship of one person within the context of a group, because this group concept is at the heart. If you behave in a manner that is unbecoming, really you are not only disgracing yourself, you are also disgracing your peer group, you're also disgracing your gender, you're disgracing your cultural group or your tribe or ethnic group, your clan, even the family's reputation and good name, the black people, humanity itself. It's like the time I used to have some rough exchanges with a friend of mine who is now a radio journalist. Sometimes we would tease each other when one of us had made a political mistake. We would say, "You know Nana, you are a disgrace. You are a disgrace not only to humanity, you have disgraced us and the house that you are in and its walls all together and the roof on top." So it's like the totality of your surroundings.
>
> PR: It's you in the environment?
>
> NK: Yes, so you have made the environment impure by your transgressions.
>
> PR: And what should you do about that?

NK: You laugh, but in a manner you try to defend yourself, but even though you go into denial, you know it's just a question of pride. You know deep inside you that yes, he is speaking the truth, you've erred there. You have to ask forgiveness, really. But your forgiveness will have to be accompanied by revelations, or you have to tell what is it that you are sorry about. You see? Tell the people that you are wrong in so far as doing this and this.

Nana went on to describe a ritual of happiness to which his family had invited me and many members of the community. "No matter if this moment of happiness is short lived, the main point is not how long it will last but that we've experienced it and we've derived as much joy out of it and shared it, so that in the near future when you are overwhelmed by some tragedy and difficulties, you will still have that excess energy to tackle the other problems." Nana described, as possible sources of *ubuntu*, the nature of the family and the patterns of consideration and compassion about which children are taught. He said,

So perhaps it is those subtle and little things that you see as being insignificant that have to shape and hold the personality beyond what we think is possible. . . . So you are shaped by your experiences. And sometimes you are not able to understand the benefits of what you are doing in the short term, but the consequences of what you are doing have a bearing and a content that is bigger than what you think is possible at that point in time.

He gave a "Marxist" analysis of the damage done by colonialism and of the corrosion of values brought about by individualism. He talked, too, about learning as an activist from friends and from their mistakes and about coming to accept responsibility for one's behavior, as it could undermine the cause for which one stood and fought even if one was a very small player. We discussed the efforts security force agents made to undermine someone's trust in the shared goals of resistance. I asked what it is that holds one when one is faced with prison and torture and subtle psychological play. Nana replied,

Ja, because when I was detained for the first time at, I think, the end of July 1985. I was told—it was a revelation to me; I was never prepared; I knew that I was gonna—if you play with fire, you're gonna burn. No freedom fighter of any reputation would not expect to suffer for his convictions, but

I never knew that the apartheid security police would go so far as to know who was my girlfriend before this one, and my school performance, and that I was playing soccer, and [that] I was quite vocal in forming local choirs. So then I knew that they would go so far as to spread their tentacles and know everything about me. And now when they confronted me they told me that, "You have wasted your life when you could have done so much with it. Your school record is quite depressing. You've been number one in all your classes until now, so why are you going to rot in jail just like Mandela and your own people are going to forget about you?" and "You are a lost cause, you will fail just like your struggle," and "You know that we are cleverer than you and you are going to fail and the whole struggle will fold within a matter of two years. We hope to round you up just like we did in the early sixties, and we are going to break the back of your struggle and your own people will shun you," and "Really, it is such a tragedy. We want you to be successful in life but what can we do?" This other one made it explicit because in summary he said, "What can you do when a lamb dies, meanwhile you are busy giving it medicine?" So you begin to despair a bit. But it is in the midst of adversity that I learned to discover the hidden resources inside me.

Manufactured Moralities

Simone Weil said that Marx "was struck by the fact that social groups manufacture moralities for their own use" (2001, 147). It seems to me that the young who stood against the apartheid regime to some extent manufactured moralities. The passage in full follows:

> [Marx] was struck by the fact that social groups manufacture moralities for their own use, thanks to which the specific activity of each one is placed outside the reach of evil. There is thus the morality of the soldier, that of the businessman, and so on, whose first article consists in denying that it is possible to commit any evil while waging war, doing business, etc., according to the rules.

This prompts the question as to whether the young, supposing they formed social groups that manufactured moralities, intended to place their activities outside the reach of evil. Part of the manufacturing was imagining a future and holding to the belief that their cause was just. Reshaping does not end, boundaries shift, and present reflection reconfigures attitudes to the past.

(This process will be shown in the excerpts appearing later in this chapter, drawn from the interview with Nana about his friendship with George.) I heard no justifications for harm done to others framed thus—in the sense of a just cause, claiming that the activities were not evil—except from national leaders who claimed immunity under the guise of having fought a "just war" or for having been forced to implement draconian measures because the infiltration of informers had been used as a major tactic of war by the South African government. At the local level in Zwelethemba, acknowledgment of and responsibility for immoral actions, even those committed under duress, were more clearly enunciated if only because in small towns placed under close surveillance by security forces and by political activists few activities remained secret.

The surest way I had of coming to know how the fourteen men had, in the 1980s, negotiated the everyday under extraordinary circumstances was by paying attention[1] to their speech and to their interactions with one another and with me as we explored the past. I saw what I took to be admirable morality expressed in the thinking and actions of some of the men most of the time and all of the men some of the time. It is that strength among the young that I had sought to understand in my ethnographic work in southern Africa.

For Ludwig Wittgenstein, "Virtue (freedom and happiness) consists in our (ineffable) mode of approach to the facts" (quoted in Murdoch 1993, 103). Here I am concerned with this "approach to the facts." Plato, in Iris Murdoch's view, holds that virtue "comes as the reward of a sort of morally disciplined attention. . . . . The solitary private moral agent must be his own authority, continually doing it all, over and over, for himself" (23). From Simone Weil, Murdoch takes the definition of attention as being the "idea of a just and loving gaze directed upon an individual reality" that she, Murdoch, believes to be the characteristic and proper mark of the active moral agent (2001, 33). Perhaps it was a mode of approach and a continual process of working with disciplined attention that may have helped some of the young men to form a morality and to act morally.

There is work entailed in reaching for a moral reality. For Murdoch, "Where virtue is concerned we often apprehend more than we clearly understand and *grow by looking*" (2001, 30). Growth is a process of deepening or complicating a process of learning. Morality entails choice, and the work of attention leads up to moments of decision. The work is continuous; it imperceptibly builds up structures of value; the attainment of freedom (in moral choice) is a small, piecemeal business; and the moral life goes on continuously—it is not switched off between moments of choice (36).

According to Scanlon (1988), the morality of right and wrong contains a system of "co-deliberation," in which moral reasoning is an attempt to work out principles that each of us could be asked to employ as a basis for deliberation and accept as a basis of criticism. "Seeking such principles is part of what is involved in recognizing each other's value as rational creatures. Our needs for protection and for the assistance of others play a role in determining which principles it is reasonable to reject and which to accept, and hence in determining which actions are right and wrong at the most basic level" (268).

Given the constraints of living in Zwelethemba in the 1980s—its sole entrance and exit, a constant police presence, frequent body and house searches, telephone lines that were tapped, bright searchlights bathing the night streets—dependence on others was imperative. Youth leaders depended on their peers (for those about whom I am writing, these were initially schoolmates), slightly older leaders (senior school children or people who had recently graduated from high school or had been hounded out of the class as a consequence of police harassment and/or administrators' rejection), and comrades within banned political organizations (usually the African National Congress and/or the South African Communist Party in Zwelethemba) in the suburbs of Cape Town or the small towns of the Boland. They also depended on their families and older residents.

I remind the reader of four occurrences during which the men can be seen to have paid attention to moral behavior and the work involved in it. One used his charisma to draw many younger school children into protests, and during one intense police effort of search and arrest, he was accused by their mothers of having led them into situations that resulted in imprisonment and ill treatment, whereas he and a colleague had successfully evaded the police net. In response to their accusations, the two men walked into a police station and gave themselves up. Another one continued to accept as a comrade in leadership a friend whom all the others believed to have given information about him to the police, which led to his arrest and subsequent torture. A third insisted that his colleagues attend the funeral that he organized, in accord with the ANC format, of a comrade who had turned state witness against him (see chapter 2 for them all). A fourth gave up his holiday to accompany children who had been maltreated as laborers on a nearby farm to their homes in a town far in the north (see interlude 1). In addition, a fifth served on a Peace Forum despite having to sit next to a man who had tortured him (it was Eric, and at the first meeting he turned to him and asked, "Do you remember me?" to which the policeman replied, "Yes"). A sixth saved a man from being necklaced by an angry gathering of youth. This was Nana, who told me that the moment of which he is most proud as an activist was when he stood against the wishes of an angry crowd bent on necklacing a man who had been accused of being an *impimpi* (informer). He told the crowd that they could not kill him without allowing him the chance to speak, and the crowd gave him the chance and then set him free. Nana read an earlier version of this chapter and kindly sent a carefully considered response to me, making it clear that this incident concerned a different man from his friend who was said to have informed on him (see below). He added that later conditions suggest that the man may not have been innocent (he detailed the reasons for his supposition), yet he still believes that having saved him from being necklaced "was the best thing to do for myself and fellow freedom fighters." Nana also organized a full funeral and oration for a destitute man, who was not from the community or the area, who had been shot on a street in Worcester by a local white man.

All of the men recalled community members' bravery in helping them to escape the police: a "Coloured" man from a neighboring community who would drive them out of Zwelethemba at any hour and at great risk to himself; the many people who left their doors unlocked at night to enable them to run through the houses as they evaded arrest; the many who hid them despite having small homes that were easy to search; the many who misdirected the police or warned them of police intentions and approach; the many who covered up for them; and some who fought the police themselves, giving those being pursued the chance to escape. No incidents of retribution against those whom they suspected (or knew) had caused them harm came to my attention.

I shall mention some of the things that were said or done that still remain like splinters in the minds of the young men and to which they drew my attention. One of them, Ntando, was shot by the police as he stood watching them arrest young men who had been involved in a street protest earlier in the day, and when he regained consciousness in the hospital he was deeply distressed to find that though he was paralyzed, his wrists were chained to the hospital bed. Years later, the headmaster of the local high school assigned a classroom on the second floor that had no access for a wheelchair to the matriculating class of which he was a member and refused to listen to the young man's pleas to assign a classroom on the ground floor so that he could continue his education. The young man said he cried every day for a year and never managed to obtain his diploma. Another of the men, Zandisile, winces every time he remembers the police at the local station telling him not to mind about having had his leg amputated because it would grow again. A third, Nana, was distressed by the intimacy of the policemen's knowledge of his life and relationships that could only have been learned from the mouths of friends and lovers. A fourth, Mawethu, took a long time to regain an easy relationship with a sister whom the police beat until she agreed to spy on him. A fifth, Xolile, was shocked to see that, despite having been tried and sentenced to over six years imprisonment for his activities as an ANC cadre, the list of ANC activists held in the president's office did not include his name, yet the names of younger men from the community who had not been involved in political action at all were there. He was hurt, too, when he and his co-accused visited the Truth and Reconciliation Commission's headquarters in Cape Town to see that well-dressed and mostly white people were quickly waved through the security check while they were thoroughly searched and had to stand aside while long calls to higher authorities in the Commission were made seeking their clearance. Once that clearance arrived, they simply left in disgust.

The Philosopher

Nana was teasingly called "the Philosopher" by the others in our group. A brief sketch of his political trajectory in the 1980s follows. It is given as a context in which to place excerpts from his ideas that illustrate the considered attention he gives to difficult matters and to a reflection on self.

 Nana was born on March 20, 1968. He has a bearing that reminds one of Nelson Mandela's. He, too, is of royal heritage, though Sotho rather than

Xhosa. He comes from a strong family. His mother was a laboratory assistant in a Worcester factory until she was forced out by "Coloured" workers who claimed she had no right to the job because Worcester lay within the Coloured Labour Preference Area. Nana was top of his class throughout his primary schooling and was the best student in mathematics in the Boland area in standard five.

A senior at school introduced Nana into local politics in 1983, when he was fifteen, and for the next two years he was embroiled in protest. In 1985, he was detained in Worcester prison and held for two months. He was treated harshly, as he had already become a leader. That year, one that saw widespread protest and mass arrests, he helped to form ZWEYO. On his release from prison, Nana dropped out of school to evade the police, but in 1986 he returned to school. In June of that year, the second State of Emergency was declared, and his colleagues in Zwelethemba and Cape Town warned him that some of his neighbors and friends had been pressed into informing on him; he was told that this time the police would not simply hold him for a short while. He was persuaded to go underground.

Nana spent five months on two farms working as a laborer. The owner of the second farm had a brother in exile who was avoiding being conscripted into the army, and he, the farmer, knew that Nana was evading the police but allowed him to stay. After four months, the farm manager informed the police of Nana's presence. Farm workers warned Nana that the police had been called and helped him to escape through the fields. He spent a night on another farm and managed to telephone his contacts, and they whisked him away from the area.

Senior comrades moved him to Cape Town, from where he skipped out of the country briefly, then returning to Cape Town and Stellenbosch to continue with the struggle. Later, with support from the ANC, he completed his schooling in Cape Town at the Cape Tutorial College, Rondebosch, and the Boston House College in the city center, where he learned to speak "through my nose with a stiff upper lip." From November 1989 to June 1990, he was "in and out of Botswana reporting on the movement." On one return to South Africa, he spent a few weeks in Worcester as, he says, "an alien in my own country." In 1991, he was legally back. He signed on for a bachelor in science degree with UNISA (a distance-learning university) but was unable to study, as he was still wary of being captured. He only returned formally to Zwelethemba in 1992. He continued to be involved in ANC Youth League politics, becoming the chair in the Boland area and, from 1995 to 1998, deputy secretary of the Western Cape Province. From 1993 to 1996, he was sponsored by the Catholic Education Aid Programme for his bachelor in social sciences degree, and the Wenner-Gren Foundation sponsored his honors degrees in social anthropology (completed in 1998) at the University of Cape Town, where I taught from 1991 to 2001.

Some of his reflections on memory, trust, and politics follow. They are drawn from a conversation he had with Fiona Ross[2] and a story he told me about the way in which uncertainty around loyalty and betrayal entered his relationship with a friend. The conversation was taped and transcribed. It circled around a discussion of local politics in 1998 in Zwelethemba and was shaped by memories of local council candidates' actions in the previous decade. It began with an exploration of local government elections and the defeat of a person whose actions during the fight for liberation were held against her (see Ross 2003). The extracts I offer here allow a privileged glimpse into one activist's education of self and his valiant attempts to work out the balance between necessary action and disciplined engagement in politics.

Observing that "the discourse of remembrance is not very reliable in politics," Nana said that it is not always easy to know when past errors will be recalled in a community and come to haunt present efforts. He said,

> We have imperfections. We have shortcomings, limitations, and [we make] mistakes. At one time in the revolution, each and every one of us—there's no one who can claim he has never made any mistakes in the course of the struggle. Some of the mistakes we [made] have cost some people their lives [or have caused] some people to suffer maximum injuries. Some people are scarred for life. . . . So, in that context, we have to accept the fallibility of everyone.

He expressed his distaste for the politics of character assassination, slandering, and backstabbing. He said that local leaders among the activists in Zwelethemba felt the pressure of others' expectations that they should behave impeccably, even after democracy had been achieved. He spoke about his disapproval of an attempt by former activists in December 1997 to appropriate council housing for themselves, pushing aside people to whom the houses had already been assigned. They made claims based on their participation in securing liberation. At a public meeting, former comrades stood against one another and, in part, it became a tussle between fine oratory and the trust of the community over whether outspokenness would be taken as confrontational or as the expression of an ethical stand, even if it opposed a powerful group's interests. Nana continued, "I've always been a rebel. I'm not a person who accepts. I always question this institution called leadership. And that put me in trouble. Not only in Zwelethemba, even in the Movement. I'm always having this disquiet about leadership." He talked about ways of inhabiting the denouement following a time of exception. He continued with a description of the changed expectations of young leaders and, in doing so, outlined, with irony, the character of leadership in the 1980s.

> NK: In the '80s you were a leader in so far as how defiant are you? How much are you able to resist oppression by the police? How much ability do you have to come out of detention with your spirit undented, emerging victorious because you've been able to outmaneuver the police: instead of subduing you, you've emerged victorious because you did not tell them what they interrogated and tortured you for. . . . Yes, how many stones did you throw? How much were you in the forefront of throwing stones? How much were you really up front when there was action, things to be burned, or violence to be meted out? How articulate were you in terms of *toyi-toyi*ing? How good were you in terms of memorizing all the freedom songs? How good are you in terms of articulating the positions of the Movement? That was the yardstick. . . .
>
> So much so that some things have been [unpacked from] the baggage . . . of leadership [since the end of conflict]. This thing of defiance. This thing of freedom songs . . . now you are supposed to be able to analyze the situation. You must be able to be proactive. You must be able to formulate policy. You must be able to unpack transformation. Critique it, critique transformation, provide alternatives, you see. And it's more like intellectual work. Besides, you must also be able to root yourself among the masses, understand their needs. Be where they need you. Be among them, suffer with them, advise them, and so forth and so forth. So that's what makes you a leader. Besides that, in addition to that, you must acquire education. Education is also important. So, if you have all those skills and in addition education, then it puts you on, yes, on a broad

path, as the Xhosas say, *Ikubeka endleleni ebanzi*. So you are able—it opens a space for you, for you to maneuver. With education and all the other qualities and skills that all the comrades have, you are now one step ahead. Sets you on a broad path, free to maneuver without any hindrance.

FR: So in a sense, the kind of qualities that would have been required from a leader, a young leader, in the '80s would have been a deep emotional attachment to the Movement; an ability to outwit the state, to be a trickster in a sense, whereas now the qualities that are required are actually much more intellectual?

NK: Yes, some of us sort of summarize. We say, "Hey, must be middle class" [laughs]. But really it's more than just being middle class—to be termed middle class among us is a derogatory term. Even to be called bourgeois, "Ohh, it's something else! Thou shall not call each other bourgeois!" So if you, and the community say, "*Ja*, why do you compete against Nana? You don't have university education. After your struggle you became frustrated, you drank a lot, and Nana has more information than you. He has read *big* books, and you did not read all the other books that he read." It's that type of regrettable thing because not everyone has had the opportunity to go to university. Not everyone after the struggle was still intact mentally. Some have emotional scars that make it impossible for them to progress academically or at school. So the university or college or post-matric education is not an option. . . . We are obsessed with this notion of wanting to achieve whatever we set for ourselves. We are not ambitious [about taking a] risk. Perhaps we have risked too much: more than our share. So much that our bags are empty of risks.

A final excerpt from Ross's interview with Nana touches on differences between the experiences of young men and women during that time in that place and on their relations during the struggle, especially regarding trust. Nana assumes the voice of a generic male and implicates himself in attitudes and actions that may not accurately represent his: there is self-mockery and playfulness in his talk. I have included Fiona's part in the discussion because she was reflecting on her work with young women activists there.

FR: Tell me about marriage.

NK: So, in some other families, when you are married you have to be a housewife. Nothing more. "Let go of your struggle attire. Become a full-time homemaker. We cannot share our mother or our wife, our daughter in law, with the struggle. She is ours."

FR: I am writing the very last chapter of my thesis on young women activists and the fact that there doesn't appear to be a great deal of public acknowledgment in the country for the roles that young women took. In part because they weren't as active as young men, in part because there were fewer numbers of girls who were involved compared to the male youth, but I'm also arguing that it had a great deal to do with marriage and expectations of marriage. And I suppose what I am asking you to do is to check if I am analyzing this correctly? It seems to me that in some ways young women in the '80s [in Zwelethemba], and I'm talking about the '80s because that's the period I know, were able to be politically active because they were young women. And once they were married they fell under almost a different classification that did not allow them to be free radicals. . . . After that, they could only become politically active through the activities of their children—as mothers they could be politically active, but as women their roles were constrained pretty much to the women's movements. Do you think that that's a fair assessment?

NK: Yes, that's fair. There's more to it than that. Marriages, in themselves, during the struggle, were restrictive for the newlyweds, more especially for the women. You have roles in marriage that are highly conservative. [They left no time for the previous role in which she may have been] outspoken and different and [involved in] resistance during the struggle because to be a newlywed you must act in a dignified way—be docile. Yes, this word "dignity," *umfazi funeka abenesidima* [a woman must have dignity], this word is the one that restricts your freedom as a newlywed because *isidima* says that you must have dignity, that depth of character that makes you respectable. In Zulu it's called *isithunzi*. In seSotho we call it *seriti*. It's very difficult to translate into English; it's a *heavily* emotive word: *isithunzi*. African men must be respectable, they must command respect, and African women must also command respect: you command respect in so far as you are able to observe the marriage laws, rules, and regulations and in so far as you are able to perform the duties [implicit in this] very rich and emotional term. It is used as if it represents your full humanity. A housewife must *exude* it, express it by observing a dignified way of doing things. And be seen to be dignified. It means that there are some things that you must not do: talk loudly, insult people, be disrespectful, be defiant. And sometimes roles clashed. Can you imagine a newlywed person, a young woman, moving on the streets, shouting and insulting the police, daring and challenging them? [Laughs]

FR: But who would stop them? Is it the force of culture? The weight of society? In other words, say Nolwazi got married tomorrow, but say this was the 1980s: what would stop her from being at the forefront of the struggle?

NK: Community pressure, understanding convention, rather than pressure. Convention is one of those things that you take for granted, that is part and parcel of the package of being a newlywed woman. You have just got into marriage, you have received this orientation; the old women gave you some instructions, rules, and regulations, do's and don'ts. You know how we conducted ourselves in struggle—sometimes it was in direct contradiction with those rules and regulations, and therefore it made it almost impossible for young women who've just become married to express themselves in the way or manner that they had grown used to when they were unmarried and had joined the struggle as, in your words, "free radicals." Marriages restricted the participation of activists. She had to pigeonhole herself [laughs] into this code of conduct of womanhood, *ubufazi*, because you are not married to an individual, you are married to the whole family, to the whole clan, to the whole ethnic group, because you represent them in that you are a good mother.[3] [Unclear] So you can see the conventions.

FR: . . . This is the generation that confronted the elders. This is the generation that generated a revolution against the state. This is the generation that broke all of the boundaries of what the state called law. This is the generation that broke the boundaries of what the state defined as its edges, and they skipped the country. You know, this is a generation which is characterized in many ways by being able to break very, very rigid boundaries and yet somehow, "culture" almost coalesces as a weight around young women's identities when they marry. . . .

NK: It clips her wings. She cannot fly. Culture clips the wings of young women. Young women who got married while they were still activists had to settle. [Culture] cannot allow the situation in which [a] woman can become a newlywed who is *toyi-toyi*ing, lifting her legs ninety degrees [both laugh]. . . .

I can never imagine a woman move [*toyi-toyi*] on the side of the road, when a police van is there, taunting politically. That is unheard of, it seems, no matter how radical you are. . . . You will be questioned as a radical. "What kind of revolutionary are you? We aren't revolting against our own culture. We are revolting against the system. The system seeks to undermine our culture, while the revolution seeks to affirm that culture and to transform it for the better." There's another debate whether that culture is sort of restricting the freedom of women, but we had to fight one fight at the time; fight the system and then after that we can afford an opportunity to look into our cultures, really, really do some other things, give opportunity for quality of freedom to be exercised [unclear].

I'm not trying to imply that the women's struggle was suspended until we defeated the enemy, but their part . . . because of the intensity of our hatred of the system [we stood], sort of, for women's rights, and [we] were even against, on the whole, patriarchs in the struggle, but they were part and parcel of the revolutionary fabric. But we gave . . . precedence to confronting the system. . . . So, yes, the struggle intensified, and women's issues came to the fore because some of them were outspoken about the need not only to look at the state but to address us. We comrades have violated our fellow female comrades in the struggle. We disrespected them, yes, we abused them, yes . . . we lied and cheated. We used our status to have access to their hearts and to their bodies, to sleep with them. It was not uncommon. There were some of us as comrades who had plenty of women because our status gave us access to their bodies.

FR: And it's not uncommon for some of the comrades to now call those same women prostitutes!

NK: Yes. You see, because really, that's regrettable. Uhh. Yes, women would fight over a comrade. "This one is mine! You must have your own comrade!" There was a time in '85, in those days, [when] to be a comrade was a ticket to have a woman. So that's how some *comtsotsis* [gangsters] also derived this joy of being a comrade. . . . Regrettably, we wish we had taken heed of the words of Kwame Nkrumah [the first president of postcolonial Ghana] that the struggle should not be a means to exploit women. We sort of wanted emotional comfort, while we did not trust them. That's the, you know, irony of the situation. We wanted them to comfort us, to sleep, have sex, and feel relieved of the pressure, and at the same time we did not speak to them about what is troubling us, the emotional traumas that were burning inside us. Women were seen as potential informers.

FR: That's quite a thing to say, Nana.

NK: Yes. That was the perception. I am not saying that women were. Yes. There was a perception. . . .

FR: Why?

NK: . . . Perhaps if I can speculate I can say that because we were assuming that women cannot stand the pressure of interrogation and torture. They will let go of the information. Meanwhile, not all of us could stand torture. Just one smack on one of the guys can cause the whole confession. But we became extramoral when we dealt with women. Don't trust a woman with the most deep, dark secrets of the struggle. You must limit the kind of information that they have access to . . . because women gossip.

Nana's comment that "The system seeks to undermine our culture, while the revolution seeks to affirm that culture and to transform it for the better" is a key to an understanding of the way in which women activists in this small town were viewed by many of the men. Nana adds, "Despite the *disapproval* of many male activists women were not defeated." The women continued to fight on both fronts and secured the rights that are entrenched in the South African constitution. Nana repeated to me his regret that young activists had not taken heed of Nkrumah's words. Ross's book documents the high cost for women in Zwelethemba of their participation in the conflict. One of the most senior leaders among the youth in the mid-1980s was a young woman who entered the fray as a schoolgirl and only left some years later, when she married. She was Nana's close and trusted colleague. Of the top layer of local leaders, 32 percent were young women, and of the second layer, 44 percent were.

Contaminated Truth

Nana told me a story that he is still telling himself. In the following interview, he is shaping that story into a public one. He weighs my responses, reflects on the manner in which he reacted in the past, and consciously reconsiders the judgment he made then against the one he puts forward now, from a very different vantage point of freedom and success. It is a story about a break in a friendship caused by suspicions of disloyalty that circulated widely at the time—or it is actually about betrayal. Betrayal wove a constant thread through the lives of young activists (see chapter 3). The South African government used sophisticated tactics to spread an insidious net of informers across the country and beyond. Nana's tale is a remarkable one about hurt and reflection, and I use it to suggest the challenges that had to be faced and the process of questioning that continues. I quote from a conversation he and I had that was taped and transcribed. I have used pseud-

onyms for people mentioned in the discussion, including Nana's friend. In
the transcription, there is an example of the black humor Nana sometimes
used, and the context requires some explanation. The widespread use of informers led to accusations of betrayal and, sometimes, as we have seen, those
accused were put to death in a terrible way called "necklacing": a tire was
filled with gasoline, placed around the person's neck, and then set on fire.
Much has been written about it, and the Commission dealt quite comprehensively with it (see chapter 3). During the height of the conflict in 1985,
word spread that Nana's friend, whom I shall call George, had become an
impimpi to the security forces and that he was giving them details of Nana's
actions and movements. Nana was, at the time, alerted to the accusations. I
asked him to tell me about it.

> NK: The question of George is very complicated.
> PR: Betrayal always is, isn't it?
> NK: Yes. But what is essential is that I was able, over time, to put myself in
> his shoes and ask myself: why would a friend deliberately betray his own
> friend?
> PR: Why did he do it? What were the circumstances?
> NK: The circumstances around it: George was an orphan. He was raised
> by . . . [relatives], and when the man and his wife passed away, George was
> left to be taken care of by [younger kin]. Well, they ill treated him, really.
> You see, he was never given the basic necessities that you take for granted
> as a child. Pocket money for school, shoes, books, school fees, basic things,
> [and the lack left] psychological scars on him. He was always dressing [in
> a] drab [way], not given the best of clothes. He would have to wait for the
> left over clothes from his family and friends, and it was a struggle to make
> ends meet from the very outset. He had a very tough life. Sometimes,
> when my mother gave me money, I would say, "Give me some more," and
> she would be worried and think that I was involved in some kind of smok-
> ing or drinking, but I would be shy to tell her the story of George. I would
> say, "No, just give me some more. I have many [needs] and I am active
> in many things—sports, choirs, you see? So please give me some more."
> And then she made inquiries, and so I said, "Okay, if you want to know."
> I related the story of George, and then my mother felt sorry for me and
> would give me that extra amount, and I would give it to him. At school, in
> my circle of friends, I [invited] him into my study group.
>
> I used to assist him in mathematics and science because I have always
> been fond of mathematics and science, and he was struggling in those two

subjects. I would assist him, and then he would scrape through. We joined COSAS together in 1983. I was never important in COSAS. I was just a rabble-rouser; I would cause problems and punch holes in theories and [query] whatever they had done. "Why do you do this, why can't you do the other things?" The kind of person who irritates and derives fun [from doing so]. In a certain way it was egotistical of me . . . I was getting my own kicks, deriving my own kind of sense of importance, saying that, *ja*, I have contributed by asking all these irrelevant questions and enjoying seeing people struggle to answer them. He was always quiet, considerate, always thoughtful. Better than me. And sometimes it would irritate me— how can you be so politically [astute] but at school [not do well]? . . .

Our friendship blossomed. We played soccer on the street and in the club together. Although he was never that good at soccer, but I enjoyed his company because our street was on the outskirts of the township, so it was lonely, and it became a site of notoriety. You become silly and naughty in those streets because they are on the periphery. It is in those streets that you learn to be extra wicked, violent, silly, naughty, all those other things that your good parent tells you not to do. You do them. And all those things that will shock your parents but your parents [on being told about them] will be disgusted and say, "No, it is not my child who would do this." But you do that, and when you go home, you say, "Why, it's not me, Mum," and your mother would say, "*Ja*, I vowed to God, really my child would never do that." And your mother believes that how you con- duct yourself in the home is not totally different from how you conduct yourself on the street. As you know there are lots of *bundu* boys around and [we learned to protect each other, and, later] he [George] would ward off police from me. In 1985, there were many developments: the leader- ship was arrested; it was topsy-turvy, really difficult times.[4] There was no order, really. In the course of all that, the [local leaders who had not been arrested] wanted to silence [my problematic critique], and they gave me a position as the secretary of the youth organization [ZWEYO]. Now I matured very quickly in that position and became respectable even in the community, even among the older generation of political activists. They began to take me into the core [of their concerns], and I became more vo- cal, acting as a unifying factor and also a controversial factor. Most of the leaders got arrested. So I was left in power with a few others. [The young man, Amos, who had drawn me into politics was then] arrested—he was much more senior than I was. We were left in the lurch . . . As I [acquired local] power, I suppose other people became envious. There were rumors

running around that there was an informer and that the police were
moving around with a list of people who had attended the funeral [of the
Cradock Four], and George [had fallen under suspicion].[5]

Nana went on to describe George's involvement in a local church, at
which George sometimes preached, and the suspicions of betrayal that
were cast on one of George's neighbors who used to help him. Suspicion of
George spread, and Nana was cautioned to be wary of him. After some time,
George left home and was not seen again in the Cape. Nana, in his interview
with me, put forward his theories as to what may have happened, although,
at the time, he suspected George. He continued:

NK: There were two members of the Special Branch [the Intelligence Ser-
vice] who belonged to the same church and were on the church council.
Perhaps . . . [they] blackmailed George . . . wanting him to confirm and
double-check information and perhaps he refused. Perhaps they gave
him an offer that he [found unacceptable]. And then, in desperation or in
[retaliation], they said, "Okay, we are gonna show you, don't mess with
us." They spread the rumor that George is an informer to get back at him.
And in those times it was difficult—there was no time for reason, really,
it was a time of emotions. When we heard that someone was an informer,
that was a trigger—we could kill the person on the spot and ask later,
"What did you say?" So that was the problem. Perhaps George protected
us, really, he didn't give information, and when he was confronted in fact
he didn't run away because he was guilty—he ran away because he felt
betrayed, you see? So rather than allow our hands to drip with his blood,
he chose to run away so as to deprive us of the opportunity to kill him.

PR: That's a supposition? You don't know?

NK: Yes, that's a supposition. [After he left home] he wrote a letter to me. I
did not even read it; I tore it up. I don't know why. Perhaps I was still full
of anger [at the thought that he had betrayed me]—understandable in a
person of my age, seventeen to eighteen years at that time. At that age you
are driven more by emotions than by your brains and thoughts. That's
a theory that I'm having about him. I met George at the funeral [in Jo-
hannesburg] of Comrade Chris Hani.[6] He was all raggedy and he was a
vagrant, really, more like a hobo. And he tore my heart apart.

PR: I remember you telling me that.

NK: I've never been the same. I felt so guilty. That's when I began this
process of interrogating myself, trying to put everything into proper per-

spective. But one can never understand the truth, even if I were to meet him again. The time—time has also contaminated a better version of the truth, so we are going to get truth of a lesser quality now. Contaminated. The experiences he went through after he ran away from Worcester would shape how he would relate his story now.

PR: But was there any evidence of him having caused harm? Were people picked up as a consequence of the information he gave the police, or doesn't one really know?

NK: No, there was no proof.

PR: But there was an informer in the area, that was all?

NK: There were many informers; people were being picked up at the time. If George was an informer, how [was it made known]? If he was a vital cog in the supply [of information] because he was so close to us in the center, why would the police give away their winning ticket?

PR: Even the police were informed on by informers. It was complex, wasn't it?

NK: Yes. George was close to me, and the police were interested in me. People were promised houses [to inform on me]; I know some people in my neighborhood were being paid money to keep check on my family and check when I popped home, and as soon as I did, they may have phoned [the police]. I know it was part of the procedures, and it is [often] rife in a country that is in a civil war or a country that is in strife. The state won't be shy to invest money checking who its enemies are and where they are. It makes sense that George would be an important cog for them. . . . There never will be any proof. That's the question, that's the main point. To be able to rise above that brutality—it drains the energy levels. You have to rely on your moral fiber [and] from all those good teachings that human beings are inherently good and that they learn to be bad and that they are corrupted by conditions.

The story of George shows how difficult it was to know truth from lies during the conflict. George is the loved one who left. He brings dark morality into the scheme of things. It is an archetypal tale. Did he betray Nana? Many people were sure, at the time, that he had. Did the security forces implicate him falsely? Is Nana right in thinking (or hoping in retrospect) that George left town to prevent Nana and his comrades from making a mistake if they harmed him?

The story shows how Nana is living with his thoughts after the conflict is over. Is George the shadow, the projection of Nana's achievement? The business of being a leader is complex, as all moral projects are.

I have suggested that some of the young who stood against the apartheid regime strove toward self-knowledge and attempted to act in relation to an ethic that they consciously formulated with regard to political activism. (In interlude 1, I talked about their introduction to politics, and I touched on the emergence in childhood of their ideas of justice and loyalty.) I have drawn on interviews with one young man, showing that he continues to reflect on the experiences he and his close comrades had and the decisions they made during difficult times. His remarks on past attitudes toward and treatment of young women show some of the complexities with which they were faced. He recalls the attitudes while being aware that, at least in terms of discourse, they have changed, and in so doing he lays himself open to the charges that can be made against many of the young men at that time; he makes no attempt to exempt himself. As a member of the top layer of local leaders, Nana worked in close cooperation with women. The interview about the break in his friendship with George shows the strain under which they operated and the continuing cogitation around recall of the past.

Norms and Normalization

In his 1974–1975 lectures at the Collège de France, Foucault talked about "the government of children," which, he said, developed in the eighteenth century, or the Classical Age, when the "art of governing" emerged in the sense in which "government" was then understood as precisely the "government" of children, the mad, the poor, and the workers (2003c, 48–49). Foucault takes from Georges Canguilhem a set of ideas to do with norms and normalization (Canguilhem 1978). The first relates to the general process of social, political, and technical normalization during the eighteenth century and the multiplication of its effects regarding childhood and other facets of society. The second is the idea that the norm is defined by the exacting and coercive role it performs and so claims power: it is "not simply and not even a principle of intelligibility; it is an element on the basis of which a certain exercise of power is founded and legitimized" (2003c, 50). And the third idea is that the norm's function is "not to exclude and reject," for it is "linked to a positive technique of intervention and transformation, to a sort of normative project" (50). It is an important passage in Foucault's thinking, as it leads up to his description of a "type of power that is not linked to ignorance but a power that can only function thanks to the formation of a knowledge that is both its effect and also a condition of its exercise" (52).

I draw on Foucault here because we seldom talk quite so clearly about the "government of children" and because his notion of the norm as a project not to exclude and reject but to intervene and transform sadly throws into relief the apartheid project, which had a "norm" for black children that was a subnorm or an unnorm (i.e., neither subnormal nor abnormal) for children seen as remainders, rejects, undesirables, servants, laborers. Against this, the young rebelled and, I have argued, somehow managed to hold to an ethical project superior to that of the apartheid state.

FIVE

Neutralizing the Young

> Had never expected hope would form itself
> completely in my time . . . was never so sanguine
> as to believe old injuries could transmute easily
> through any singular event or idea . . . never
> so feckless as to ignore the managed contagion
> of ignorance the continued discontinuities
> the felling of leaders and future leaders
> the pathetic erections of soothsayers
>
> —ADRIENNE RICH, "MIDNIGHT SALVAGE"

This chapter is about the difficulties of recording the role that the young play in wars and of describing their action and practice during conflict. It is a contribution to the critique of a system of knowing or causing to know (see Last 1981). By obscuring reality, we excuse ourselves from knowing the consequences for the young of war and oppression and from acknowledging the profundity of their understanding and the courage entailed in their engagement in conflict.

Adrienne Rich has, as poets do, seen clearly that a single event or idea like a truth commission is unlikely to transmute harm done. Nor can it compensate for the felling of leaders and the inability to build on the trust, political wisdom, and moral strength of those who fought on the streets of the "earth made wretched under apartheid." At the time of the conflict, the role of young activists in the fight for liberation was internationally acknowledged; within South Africa, it is now accorded due honors on a specific national holiday and in minor ways, often as part of rhetoric. However, the details

of the contribution of young activists and the description of their fight, despite the efforts of the Commission, have not been fully recorded. Few of
them received reparations, and there has been put in place a minimum of
assistance in care, training, education, or employment opportunities. Here,
I begin by harvesting details of what was done to thousands and thousands
of the young under apartheid, drawing on data gathered during the time of
conflict by brave and admirable nongovernmental organizations. The findings of the South African Truth and Reconciliation Commission, as given
in its initial five-volume *Report*, follow. The chapter examines one aspect of
the TRC's account of the South African war for liberation between 1960
and 1994. It looks at how casualties are listed, classified, and classed between
"civilian" and "soldier." It is hard to know how the Commission will be
judged as time goes on. Some of its shortcomings are already clear, and one
of them, in my opinion, lies in the manner in which its concentration on violations obscured the part played by the young in securing democracy. The
following account is a warning tale: it suggests that definitions themselves
can exclude and occlude.

An ethnographic study of the Commission constituted a strange piece
of fieldwork. Being a detached observer of the TRC hearings was distressing. I knew but a few of the testifiers and made no attempt to meet others,
not wishing to intrude during anguished times. The hearings filled me with
ambivalence about the Commissioners' roles and my own. I was particularly
troubled by the realization that the testimonies were like snippets from a
collage, cut out of time, place, history, relationships, contingency, choice,
and pattern. The general subsumed the particular. It soon became apparent
that few young activists were testifying and that little would be documented
about the nature of their fight.

A Subtle Form of Neutralization

Some statistics about the numbers of the young who were involved in the
struggle against apartheid were compiled during the conflict and were available before the Commission began its work. It is still not known how many
of the young were directly involved from 1960 to 1994. No liberation organization has figures available. A senior officer in the ANC, in response to our

request for them, said, "I shall be delighted if anyone has the information." He doubted the usefulness of Youth League or Youth Congress figures, as they were largely based on attendance at rallies. Neither the Pan Africanist Congress (PAC) nor the Azanian People's Organization (AZAPO) had figures. None of the liberation organizations had, at the time, accumulated and sorted their archives. It is not surprising that membership was not recorded, given the broad support for liberation, even if, for many, it was not acted on—and given the danger of flouting laws that made it a crime to belong to or promote the activities of banned organizations. The ANC and the PAC were banned on April 8, 1960, and their military wings in 1963. AZAPO was banned later. In all, ninety-eight organizations were banned, of which 43 percent were youth and student organizations (HRC 1990, 23; see also Coleman 1998, 91).

Prison officials in the Northern and Western Cape responded to my request for figures of the young held in their jails from 1960 to 1994, and I was sent numbers of all prisoners for the years in question. However, the figures were not differentiated in terms of age, nor did they show under what legislation, for what length of time, or how many times each person had been imprisoned. On further enquiry, it was suggested to me that I visit each prison. My attempts were thwarted either by a refusal of access or by the fact that data relating to "periods of unrest" had been shredded or lost.

Government statistics on the detention of children and youth are Monty Pythonesque in their obscurantism. House of Assembly Questions and Answers on Detention show how the actual figures were disguised under a battery of legislation and by varying the boundaries of categories. Frequently, those questioned simply refused to answer.

The estimates made during the years of conflict by independent organizations like the Black Sash, the Detainees' Parents Support Committee (DPSC), the Human Rights Committee (HRC), and the South African Institute of Race Relations (SAIRR) are invaluable resources. However, their figures often differ. For the year 1986, for example, the number of children under eighteen held in detention without trial ranges, according to three sources, from 2,677 (Thomas 1990, 439; source, Hansard Government Statistics) to four thousand (ibid.; source, DPSC) to 8,800 (UNICEF 1989, 87, in Hansard). For the period July 21, 1985, to August 7, 1986, Hansard House of Assembly documents (1960–1994) give detention figures for "ju-

veniles" (people under the age of twenty-one) as 3,681 and for children under sixteen as two thousand: 46 percent and 25 percent of the total number
of detainees, 7,996, held during those seven months.

The HRC (Coleman 1998, 43) conservatively estimated that during the
apartheid era eighty thousand people were held in detention without trial:

> A number of observers and students of repression around the world have
> commented that the repression in South Africa during the apartheid era
> pales into insignificance when compared with some Latin American coun-
> tries if the numbers of political disappearances and assassinations are used
> as the criteria for making such judgement. For example, disappearances and
> assassinations in Argentina were said to total around 30,000 while in South
> Africa the figure was but a few hundred. However, in South Africa this
> terminal method of eliminating political opponents has never been the main
> weapon, but rather the weapon of last resort when all other methods have
> failed. Apartheid's big gun has been detention without trial and this is where
> we see the big numbers—conservatively 80,000 people have been subjected
> to this subtle and sophisticated form of neutralisation. It has the advantages
> of maintaining the semblance of legality (all detentions are made in terms
> of legislation); it can be aimed not only at individuals, but at families, groups
> and organizations and even at whole communities, including women and
> children; it can be used to extract information to draw others into the net;
> it can be used to force confessions leading to conviction and permanent
> incarceration; it can be used to break political activists both physically and
> psychologically; it can be used to recruit informers and sow suspicion and
> confusion within communities; it can be followed by a banning order which
> effectively extends the victim's detention to within his or her own home; and
> finally it can, if need be, set the stage for permanent removal from society.

The most frequently quoted figure for the detention without trial of children under eighteen years old between 1960 and 1988 is fifteen thousand:
it is an estimate based on numbers published by the HRC in the document
"Detention Without Trial," published in November 1988 and included in
Coleman (1998, 43–53). By their own account and with reference to their
other data and estimates, the figure slips beyond the conservative into timidity, an understandable timidity given that the document was published
during the apartheid era and taking into account the ferocity of government reaction to the slightest inaccuracy they could detect. They take as the
base seventy-five thousand detentions, then say, "Official figures released

in an affidavit to court by the South African Police during April 1987 revealed that of a total of 4,224 detainees being held in Emergency detention on 15 April 1987, those aged 18 or less (down to 12) numbered 1,424, or 34 percent of the total. If one accepts the extremely conservative estimate of 20 percent under 18s for all detentions since 1960, then about 15,000 children under 18 experienced detention" (Coleman 1998, 51–52). The same figure is quoted by the HRC publication *Children and Repression in 1987–89* (1990, 4) in which the following figures are also given:

Detention without trial for children under 18 from:
1984–1986: 10,000
1986–1987: 8,500
1987–1988: 1,000

The number from 1984 to 1988 of children under eighteen detained is 19,500, that is, 37.5 percent of the total number of detainees, fifty-two thousand. If 37.5 percent of the seventy-five thousand detainees held from 1960 to 1988 is assumed, then the number of children under eighteen is 28,125. The official government figure released for the period of July 21, 1985, to March 7, 1986, was that 25 percent of the detainees were under sixteen years of age; that is 2,016 out of 7,996 (Coleman 1998, 51). If it is supposed (however unlikely the supposition may be) that 25 percent of the fifty-two thousand detainees held between 1984 and 1988 were children under sixteen, then thirteen thousand children aged thirteen through fifteen were held. Hansard records that twenty-nine children aged thirteen, ninety-one aged fourteen, 2,287 aged fifteen; and 357 aged sixteen—a total of 2,764—were detained (SAIRR 1960–1992). Almost three thousand were considered to have been a direct threat to the state. These sets of figures suggest that the estimated fifteen thousand children detained from 1960 to 1994 is probably conservative. The estimate made by the Black Sash that during that period twenty-four thousand children under eighteen were held in detention under emergency and security laws seems more likely to be closer to the actual number.

It is important to note that officials adopted a number of means to disguise their incarceration of children. The law only obligated the government to release figures of those detained for over thirty days: many thousands were held for fewer days (they were often released just before they had spent thirty days in prison) without being charged or brought to trial (Coleman 1998, 52). Figures were released pertaining only to detentions under State of Emergency and security legislation, but children were held under many other pieces of legislation, including those having to do with crime and public violence (see appendix 6). Many of the young were detained without trial over and over again. Local police and prison officials were, at various times (to phrase it most conservatively), given loose rein over the treatment of the young. There was no control over management and security of their record keeping. Masses of documents were shredded or lost from police stations and prisons throughout the country. Furthermore, many of the young who were held in cells did not tell their families what had befallen them.

Other figures on what was done to the young suggest the nature of the force that was aimed at them. Eight people aged twenty or younger died in detention between June 1986 and 1989; eighty-four prisoners aged fourteen to eighteen were hospitalized; thirty-nine children under eighteen were placed under restriction orders; and one thousand people aged on average fifteen to eighteen years were on the run, some for five to six years (HRC 1990). Elizabeth Floyd (herself detained) said, "death is clearly behind the detention system" (HRV hearing, May 2, 1996, Johannesburg).

Youth and students were "at the forefront of resistance to apartheid since 1976, and have as a result borne the brunt of repression" (Coleman 1998, 24). They became one of the main target groups of the security police (50). In 1988, 46.5 percent of detainees were students or scholars, and in the first three months of 1989, 75 percent were (HRC, 17).

There are at least five reasons for worrying about how many children were imprisoned: because the numbers involved reflect the part played by children and youth in securing the end of apartheid, because that part is poorly documented (despite the sterling work of organizations like the Black Sash and the HRC), because there is an inadequate accounting of even the most extreme of children's experiences, because the young called down the wrath of an armed state on their heads, and because impunity and disregard has followed.

One to Two

> For almost every adult that was violated, probably two or more children or young people suffered
>
> *Truth and Reconciliation Commission of South Africa Report*

The writing in this chapter comes from my indignation. Scanlon (1998, 271) says that it is the "violation of the requirements of justifiability to others that makes it appropriate for a third party to react with indignation rather than merely dismay or pity for the victim."

The Human Rights Violation Committee of the Commission received 21,298 statements (1:166—the number is 21,297 on page 168 and 19,524 on page 169; the reason is unclear) about gross human rights violations (GHRV), of which 37,672 allegations were made, including ten thousand killings (1:170–171). The *Report* says that 3.5 million suffered directly, of whom 90 percent were African. And, the *Report* says, a "truth" was arrived at: "the state sanctioned murder." The Commission's statistics, based on their own evidence only, are that 9,043 people were killed, 2,900 were tortured (and in the testimonies of those tortured there were 5,002 instances of torture recorded), and 17,150 were severely ill treated. (See the *Report* for a discussion of the definitions, codes, and database used by the Commission.) The *Report* says that half of those tortured were men under twenty-four, and the majority of victims of killings were young men between the ages of thirteen and twenty-four (4:259). The Commission performed no census and made no sample because, the Commissioners said, they lacked the resources and the money.

If we follow the other statistics that are widely accepted and take the number of people who were detained without trial for political reasons during the 1960 to 1994 period (the period covered by the Commission) to be eighty thousand (a figure that leaves out all other forms of gross human rights violations, including acts committed by vigilantes, security forces outside jails, liberation organizations, and members of communities against one another) and place the Commission's findings beside that figure, we see how few of the records of those harmed are in the TRC archive. The statements from 21,298 people represent 26 percent of the eighty thousand detained without trial. Of these statements, 17,150 were declared to represent severe ill treatment (81 percent) and 2,900 experiences of torture (14 percent). Supposing that these percentages can be taken to be representative of the eighty thousand people detained, of whom twenty-four thousand were under eighteen, then it is possible that 15,552 children aged seventeen or younger were severely ill treated—the Commission agreed that "detention without trial itself constituted severe ill-treatment" (Burton 2000, 81), and 2,688 were tortured. That is to say, a total of 18,240 children endured severe suffering in detention. The point is simply a reminder that the findings given in the *Report* are no more than a scrap of the whole cloth.

The Report *on "Children and Youth"*

There are many caveats in the *Report*'s statements about youth and children, and a series of defenses are proffered. Volume 4, chapter 9 is on the Special Hearing Concerning Children and Youth. An early paragraph in the chapter reads as follows:

> When considering the experiences of children under apartheid, it is impor-
> tant to remember that the Act provided for victims of defined gross human
> rights violations to testify and make statements to the Commission. This
> chapter therefore concerns the statements and testimonies of deponents
> who were defined as victims in terms of legislation. This focus on victims
> is not, however, intended to diminish the active role of children and youth.
> Children were agents of social change and harnessed vast amounts of energy,
> courage and resilience during the apartheid era. For many young people,
> active engagement in political activity resulted in the acquisition of skills
> such as analysis, mobilization and strategizing, as well as the ability to draw
> strength from friends and comrades in times of hardship. Many of today's
> leaders come from a politically active history and have displayed a remark-
> able capacity for forgiveness and reconciliation.
>
> *(4:268–269)*

In volume 5, it is said that "the Commission received few statements from ANC leaders, past or present. Almost none of the ANC's senior leaders in exile came to the Commission to give first-hand details of what had led them into exile or of their experiences at the hands of cross-border intruders. . . . Few *Umkhonto we Sizwe* (MK) cadres or underground activists, aside from those who applied for amnesty, made statements to the Commission" (5:199). The *Report* continues:

> Thus, while the Commission tapped a rich seam of experience from rank and
> file supporters of the ANC, its knowledge of those who led and those who
> worked in its structures for lengthy periods of time is largely non-existent.
> This has severely constrained the Commission's capacity to provide the "full
> and complete" picture that the act demands. . . . The Commission accepts

that its framework may have been problematic to some. *Many refused to regard themselves as victims.* The consequence is, however, that the historical record of violations in this country and outside it has suffered grievous omissions, particularly in regard to the 1960s and, more broadly, in relation to torture [emphasis added].

They note that few underground activists gave statements, that their knowledge of leaders and workers over time is largely nonexistent, that the lack severely constrained the fulfillment of their brief, and that the record suffers grievous omissions. They observe that "Scarcely any former UDF [United Democratic Front] regional or local leadership figures gave statements to the Commission. In some areas they were openly cynical. The UDF played a central role for a significant part of the 1980s, the period that saw a considerable intensification of conflict and abuses. Thus again, an important and crucial input has been denied to the Commission" (5:200). The PAC is roundly scolded for the "flimsiness and lack of coherence" of its leadership in responding to requests from the Commission: they "repudiated" it, yet members applied for amnesty (5:201). The IFP "made no pretence of co-operating" (5:200). Elsewhere in the *Report*, the chairman, Archbishop Tutu, confesses that it was "a flawed Commission," though the best possible under the circumstances.

Indeed, the Commission bemoans the lack of cooperation from many sectors. They cite the defensiveness of many who appeared at the special hearings, the refusal of judges to attend the hearings on the legal system, and the low number of magistrates who responded to the invitations. The Commission chose not to subpoena them, although they had the power to do so. They say that given "the difficulties and restraints in accessing information," they relied, to a large extent, on amnesty applications. Revelations by members of the security forces brought forth applicants from security police members, but the South African Defence Force (SADF) ranks kept silent: some information was gleaned from former members of Military Intelligence (MI) and Special Forces. The National Intelligence Service (NIS) members made no application and denied responsibility for actions that arose from the information they handed to operational units in the South African Police (SAP) and SADF. "The Commission," the *Report* adds, "rejects this position." The bulk of ANC, PAC, and APLA applications for amnesty related to the post-1990 period (5:200–203).

On their access to documentation and information held by "primary role-players," the *Report* says,

> It needs to be stated at the outset that the former state deliberately and systematically destroyed state documentation in an attempt to ensure that a new democratic government would be denied access to incriminating evidence. Hundreds of thousands of classified records—literally scores of tons—were destroyed. Much of this documentation related to the inner workings of the security forces and intelligence agencies, covert projects, informer networks, personnel records of security force members, and material confiscated from institutions and individuals. The destruction of the documentation deprived the Commission and the country as a whole of a rich and valuable source of material for its investigation into the conflicts of the past.
>
> *(5:203)*

The "series of filters and blocks" to the Commission's free and open access to materials are listed in regard to the South African National Defence Force (SANDF) and the National Intelligence Agency (NIA) under the new government (the SANDF and NIA replaced the SADF and NIS, respectively). The Commission confesses to having "erred in not conducting a search-and-seizure raid in the [military] archives" (5:204). The NIA established a "TRC desk," but it failed to respond to the Commission's requests.

The Report *on What the Apartheid Government Did to the Young*

The Commission reaches a series of conclusions about the direct and vicious attack by the state on the young. The following findings are drawn from volume 4, chapter 9, on the Special Hearing: Children and Youth. It is admitted that few, even at this series of hearings, spoke about the role of young people: the focus was on their suffering. (The statements that follow, up until the next subheading, are direct quotations from chapter nine. They have been run together as continuous text, and page numbers are given in brackets.)

> Very early on, the former state became aware of the pivotal role of children and youth, identifying them as a serious threat and treating them accordingly. Dr. Max Coleman spoke of the waging of an undeclared war against children and youth, in which they became the primary targets of detention,

torture, bannings, assassination, and harassment of every description [252]. Children and youth faced the full force of state oppression as they took on their role as the "foot soldiers of the struggle" [253]. The threat, which the youth presented, is evidenced by the backlash from the former state that used its oppressive armoury against the young [253]. Many . . . student and youth organizations emerged, based on differing political ideologies. They too became targets of state repression [253]. The state used various means to suppress dissent. Arrests and detentions removed opponents from the political arena. Courts were used to criminalise political activity. In the 1980s, in particular, students and youth organisations were banned, as were the possession and distribution of their publications. From 1976 to 1990, outdoor political gatherings were outlawed. From 1986, there was a blanket ban on indoor gatherings aimed at promoting work stoppage, stay aways, or educational boycotts.

The security establishment engaged in the informed repression of children by hunting down "troublesome" youth and developing an informer network. This latter had dire consequences for youth organizations [254].

Until 1985, casualties were mainly the result of security force action. From 1987, however, vigilantism began to make an appearance. Dr. Max Coleman, who made a presentation at the hearing in Gauteng, argued that:

The destabilization strategy was cold-blooded, calculated, deliberate . . . it was about a collusion between various elements who had an interest in maintaining the status quo or at least retaining the power which they had from the apartheid system [254–255].

Many vigilante attacks were rooted in intergenerational conflicts. Some men saw the dramatic surge of women and youth to political prominence as a threat to the patriarchal hierarchies of age and gender. Young people were perceived to be undermining the supremacy of traditional leaders who saw it as their duty to restrain them. Vigilantes mobilized around slogans such as, "discipline the children," and frequently described themselves as "fathers" [255]. Vigilantism coincided with the state strategy of creating "oil spots"— that is, establishing strategic bases in townships as a means of regaining control of the population. A second aspect of the strategy involved the co-option of leaders, the counter-organization of communities and the formation of counter-guerrilla groups. The state supported many vigilante groups by providing funding and training.

Large numbers of youth, whether politically active or not, were affected by the violence, especially those who lived near the hostels [for migrant men] [255].

Many of South Africa's young people grew up in an atmosphere of imminent danger. They lived with the painful reality of losing loved ones and family members and were often conscious of the burden of responsibility they carried for the lives of others. Their lives were characterized by fear and insecurity. Because the state made no distinction between public and private space, their homes did not provide them with a safe haven. Many children were on the run because they feared for their lives and suffered grave disruptions to their education and development [257].

On the Role of the Young

The *Report* says little on the actual part that the young played. The following is culled from the same chapter:

According to testimony at the Athlone hearing, children had to make choices about whether to avoid, participate in, or lead the resistance. Many of South Africa's children did not stand passively by, but actually disputed the legitimacy of the state. In doing so, "they contributed to the dismantling of apartheid" [252]. The role of children and youth was crucial in opposing the apartheid system. However, in the process, they were drawn into an arena that exposed them to three particular kinds of violence: state oppression, counter-violence, and inter- and intra-community violence [252]. The role of youth in resisting apartheid dates back to the formation of the militant African National Congress (ANC) Youth League in 1943. The militancy of the youth provided the impetus for the Defiance Campaign of 1952 and the drafting of the Freedom Charter in 1955. In the 1960s, students were amongst those who rose up in their thousands to protest against the pass laws. The state's response to these peaceful protests was mass repression. Many youth saw no option but to leave the country in order to take up arms and fight for liberation. Umkhonto we Sizse (MK), formed in 1961, drew many of its recruits from the ranks of the youth [252–253].

In June 1976, the student revolt that began in Soweto transformed the political climate. One hundred and four children under the age of sixteen were killed in the uprising and resistance spread to other parts of the country. Dissent by the children and youth of South Africa cast children in the role of agents for social change, as well as making them targets of the regime. Classrooms became meeting grounds for organisations such as the Congress of South African Students (COSAS), which was formed in 1979 and ultimately boasted a membership of over a million students. The security police clampdown on COSAS resulted in the arrest of over 500 of its members by the time of the declaration of the state of emergency in July 1985 [253]. In many cases [of state sponsored vigilante action in townships], the responsibility for protecting their homes and streets fell on children. Some young people turned their attention to the defence of their communities, redirecting their energies into the formation of self-defence units that were, in their view, justified by vigilante attacks [255].

Children were agents of social change and harnessed vast amounts of energy, courage, and resilience during the apartheid era [268–269].

The Commission's Evidence of What Was Done to the Young

In volume 4, chapter 9 (to which the page numbers refer unless otherwise stated), in a section entitled "Evidence and Emerging Themes," the *Report* gives the findings related to the harm done to the young (258). The *Report* cautions against taking them as reflecting "a universal experience of violations": they should be read within the framework of the Commission's experience (259). The *Report* presents the evidence in four figures (reproduced in appendix 5):

> Figure 1. Number of killings, by age and sex of victims. [It is noted at the bottom of the figure that the "age and/or sex of the victim [is] missing in 61 percent of the violations." The figure does not reveal where that 61 percent lies, as there is no category for people of neither age nor sex.]
> Figure 2. Number of acts of torture, by age and sex of victim. [Only 14 percent of the violations are not identified as having been committed on bodies of specified age and/or sex.]
> Figure 3. Number of abductions, by age and sex of victim. [Fifty-seven percent of victims are unidentified according to age and/or sex.]
> Figure 4. Number of acts of severe ill treatment by age and sex of victim. [The age and/or sex of the victim is missing in 22 percent of the violations.]

There are a number of serious problems in the documentation and presentation of findings on violations experienced by the young. Did statement takers fail to note the age and/or sex of as many as 61 percent of those killed and 57 percent of those abducted? Further, the fact that 22 percent of acts of severe ill treatment and 14 percent of acts of torture could have been identified without notice of sex or age of the person suggests inadequacy in data collection. In volume 5 of the *Report*, the paragraph that prefaces the findings on children and youth states:

> The Commission endorses the international position that children and youth under the age of eighteen are entitled to special protection from government and society. As the Commission's statistics have shown, the greatest proportion of victims of gross violations of human rights was youth, many of them under eighteen.
>
> *(5:254)*

Despite that endorsement, the Commission chose to conflate statistics of children between the ages of thirteen and eighteen with those of youth between nineteen and twenty-four. In volume 4, chapter 9, the following rationale is given:

> By far the largest category of victims to report to the Commission fell into the twenty-four age bracket (see figures 1–4). *For this reason*, some adaptations to the accepted definition of children and youth were made for the purposes of this report. Children between the ages of thirteen and eighteen experienced violations *equivalent* to their nineteen to twenty-four year old counterparts, and it was considered that a *more appropriate* unit of analysis could be achieved by combining these age categories to include young people between thirteen and twenty-four years of age. This reflects, first, the fact that this age group was a clear target for gross human rights violations in South Africa and, second, the fact that those who were more likely to be victims of random violence were those who found themselves in exposed situations. Younger children were victims of random violence but were less likely to attend marches or demonstrations, which is where the largest number of random violations occurred.
>
> *(258–259, emphasis added)*

In effect, the Commission undermined the possibility of recording accurate data for the archive and of contributing to the international position with regard to the protection of children. The question of "equivalence" of violations experienced by young people under or over the age of eighteen years begs for analysis. One may ask how "random violence" can be firmly identified: the intimacy of knowledge by security force members of the identity of local youth leaders could have led to carefully targeted violence. The question of age is a complex one in relation to statistics. The Convention of Rights of the Child refers to children under the age of eighteen, the Commission's statistics refer to children from zero to twelve and to children and youth from thirteen to twenty-four, and the ANC defines the category of youth as anyone under thirty-five. The *Report* gives a disingenuous reason for the small number of violations documented as having been committed to children under the age of twelve: "It is unlikely that this was a result of under-reporting, as violations perpetrated against the very young have tended to invoke the strongest condemnation" (258). Who, we might wonder, was listening to and acting in accord with such condemnation?

The figures in the *Report* are poorly drawn, too small, and give no totals, so that the only recourse is to measure with a ruler against the baseline to find totals for particular age categories. (Commission data on the total numbers of those killed, tortured, and severely ill treated have been quoted above.) It is hard to countenance the absurdity of devising figures that place men and boys on the plus side of a divide and women and girls on the minus side: that is, female victims are represented as being from minus 1 to minus 500 on the figures. Estimates based on the use of a ruler on figure 1 suggest that 45 percent of the total number killed were people under twenty-four years old. Figure 3 shows that 42 percent of abductions were of people in this age category. Figures 2 and 4 show that 53 percent of all acts of torture and 30 percent of all acts of severe ill treatment were committed on the bodies of people younger than twenty-four years.

The chapter ends with a section on the consequences for the young of apartheid and gross human rights violations. Here, the *Report* acknowledges that the focus on the young as victims is not "intended to diminish the active role of children and youth" (268–269). The "largely positive role" they played is recognized, yet the Commission's evidence reveals "the generally negative consequences of repression in the period under review" (269). Appendix 6 gives the Commission's findings on children and youth (5:254–256). Curiously, the five "recommendations" (5:321; see appendix 7) made in relation to children and youth begin thus: "CHILD LABOUR IN ALL FORMS BE ELIMINATED THROUGH APPROPRIATE LEGISLATION" (the *Report* uses small capitals in bold for Recommendations). Curious, because children's work is neither the focus of any of the Commission's proceedings, nor are there any findings related to work—unless fighting the apartheid state is considered to have been labor.

Misreading the Nature of the Conflict

There is a continuing problem: how to arrive at an adequate description of the nature or the kind of conflict from which South Africa has just emerged. It was, surely, a different kind of war. The *Report* (2:26) uses the following definition of guerrilla warfare as the government understood it:

> The government understood the onslaught [the concerted effort to over-throw the government of South Africa] as being in the tradition of guerrilla warfare. This type of warfare is characterised by the relative unimportance of military operations in the sense of combat operations carried out against opposing armed forces. Rather, the aim of the revolutionary forces is to gain control of government by gaining the support of the people through a combination of intimidation, persuasion, and propaganda.

It is a definition that leans on the negative, that supposes two forces in opposition to each other, and that places "the people" in a passive state as receivers of intimidation, persuasion, and propaganda. The people with whom I worked would reject that characterization.

The positing of a revolutionary force leads the authors of the *Report* into particular definitions of membership, command, and accountability. Thabo Mbeki, then vice president of the newly elected government, in giving evidence during the first ANC submission to the Commission, defined the ANC as having a specifiable force. "The political and operational leadership of the movement is ready to accept collective responsibility for all operations of its properly constituted offensive structures, including operations . . . that might have been outside the established norms" (5:240). The *Report* notes that the ANC, with hindsight, claimed credit for the development of the strategy of the people's war and for "rendering the country ungovernable." The authors of the *Report* query the claim and suggest that "the ANC was responding to violence that had already erupted and was spreading largely spontaneously around the country. The pamphlet released on 25 April 1985, calling on people to 'Make apartheid unworkable! Make the country ungovernable!' was an attempt to keep up with the rising militancy in the townships" (2:34–35). The *Report* observes that by the second half of 1985, unrest had spread throughout South Africa and that in the post-1985 period it became more sustained, surprising not only the government but also the ANC (2:34). In the same volume, the relationship between the ANC and the internal mass organizations that became central to the resistance movements in the late 1970s and 1980s is described as having been complex:

> They were tenuous in that the internal underground structures of the exiled ANC, for most of the period, were weak. This meant that lines of communication and decision-making between those "inside" and those "outside" were often ineffective. The relationship was strong in that there was an extremely dedicated core of activists inside the mass movements who owed loyalty to the ANC. Even where they were not formally linked into decision-making structures via underground cells, they communicated with the ANC in exile and on Robben Island through an ingenious variety of methods. Through this complicated and uneven process, activists inside South Africa interpreted what they understood to be "the line" of "the Movement." There were, however, many occasions where activists themselves were, in practice, determining "the line" and where the ANC in exile was bound to accept their interpretation of events "on the ground."
>
> *(2:339–340)*

The description constitutes a subtle account of interrelationships between the exiles and internal activists, one that reflects interdependence and cyclical influences that shaped policy and strategy. It is, however, a general description and seems not to have been drawn from detailed testimonies of individuals or organizations.

In the *Report*, it is said that the Commission "has always been violation driven" (5:211). This drive and the task it assigned itself of establishing accountability called for tracing lines of command, so that a party or organization could be held morally responsible for violations committed by its members. To be awarded amnesty, an applicant must establish that the abuse perpetrated was done in pursuit of the aims of a recognized political organization. Those who had been violated and made statements to the Commission were not asked on the form to which political organization they had belonged at the time. Membership or affiliation matters. However, lines of command and membership among those who fought within the country are difficult to establish. The conflict was long, and the liberation organizations were banned for many years, so that their activities were dangerous, clandestine, largely unfunded, and carried out against the force of a sophisticated and fully armed state. It is possible to trace the patterns of lines in command and to establish membership of liberation movements by careful recording and analysis at community levels, but no attempt has been made to do that on a national scale by the government, the Commission, or liberation organizations. In consequence, many people, including the young, who fought over years and years and who suffered strings of violations and great losses in many aspects of their lives remain unacknowledged and have received no compensation. The ANC had initially excluded most young activists from their demobilization and pension schemes.

In deciding what manner of conflict the country had been through, the Commissioners decided to follow the guidelines provided by the norms and rules contained in international humanitarian law, particularly as laid out in the four Geneva Conventions of 1949 and the two Additional Protocols of 1977. They adopted the two essential concepts of "combatant" and "protected person."

Article 43 (paragraphs 1 and 2) of Additional Protocol 1 of 1977 defines combatant as follows:

> The armed forces of a Party to the conflict consist of all organised armed forces, groups, and units that are under a command responsible to that Party for the conduct of its subordinates. . . .
>
> Members of the armed forces of a Party to the conflict are combatants; that is to say, they have the right to participate directly in hostilities.

Protected persons include the following categories of persons:

> wounded; sick and shipwrecked members of the armed forces and civilians; prisoners of war; civilians, including those interned and those on the territory of the enemy or in occupied territories (1:73–74). [References in the above text are made to the Geneva Conventions and Protocol 1.]

As a result, the Commissioners excluded soldiers or members acting as soldiers from the SADF, the SAP, Umkhonto we Sizwe, and the Azanian Peoples Liberation Army from consideration as "victims." In determining whether a person was a member of an "organized force . . . under a command responsible to [a] Party to the conflict" (Additional Protocol 1, Article 43, paragraph 1), the Commission was faced with the problem of how to categorize "members of a variety of more or less organised armed groupings," including those who were "little more than bands of politically motivated youth, acting on example and exhortation" (1:77). The *Report* has this confession:

> In the end, given the lack of information on the degree of control and the nature of the combat situation, it [the Commission] decided to employ the narrow definition of combatants. This meant that, in general, cases involving members of the above organizations were treated in the same way as non-combatants.
>
> (1:77)

A decision was made that has had far-reaching and devastating effects on young people who fought against the state, effects that ricochet through society now. *In effect, thousands and thousands of fighters within South Africa were treated as civilians.* One might have supposed that "the lack of information" identified by the Commissioners might have led them to fill in the gaps, not step over them. Old definitions condemn modern participants in the interests of clarity. The Commissioners' admission in their *Report* that "Many refused to regard themselves as victims" is a very serious admission with regard to their failure to document the role of the young (5:199). Many of the testimonies about children and youth were made on their behalves, usually by kin, most often by mothers, and relatively few of them were about the young who had committed their lives to the struggle. Many testifiers who told of gross abuses committed against their kin did not know whether they had been politically active within a liberation organization partly because they were shielded by the young from full knowledge of what they had endured. Soon after the hearings had begun, I (and no doubt others) pointed out to the Commissioners that those who had fought against the apartheid regime inside the country were refusing to apply for reparations or to tell their histories to the Commission because they rejected the label "victim." The Commissioners made no change in their rhetoric or the design of their hearings to address this objection. They could have. Perhaps the idea that the liberation forces in the conflict in South Africa had command structures that actually directed fighters' actions and to which fighters were accountable for their every action reflects notions of war that now apply to only a specific kind of fight.

Affiliation and Accountability

The authors of the *Report* admit that they had "difficulty in attributing precise responsibility for human rights violations" (2:4). It is interesting to see how the Commissioners' findings determine responsibility, despite their stated difficulty in identifying affiliation. In trying to assign responsibility, the writers of the *Report* have trouble in referring to members of liberation organizations within the country: they refer to "*civilians who* saw themselves *as ANC supporters and acted in line with what they* perceived to be *ANC's strategic direction*" (2:9), gross human rights violations that were perpetrated not by direct members of the ANC but by "*civilians who saw themselves as ANC supporters*" (2:241), gross violations that were carried out by "*members of South African society* acting in what they considered to be the pursuit of a political aim" (2:4), and the "*blurring of boundaries of these allegiances*" (2:340; emphasis added throughout).

Despite the Commission's difficulty in assigning "precise responsibility," a high moral stance was taken in holding the parties to the conflict accountable: "the Commission is of the view that gross violations of human rights were perpetrated or facilitated by all the major role-players in the conflicts of the mandate era. These include . . . Liberation movements and organisations" (5:209). In evaluating the role played by those who were involved in the conflicts of the past, the Commission was guided by its endorsing act. In the light of this and of the evidence received, the Commissioners conclude that "gross violations of human rights were perpetuated or facilitated by all the major role players in the conflicts of the mandate era" (5:209). All the parties they list are not "held to be equally culpable. . . . The preponderance of responsibility rests with the state and its allies" (5:210). They identify sectors declared to be guilty of "acts of omission," whether out of fear or because they were the beneficiaries of the state system and contributed to a "culture of impunity" (5:209–212). We have yet to see whether the Commission's contribution undermined that culture of impunity.

The Commissioners add that not all the parties "can be held to be equally culpable"; indeed, they say, "this was not the case. The preponderance of responsibility rests with the state and its allies" (5:210). It grants that the liberation movements pursued a "just war," but it draws a distinction between a "just war" and "just means" and holds them "morally and politically accountable" for gross violations of human rights (5:239). The Commission observes that "No major role-player emerges unscathed" (5:257).

I referred above to the finding that the ANC was morally and politically accountable for creating a climate in which supporters who were not directly under ANC command committed violations. The UDF is similarly held accountable and, moreover, one in which violent actions "were considered legitimate" for creating a climate in which members of affiliated organizations "believed they were morally justified in taking unlawful action" (2:246). Both quotes are emphasized in bold and are capitalized in the *Report*. The UDF and its leadership are accountable for having "failed to exert the political and moral authority available to it to stop" violent practices, especially "necklacing" (5:247).

Clearly, the best tactic in terms of avoiding being held accountable and having the details laid out was to have said little and to have proffered few documents. The Commission notes that it has made a more detailed finding and comments more extensively on the ANC than on the PAC, but it also says that does not mean that the former was responsible for more violations. Rather, it reflects the ANC's openness in contrast with the PAC, which offered very little by way of information on any of its activities, including exile abuses, and supplied no documentation. The Azanian National Liberation Army's activities, in the section on "The Liberation Movements from 1960 to 1990," are described in under one page (2:377). They are held accountable for having committed gross human rights violations. The former SADF and the NIS are castigated for lack of cooperation. The Commission's evidence on the deliberate and systematic destruction of state documentation is an important contribution to the archive.

In assigning accountability, the Commissioners acted in accord with their brief in the Act as they interpreted it: "The primary task of the Commission was to address the moral, political, and legal consequences of the apartheid years. The socio-economic implications are left to other structures" (5:258). I do not understand how that division can have been made within the brief of the Commission.

Precaution of the Subject

Walter Benjamin believed in the necessary "precaution of the subject" (1979, 305), which is entitled not to be sold cheaply. The Commission took seriously the precaution of the subject in listening to people's accounts of their experiences in the past. The drafters of the endorsing Act of the Commission could, I believe, have taken other precautions to ensure that the design included the possibility of documenting the political action of children and youth more directly and more accurately and to ensure that resources were secured for reparations before the Commission began to operate.

The chapter calls for careful efforts to be made to ensure that the role of the young is placed accurately on record. Fuller documentation of the nature of the participation by the young in the fight for democracy may have contributed more to the Truth and Reconciliation Commission's ambition to move toward the promise of a just society.

A more careful analysis of the role of the young in conflicts could contribute to a more accurate description of the nature of war and of the international rules that are established to contain it and to respond to its aftermath.

Epilogue

> It is present this past . . .
>
> — PASCAL MERCIER

The project that the fourteen men of Zwelethemba and I had begun subsequent to the Boland Human Violations Hearing of June 24–26, 1996, in Worcester came to a formal end on October 21, 1999. However, we kept in contact and have met as a group seven times across the years when I have returned to Cape Town. Four of the men have died: Ntando in February 1999 as a result of the bullet wound from the vigilante's gun; Zingisile in September 2003; Paulos in February 2005, and Sox in February 2007. We mourn their passing.

During the dozen years since our last formal meeting, half of the men were employed for the majority of the time. The other seven had been unemployed for a good proportion of that time, or they had held a variety of temporary jobs. In June 2011, among the ten men left, eight had jobs. Between them, the men have had some twenty-five children (I did not collect details of marital changes). Seven of them still live in Zwelethemba, two in another suburb of Worcester, and only one has left the area and is currently working in the Eastern Cape.

Without close engagement, one cannot untangle the vicissitudes of life from the consequences of their experiences of conflict. It is clear that the past is present in some form for all of them.

The book shows that it takes close attention over time to analyze a fight of the kind in which the young engaged in Worcester and to detail the manner in which power can be used to harm and terrorize children. Acknowledgment is important in assisting fighters to craft another form of life following conflict, and, if the nature of the experiences undergone is not known, then due recognition is unlikely to be given. Marilyn Strathern says, "A social anthropologist stands for a lay interest in the fate of authorship" (2004, 5), and, in her writings on violence, Veena Das demonstrates for anthropologists what it means to be responsible to suffering and to engage in an ethic of responsibility (2007, 207–211). I utilized anthropology's approach to the world to relate the fate of the men in Zwelethemba as they described it.

To make broad social and political claims about rights of protection and entitlements, Judith Butler argues for a reconsideration of certain issues that include "precariousness, vulnerability, injurability, interdependence, exposure, bodily persistence, desire, work and the claims of language and social belonging" (2009, 2). Her call is to focus anew on and expand the political critique of state violence and the differential distribution of resources (32) and to find ways of checking destructiveness (49).

Appendixes

Worcester

Worcester is the largest of the Boland towns that include Ceres, Montagu, Robertson, and Tulbagh. The 1991 census gave a population of 243,550 in the Boland, 7.1 percent of the population of the Western Cape. The major products of the area include wine, table grapes, apricots, and peaches. Worcester is the most industrialized of the towns; it lies 110 kilometers northeast of Cape Town. The Boland towns were divided strictly according to apartheid criteria, with areas set aside for Africans set a short distance outside the town. Zwelethemba is four kilometers from the town center of Worcester. Unemployment in the region in the 1980s and 1990s was high, often over 50 percent. Many people were, and are, seasonally employed for only four months of the year. Worcester had, at the time of writing, a provincial hospital and a state-run clinic but no provision for state mental health services.

The Trauma Centre for Victims of Violence and Torture in Cape Town published a book, *Apartheid's Violent Legacy: a Report on Trauma in the West-*

ern Cape, written and edited by Donald Skinner (1998). Its aim was to record
the problems experienced by victims of violence in greater Cape Town and
in the Boland. It gives a survey of conditions in the 1980s and early 1990s. I
draw here on the findings for Zwelethemba (Skinner 1998, 184–188). Sixty
households were surveyed, of which forty-two reported having experienced
political violence; forty-five questionnaires were completed; and nine in-
depth interviews with people directly affected by violence were conducted.
The *Report* states that opposition to the apartheid state began among Africans before the 1950s, and some people were detained and arrested in the
1960s and 1970s. Violence peaked in Zwelethemba in the 1980s. The 1984
to 1986 period appeared to be the worst, characterized by many arrests and
detentions. There were seventy-one ex-detainees and eighteen ex-political
prisoners. Most had been between the ages of eighteen and thirty years at the
time of trauma. Twenty percent of the ex-detainees were women. It should
be noted that the study reports only those who experienced detention periods of longer than forty-eight hours. There were regular street battles between the security forces when the latter entered the area. According to the
survey data, thirteen deaths occurred between 1983 and 1987. School pupils
and their Student Representative Councils (SRCs) were the main victims of
the repressive violence. Details of the violence are given in the report, and
subsequent medical and psychological problems are described, as are the
respondents' expressed needs.

The South African Truth and Reconciliation Commission:
A 1996 explanatory note from the TRC for the public

The Truth and Reconciliation Commission has been established by an Act of Parliament: *The Promotion of National Unity and Reconciliation Act, number 34.* It was passed into law on 27th July, 1995. The preamble of the Act states that,

> . . . it is deemed necessary to establish the truth in relation to past events as well as the motives for and circumstances in which gross violations of human rights have occurred and to make the findings known in order to prevent a repetition of such events in the future.
>
> *(Promotion of National Unity and Reconciliation Act, number 34 of 1995:2)*

In addition, the Act states that the aim of the Commission will be reconciliation, based on,

> a need for understanding but not for vengeance, a need for reparation but not retaliation, a need for *ubuntu* but not for victimization.
>
> *(ibid.)*

Finally, the Act makes provision for the granting of amnesty "in respect of acts, omissions and offenses associated with political objectives committed in the course of the conflicts of the past" (ibid.).

Background to the Formation of the Commission

The Interim Constitution marked the end of the *Apartheid* government's rule in South Africa and it guarantees provision for the granting of amnesty to perpetrators of human rights violations. The Commission was developed through a process of consultation with civil society. It was decided that amnesty should be accompanied by a process in which victims and their families would be able to tell their experiences of human rights violation, and that mechanisms through which reparation and rehabilitation could be implemented would be established. The process is aimed at acknowledging people's experiences of gross violations of human rights and at restoring what the Act calls people's "civil and human dignity."

Additional impetus was given to the formation of the Commission by the two investigations into alleged abuses in the ANC training camps conducted in 1992 and 1993 (Motsuenyane, 1993; Skweyiya, 1992).

Conferences mooting the notion of such a Commission were held (see Boraine, Levy and Scheffer, 1994; Boraine and Levy, 1995) and opinions were sought from national and international scholars.

The Parliamentary Standing Committee on Justice was tasked with finalising the bill to appear before Parliament. After several changes, the bill was debated and passed in Parliament in May 1995.

The Act provides for seventeen Commissioners to be appointed by the President. The head of the Amnesty Committee is required by the Act to be a judge. The President decided to create a more democratic process and appointed a selection panel. The panel held public interviews with candidates proposed by political parties and civil society. A short-list was compiled and presented to the President, who, in consultation with his Cabinet, made the final selection. Not all of the Commissioners finally selected, nor all of those who are tasked with facilitating amnesty, were on the short-list presented to the President. Commissioners were required to have sound human rights records and were not allowed to occupy high political posts.

Aims and Objectives

The Commission aims to create a human rights culture in South Africa, and to promote reconciliation.

The objectives of the Commission are:

- to establish as complete a picture as possible of the human rights violations which occurred within and beyond South Africa between 1st March 1960 and the cut-off date (presently 5th December, 1993);
- to facilitate the granting of amnesty for those who make full disclosure of human rights violations;
- to establish the fate or whereabouts of victims and to restore the dignity of such victims by granting them the opportunity to relate their experiences of violation;
- to make recommendations regarding reparation and rehabilitation; and
- to compile a comprehensive report of findings and recommendations to prevent future violations.

The Commission has a statutory life of 18 months, which expires in June 1997. The Act provides for a further extension of six months. After the completion of its work, the Commission has three months to prepare a final report which will be presented to the President and thence Parliament.

Structure of the Commission

The Act provides for three committees. They are: the Committee on Human Rights Violations, the Committee on Amnesty and the Committee on Reparation and Rehabilitation. Commissioners are supported by additional Committee members, professional and administrative staff and an Investigative Unit, which is headed by one of the Commissioners. The Unit, with its 48 investigators, is required to investigate any matter falling within the scope of the Commission. This includes verification of testimonies made by perpetrators and victims. The Unit has extensive powers of subpoena, search and seizure and entry, and will also make use of a database. It can institute strong penalties for those who fail to comply with it. A limited witness protection programme is also included in the functions of the Commission. A research department has the task of conducting research on the cases presented to the Commission, and writing the final report.

South Africa has been divided into four regions for the purposes of the Commission. Each region has a central office, and the head-office of the Commission is in Cape Town.

COMMITTEE ON HUMAN RIGHTS VIOLATIONS

The Committee aims to investigate gross violations of human rights; to find out who was responsible for them; and to determine how and why human rights violations happened.

The definition of Gross Violations of Human Rights that informs the work of this committee is laid down in the Act:

(a) killing, abduction, torture or severe ill-treatment of any person, or

(b) any attempt, conspiracy, incitement, instigation, command or procure-
ment to commit an act referred to in paragraph (a), which emanated
from conflicts of the past and which was committed during the period 1st
March 1960 and the cut-off date [presently 5 December 1993] within or
outside the Republic, and the commission of which was advised, planned,
directed, commanded or ordered, by any person acting with a political
motive.

The Committee has invited people to make submissions before it in the language of their choice. Written statements are taken from victims and from eyewitnesses. A sample of those making statements is selected for public hearings. The criteria on which the sample is selected have to do with presenting the public with as broad a range as possible of victims, violations and perpetrators. Victims, defined as either the person who suffered the violation or their family members or dependents, are referred to the Committee on Reparation and Rehabilitation. Victims are to be treated with respect and compassion and without discrimination. The Commission must protect their privacy and ensure the safety of both witness and the family.

Public hearings are held throughout the country and are televised, broadcast and recorded in the print media. The hearings focus on individual experiences and on events that affected whole communities (such as the youth uprisings of Soweto in 1976). Provision is also made for political parties to present context papers which describe the context within which parties acted.

The Amnesty committee is required to hear applications for amnesty from those who committed crimes with a political motive. Amnesty shall be granted where full disclosure is made. Names of those granted amnesty will be published in the Government Gazette. Applications for amnesty have to be made before the 15th December 1996.

The Amnesty clause of the Commission has come under considerable scrutiny and criticism. Some critics hold that the amnesty provisions contravene international law. International law finds that governments are responsible for the prosecution of those who committed human rights violations except in cases of "public emergency." Proponents of the Commission argue that a provision for amnesty was a prerequisite to the ending of conflict in South Africa. The amnesty clause was tested in the Constitutional Court recently. A case was brought against the Commission by relatives of victims who claimed that the amnesty provision violated their right to civil and criminal redress, and was therefore unconstitutional. The Constitutional Court found that the facilitating of the granting of amnesty was a provision of the Interim Constitution, and found against the plaintiffs.

At the time of writing there have been approximately 2 000 applications for amnesty. The Commission is required by the Act to attend to those applicants who are currently serving prison sentences for the crimes for which they are requesting amnesty. More than 1 600 of the applicants fall into this category. There have been indications that a number of high ranking officials of the *Apartheid* government will apply for amnesty.

The function of the Reparation and Rehabilitation Committee is to make recommendations to the President regarding reparation for victims and measures to restore their human and civil dignity. Additionally, it is required to make recommendations regarding urgent interim relief for victims.

This committee is also responsible for the psychological briefing and debriefing of witnesses appearing before the human rights violations committee.

Unique Features of the Commission

There are a number of features which make the Commission unique among the commissions held to date.

- Promulgation
  The Commission has been established through an Act of Parliament, passed after Parliamentary debate. It is the first Commission of its kind to have been put in place by a democratically-elected government.
- Selection
  A committee of seven people, representing the major political parties in the Government of National Unity, Labour and the Churches, was appointed by the President to select 25 people from whom the President would appoint the final 17 commissioners. Commissioners were required to have a sound human rights record and were not to have high political profiles. Further appointments were made by the President without a public selection process.
- Powers
  The Commission has been invested with powers of search and seizure and subpoena. The Commission has its own investigation unit.
- Amnesty
  While the amnesty clause has been hotly contested, the amnesty that is offered is not blanket. In other words, individuals must apply for amnesty, and, in order to qualify, must make full disclosure of the acts committed. Applications for amnesty are screened by a panel which is headed by a judge of the Supreme Court (the highest court in the land). Amnesty is granted according to the Norgaard Principles (established in brokering the peace in Namibia). Included in these principles are notions of proportionality; that is, the act, omission or offense must have been proportional to the political end for which it was committed. In addition, motives, the nature of the act and its objective are taken into account. Amnesty is therefore not automatically granted. Applications for amnesty must be made by 15th December 1996.

- Public Hearings

    A proportion of the submissions, both of those testifying about human rights violations and those applying for amnesty, are held in public.

- Publication of names

    The South African Commission is required to promulgate the names of those who receive amnesty in a Government Gazette. Most other truth commissions, notably those of Latin America, have published only the names of those who experienced human rights violations, and not the names of perpetrators.

The Boland Hearings

At the hearings held from June 24–26, 1996, in Sohnge College, Worcester, twenty-four accounts of the past were heard. Twenty were given by men and four by women, of which two-thirds were by or about people who were under thirty years of age when they had been violated and of whom seven were under eighteen. All but one were later declared to be victims, and their names appear in volume 7 of the Commission's *Report*. Half of the accounts were about people from Worcester (six of whom were young activists), and they included testimony from Amos Dyantyi (spelled Dyanty by the Commission staff), Xolile Dyabooi, Zandisile Ntsomi, and Pringle (Ntando) Mrubata. I had worked with Amos during a previous study, and the other three worked with me on this project.

Of the testimonies, seventeen were delivered by the person affected (thirteen men and four women) and seven close relatives (two fathers about their sons, one man about his father, two mothers about their sons, and two women about their husbands). One man's wife and son spoke about him, and another man's mother and wife testified on his behalf. The accounts were about deep violation and great pain. Five were about a kinsman who had been shot dead, and one was of a kinsman who had died as a consequence of torture and detention, under suspicious circumstances. The range in age was from the very young (a boy aged eleven) to the elderly. A variety of persons was represented, including innocents caught in crossfire, a long-term Robben Island political prisoner, and one who had been accused of being an *impimpi* (spying for the security forces). Among them nine were detained and tortured, five shot and seriously injured (of whom two were also tortured), and four severely beaten. Of the perpetrators, eighteen were said to have been members of the security forces, one was a municipal policeman, five were vigilantes, one was a civilian, and one was a political activist. Mention was made of two houses that had been burned down.

The three days of hearings reflected the complexities of community relations under oppression and in the face of revolt. The themes that emerged include betrayal, death, extremities of pain, torture, cruel treatment of children, the failure of medical personnel, and sexual abuse. The list of consequences included mental breakdown, physical harm (paralysis, loss of a leg, an eye, hearing), and loss of education, jobs, houses, and the ability to work. It was a sampler of the devastation apartheid wreaked and of the targeting of the young.

The Commission's Findings on Violence in the Western Cape: An excerpt from Fiona Ross (2003, 103–106) with her generous permission

The Cape Town office of the Commission received 1 780 statements that represent 8.4 per cent of the total number of statements received by the Commission. The statements reported on 4 267 violations, of which 3 122 constituted gross violations of human rights and 1 145 were "associated violations" (violations that did not fit the categories as established in the Act and elaborated in the Commission's work. See Volume Three: 3, note 1. It is not clear what these were: no reference is made to "associated violations" in the section of the Report dealing with definitions or in the Act). The statements identified 2 350 victims; on average 1.3 victims were identified in each statement and each victim suffered 1.8 violations. (Volume Three: 3). In other words, a large number of those who testified in the Western Cape, as elsewhere,[1] described more than one event of violation and identified more than one victim in each instance. Most deponents in the Cape were young men. More than one-third of statements concerned violations committed in 1985 and young men between the ages of thirteen and twenty-four were the primary victims (Volume Three: 393).

For the period 1983–1989, 53 percent of violations reported in the Cape concerned severe ill treatment; sixteen percent concerned torture; fourteen percent concerned killings and twelve percent described associated violations. Three percent of statements concerned attempted killing and one percent of statements concerned abduction (Volume Three: 393). Age and gender analyses of the data by year and by sub-region are not provided in the Report. It is therefore not possible to describe local variations or particularities in patterns of violation or reporting or consequences.

Seventy-seven residents of Zwelethemba made statements to the Commission. Twenty-six women (representing approximately one-third of Zwelethemba deponents) made statements. As far as I have been able to ascertain,[2] nine of the women made statements concerning their own experiences of violation.

In addition to numeric data about violence, the Report provides a narrative description of events in each region. Describing events in the Cape in the 1980s, the period on which my research in Zwelethemba focused, it states:

The political revolt unfolding in the rest of the country reached the western Cape in 1985. The first six months of 1985 saw extensive unrest in the rural areas of the southern Cape, Karoo, Boland and the northern Cape . . .

With some notable exceptions, the high levels of open street confrontation seen in 1985–86 generally subsided during 1986. The countrywide state of emergency imposed in June 1986 [*sic*] led to large-scale detentions in both rural and urban areas . . .

The period 1983–89 generated the highest peak of violations in this region, in both the urban and rural areas (Volume Three: 419).

In a section dealing with rural violence (Volume Three: 428–30), the Report describes violence in Zwelethemba in 1985:

During 1985, protest meetings were often broken up violently by security forces and street protests became more militant. Many towns saw at least one or two deaths of youth activists during 1985, which served to propel the townships into wider protest and attacks on those seen as collaborators . . . .

Worcester

In Worcester [Zwelethemba], the spark was provided by the killing of Mr Nkosana Nation Bahume, after which a cycle of deaths and injuries took place until the end of the year.

On 16th August 1985, student activist Nkosana Nation Bahume (CT00547),[3] aged twenty-one, was shot dead by the security forces. On 30th August, the local magistrate issued restriction orders on the funeral of Bahume, who was to be buried the following day.[4] At the funeral, police fired on mourners, killing Mr Mbulelo [Nondatsu] Kenneth Mazula (CT00528), aged twenty. An eyewitness testified that "police dragged his body to the vehicle and took him to the mortuary." People were assaulted, shot and detained by security forces in the uproar.

Mbulelo Mazula was buried on 8 September without incident. However, on 21 September 1985 Mr Andile Feni (CT08402) and two others were shot and injured by a policeman in Zwelethemba after a crowd had thrown a petrol bomb at a police officer's house after a mass meeting that had resolved to chase all police from the area following the killings.

On 1 October 1985, Mr Thomas Kolo (CT08400), aged 18, was shot dead by security forces. He was buried on 11 October and the funeral was restricted by the magistrate. The following day, security forces shot Mr Zandesile Ntsomi (CT00320). Ntsomi's leg was amputated and he was discharged from hospital back into police custody the following day . . . .

On 13 October, Douglas Ndzima (CT00821) was shot twice by police in Zwelethemba. That day Ms Martha Nomathamsanqa Mooi's house (CT03026) in Zwelethemba was petrol-bombed by UDF members. Mr Mpazamo Bethwell Mbani (Yiko) (CT03026), her brother-in-law, was shot dead and his body set alight.

On 2 November 1985, Mr Cecil Roos Tamsanqa van Staden (CT00132) was shot by police and died two days later. The following day, Mr William Dyasi (CT00823) was shot dead by police in Zwelethemba. An inquest was held and Constable Michael Phillip Luff was found responsible for the murder but he was not prosecuted. At the intervention of the Commission the case was reopened, following which Luff applied to the Commission for amnesty (AM3814/96).[5]

On 9 November, at the night vigil of one of the victims, Mr Buzile Fadana (CT00131) was shot dead after the police arrived and an 'armed encounter' resulted. His death marked an end to this cycle of killings and injuries that year.

By November 1985, an extreme environment [*sic*] of repression existed in Zwelethemba, which was declared out of bounds to all except residents. Roadblocks were set up and residents were only allowed to go to their homes on producing identity documents. There were twenty-four hour foot patrols, and searchlights swept the streets at night. Residents reported a heavy presence of Zulu speaking policemen.[6] Funerals of unrest victims were restricted to only fifty people and the family of the deceased. In one instance, forty young people were detained whilst participating in a funeral vigil.

The Report adds: "The Commission finds that the killing by police of Mr Nkosana Nation Bahume on 16 August 1985 triggered a sequence of violence in which numerous residents of Worcester were killed or injured by police and a number of persons or buildings were attacked in retaliation. The draconian response of the authorities, including curfews, roadblocks and sweeping detentions, only aggravated the situation."

The Report's description of Zwelethemba offers a litany of death, interspersed with accounts of injury and torture. Police killed six young men, one man was burnt to death, five men were injured by police fire and several people were assaulted, shot and detained. One woman's house was burnt. There is no mention of the attack on Yvonne Khutwane's house. The police and legal authorities imposed curfews, roadblocks, detentions, restrictions and surveillance mechanisms.

The Report says little about the conditions of resistance or the contexts of violence in Zwelethemba. It stipulates that violence was triggered by the death of Nkosana Bahume. In fact, Bahume's death occurred after fierce protest in Zwelethemba against the Black Local Authorities ("councillors," as they are locally known) began in 1983 and reached its zenith in 1985. Bahume's death followed in the wake of at least two school boycotts; one in recognition of the deaths of the "Craddock Four" and the other in support of children and youths in detention. There had been a heavy police presence in Zwelethemba since 1981 and a large number of young people had been detained or arrested on political charges between 1980 and Bahume's death. According to research notes compiled by members of the Commission and issued to the media during the Worcester Hearing, fifty-two people had been detained and charged with public violence on 10th August 1985, a week before Bahume's death. Twenty-five of them were under eighteen years old.

Other research findings suggest that violence was more widespread than the Commission Report implies.

Four Figures from the TRC *Report*

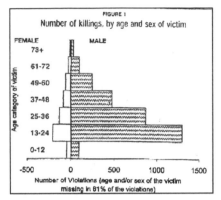

FIGURE 3
Number of abductions, by age and sex of victim

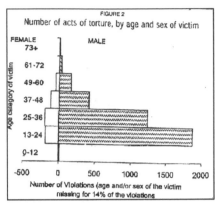

FIGURE 1
Number of killings, by age and sex of victim

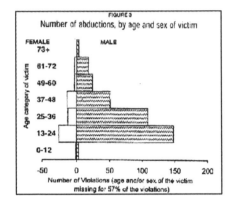

FIGURE 2
Number of acts of torture, by age and sex of victim

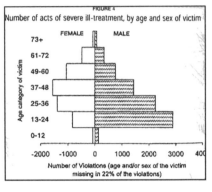

FIGURE 4
Number of acts of severe ill-treatment, by age and sex of victim

The TRC's Findings on Children and Youth
(1998, 5:254–256)

Children and youth

159. The Commission endorses the international position that children and youth under the age of eighteen are entitled to special protection from government and society. As the Commission's statistics have shown, the greatest proportion of victims of gross violations of human rights were youth, many of them under eighteen.

160. With regard to children and youth the Commission finds that:

THE STATE, IN THE FORM OF THE SOUTH AFRICAN GOVERNMENT, THE SECU-
RITY FORCES AND THE CIVIL SERVICES, WAS, IN THE PERIOD 1960–94, THE
PRIMARY PERPETRATOR OF GROSS VIOLATIONS OF HUMAN RIGHTS AGAINST
CHILDREN AND YOUTH IN SOUTH AFRICA AND SOUTHERN AFRICA.

THE POLICY OF APARTHEID RESULTED IN THE DELIVERY OF INFERIOR, IN-
ADEQUATE EDUCATION TO BLACK CHILDREN AND DEPRIVED THEM OF THE

RIGHT TO DEVELOP IN MIND AND BODY. THIS DEPRIVATION CONSTITUES A VIOLATION OF HUMAN RIGHTS.

THE BANNING BY THE GOVERNMENT OF STUDENT AND YOUTH ORGANIZA-TIONS DENIED YOUNG PEOPLE AN AVENUE FOR DISCUSSION AND PROTEST AND RESULTED IN THE CRIMINALIZATION OF LEGITIMATE POLITICAL ACTIVITY, THUS ENCOURAGING YOUTH TO TURN TO VIOLENT FORMS OF PROTEST. THE STATE IS FURTHER ACCOUNTABLE FOR THE POLITICAL REPRESSION WHICH FORCED YOUNG PEOPLE TO GO INTO EXILE, LEAVING THEIR FAMILIES AND COMMUNI-TIES. EXILE DISTORTED THE NORMAL SOCIALIZATION OF YOUTH AND NORMAL FAMILY RELATIONSHIPS.

THE STATE IDENTIFIED AND TARGETED SCHOOLS AS CENTRES OF RESIS-TANCE. SCHOOLS WERE OCCUPIED, AND STUDENTS AND TEACHERS INTIMI-DATED AND ARRESTED. THIS CREATED A CLIMATE WITHIN WHICH UNNECESSARY VIOLENCE OCCURRED. AS A RESULT, EDUCATION WAS SEVERELY DISRUPTED. MANY CHILDREN WERE UNABLE TO COMPLETE THEIR SCHOOLING AND/OR ADVANCE TO TERTIARY EDUCATION.

BLACK CHILDREN AND YOUTH WERE DEMONIZED AS THE 'ENEMY' BY THE SECURITY FORCES IN PARTICULAR AND, MORE GENERALLY, THROUGH THE PO-LITICAL REPRESENTATION OF YOUTH AND CHILDREN AS PART OF 'A COMMUNIST ONSLAUGHT', THUS FACILITATING AND LEGITIMATING THE USE OF VIOLENCE AND FORCE AGAINST THEM. THE COMMISSION HAS FOUND THAT THE SECURITY FORCES UNNECCESARILY RESORTED TO LETHAL FORCE IN PUBLIC ORDER POLIC-ING, WHERE ALTERNATIVE MECHANISMS OF CROWD CONTROL WOULD HAVE BEEN ADEQUATE TO CONTROL MARCHES, PROTESTS AND DEMONSTARATIONS. THE USE OF LETHAL FORCE AGAINST CHILDREN AND YOUTH IS PARTICULARLY SINGLED OUT AND CONDEMNED.

THE STATE WAS RESPONSIBLE FOR THE DETENTION WITHOUT TRIAL AND TORTURE, INCLUDING SOLITARY CONFINMENT, OF CHILDREN AND YOUTH UNDER THE AGE OF EIGHTEEN. SUCH DETENTION INCLUDED DETENTION IN TERMS OF SECURITY LEGISLATION AS WELL AS THE ABDUCTION OF YOUTH AND THEIR FORCIBLE REMOVAL TO PLACES WHERE THEY WERE DETATINED ILLEGALLY AND TORTURED. THE STATE WAS RESPONSIBLE FOR THE SEVERE ILL TREATMENT IN CUSTODY OF CHILDREN AND YOUTH UNDER THE AGE OF EIGH-TEEN, IN THE FORM OF HARASSMENT AND THE DELIBERATE WITH HOLDING OF MEDICAL ATTENTION, FOOD, AND WATER.

THE STATE, THROUGH ITS SECURITY FORCES, EXPLOITED AND MANIPULATED DIVISIONS IN SOCIETY AND ENGAGED IN THE INFORMAL REPRESSION OF CHIL-DREN AND YOUTH BY IDENTIFYING YOUTH LEADERS, ISOLATING THEM AND, THROUGH VIOLENCE OR FINANCIAL INDUCEMENT, INDUCING THEM TO ACT AS INFORMERS OR VIGILANTES.

IN CERTAIN CASES, PROACTIVE MEASURES TAKEN BY THE SECURITY FORCES DURING THE 1980S INCLUDED INFILITRATING YOUTH AND STUDENT STRUCTURES, POSING AS MEMBERS OF THE LIBERATION MOVEMENTS, RECRUITING YOUNG PEOPLE FOR MILITARY TRAINING AND THEN KILLING THEM.

THE STATE IS RESPONSIBLE FOR THE MILTARISATION OF YOUNG WHITE MALES THROUGH CONSCRIPTION.

THE MASS AND LIBERATION MOVEMENTS MOBILISED AND, IN THE CASE OF THE LATTER, ARMED AND TRAINED CHILDREN AND YOUTH AS PART OF THEIR ARMED FORMATIONS. THE LIBERATION MOVEMENTS AND THE IFP ARE RESPONSIBLE FOR RECRUITING YOUTH INTO THE SDUS AND SPUS IN THE 1980S AND TRAINING THEM TO KILL, THUS DEHUMANISING AND DESENSITISING THEM.

THE WAR BETWEEN THE ANC AND IFP DISPLACED LARGE NUMBERS OF YOUTH, LEAVING THEM HOMELESS. IN THIS RESPECT, THE STATE, THE ANC, AND THE IFP ARE RESPONSIBLE FOR THE COMMISSION OF GROSS VIOLATIONS OF HUMAN RIGHTS.

THE FAILURE BY THE ANC AND THE IFP AFTER 1994 TO REINTEGRATE YOUTH TO ENABLE THEM TO BECOME VALID MEMBERS OF SOCIETY AND TO DEVELOP A SENSE OF SELF-ESTEEM, HAS LED TO THEIR CRIMINALISATION AND CREATED THE POTENTIAL FOR FURTHER GROSS VIOLATIONS OF HUMAN RIGHTS.

The TRC's Recommendations on Children and Youth (1998, 5:321)

Children and youth

45. The Commission recommends that:

CHILD LABOUR IN ALL FORMS BE ELIMINATED THROUGH APPROPRIATE
LEGISLATION.

PROVISION BE MADE FOR ADEQUATE HOUSING AND EDUCATION FOR CHILDREN;[1]

TAX INCENTIVES FOR BUSINESSES AND INDIVIDUALS CONTRIBUTING TO BURSARY
FUNDS BE INCREASED.

TAX DEDUCTIONS BE ALLOWED TO THOSE WHO PAY THE PRIMARY, SECONDARY,
AND TERTIARY EDUCATION FEES OF CHILDREN AND YOUTH OF FORMERLY DIS-
ADVANTAGED COMMUNITIES.

THE GOVERNMENT GIVE CAREFUL CONSIDERATION TO THE POSSIBILITY OF IM-
POSING AN APPROPRIATE GRADUATE TAX ON THE SALARIES OF EMPLOYED GRAD-
UATES OF TERTIARY EDUCATIONAL INSTITUTIONS, AS A MEANS OF PROVIDING A
SCHOLARSHIP FUND FOR STUDENTS.

INTRODUCTION

Volumes 1 to 5 of the Commission's *Report*, published in 1998 in South Africa, are drawn on in the notes and are referenced by the number of the volume and the pages in that volume.

1. The apartheid state classified people into one of four population groups— "African," "Coloured," "Asian," and "White." The apartheid state was based fundamentally on racial (however unscientific) and ethnic groupings. Sociological and historical analysis of contemporary South Africa uses these groupings and the commission followed suit (1:168). See the reason proffered by the chairman of the Commission (1:3).

Chapter 2 of volume 2 outlines the historical context of the Commission's timeframe. It marks the major features of conflict between a minority that sought to dominate a majority, beginning in the mid-seventeenth century. Racially discriminatory practices and deep conflict existed from the beginning and, by the twentieth century, a well-established tradition of excessive or unjustifiable use of force against government opponents "had been instituted" (26). The National Party, which came into power in 1948, did not initiate discriminatory practices, but it introduced social engineering on a vast scale. Three acts are identified as perpetrating "wholesale dispossession and discrimination" by the white minority before this date. One was the 1909 South Africa Act, passed by the British parliament, granting judicial independence that transferred power in perpetuity to a minority of white voters (28). Another was passed by the first postunification government: the 1913 Land Act, which laid the basis for "the territorial separation of whites and Africans [and] it destroyed, at a stroke, a thriving African land . . . and peasant agriculture sector . . . by prohibiting land ownership outside the 7 percent of land allocated to the so-called traditional reserves and ending sharecropping and non-tenancy arrangements on white-owned farms" (27). It began a massive forced removal of African people. The third act singled out was the 1936 Representation of Natives Act, by which Cape African voters were disenfranchised (28).

The apartheid state was constructed after 1948. The *Report* observes that the system was "of a qualitatively different type" (29). It set out to segregate every aspect of life, and it "constructed a totalitarian order" (30). The *Report* says that the system itself was inhumane and degrading (34). See pages 30–33 for key legal enactments under apartheid. The Commission did not address the systemic abuses of apartheid. In the notes, I focus on the ANC, as the men of Zwelethemba, with whom I worked, belonged to that organization.

Worcester fell within the "Coloured Labour Preference Area," making it more difficult for Africans to find work, as it meant that in order to employ an African the employer had to prove to the Labour Department that no "Coloured" person was qualified for the position. Implementation of the preference took shape in the demarcating of the Eiselen Line along the Fish River in the Eastern Cape, which designated the boundary point west of which Africans were not allowed to live permanently. This resulted in numerous forced removals and an increase in migrant labor. It was deeply distressing for Nana's family when his mother, Mrs. Khohlokoane, lost her job in a factory laboratory in Worcester after "Coloured" workers went on strike against the employment of an African.

2. See Reynolds (1995a, 1995b, 1998, 2000).

3. Definitions of violations and comments on torture.

The Promotion of National Unity and Reconciliation Act, No. 34 defined victims as

(a) persons who, individually or together with one or more persons, suffered harm in the form of physical or mental injury, emotional suffering, pecuniary loss or a substantial impairment of human rights (i) as a result of gross violation of human rights; or (ii) as a result of an act associated with a political objective for which amnesty has been granted; (b) persons who, individually or together with one or more persons, suffered harm in the form of physical or mental injury, emotional suffering, pecuniary loss or substantial impairment of human rights, as a result of such person intervening to assist persons contemplated in paragraph (a) who were in distress or to prevent victimisation of such persons; and (c) such relatives or victims as may be prescribed.

The Act defined gross violations of human rights as torture, abduction, killing, or severe ill treatment. The last is defined as:

Acts or omissions that deliberately and directly inflict severe mental or physical suffering on a victim, taking into account the context and nature of the act or omission and the nature of the victim . . . [i.e.] determined on a case by case basis (1:80).

Volume 2 (187–220) contains a section on "Torture and Death in Custody," and it includes "Methods of Torture," "The Use of Torture in Arrest and Interrogation of Detainees," "Deaths of Detainees Held in Terms of Security Legislation," "Knowledge of Condonation of Torture," as well as the Commission's findings, from which the following is drawn.

The Commission finds that torture was used by the security branch at all levels and in all parts of the country, that little effective action was taken by the state to prohibit or even limit its use, and that legislation was enacted that was intended to prevent intervention by the judiciary and to remove public accountability of the security forces for the treatment of detainees in the past. "The Commission concludes that the use of torture was condoned by the South African government as official practice."

On the basis of empirical investigations Foster (1987, 117–118) arrived at this conclusion: There "is clear evidence of the extreme severity of treatment handed out to detainees . . . both physical and psychological torture is employed on a widespread and fairly systematic scale in South Africa. The number and range of health problems particularly of a psychological nature, both during and following release from detention indicate the severity of treatment at the hands of security officials."

David Dyzenhaus (1998, 63–65) gives an account of the fact that when detainees testified to having made confessions under assault it was often dismissed by the court for lack of evidence, as witnesses—the district surgeon, the magistrate, the police official—said there were no signs of recent injuries. His book is one of the earliest critical analyses of the examination of the apartheid legal order as revealed in the Commission's deliberations. In his view, apartheid was exceptional (among states that resorted to extremes of violence) in that it was implemented and sustained through law (ibid., 149). See Asmal et al. (1996, 97–110) for a discussion of the nature of state terrorism in South Africa, including torture, detention, hit squads, and vigilantism.

4. The *Report* comprises seven volumes. The first five volumes were published in 1998. An introductory volume includes the key concepts, rationale, and methods of the Commission. Volume 2 addresses gross violations of human rights from all sides of the conflict, while volume 3 considers the violations from the victims' perspectives. Volume 4 examines the nature of the society, or context, in which the violations occurred and invites self-examination of the involvement in the society. Volume 5 gives the conclusions and analysis of the Commission. Two volumes were published in 2003. Volume 6 presents the reports of the four committees, including that of the Amnesty Committee, and reports on the administration of the Commission plus a section on "Findings and Recommendations"; Volume 7 lists the names of the nineteen thousand declared by the Commission to have been victims.

5. Selected references on the Commission and related matters follow: Asmal, Kader, and Roberts (1996); Asmal, Chidester, and Lubisi (2005); Bell and Ntsebeza (2001); Burton (2000); Coleman and Human Rights Committee of South Africa (1998); du Toit (2005); Foster, Davis, and Sandler (1998); Foster and Skinner (1990); Hamilton et al. (2002); Harris (1999); Human Rights Committee of South Africa (1990); James and van de Vijver (2000); Manganyi and

Du Toit (1990); Nuttall and Coetzee (1998); Posel and Simpson (1999); Ross (2001, 2003); Sarkin (2004); Skinner (1998); Straker (1992); Truth and Reconciliation Commission Report (1998); Villa-Vicencio and Verwoerd (2000); Westcott (1988); and Wilson (2001).

6. On reparations and pensions, the Promotion of National Unity and Reconciliation Act no. 34 of 1995 recommended that reparation measures be considered to achieve unity and reconciliation. Wendy Orr, a commissioner of the TRC and a member of the Reparation and Reconciliation Committee (RRC) wrote an article, "Reparation Delayed Is Healing Retarded" (2000, 239–249), in which she discusses the purpose and process of the establishment and workings of the committee. She discusses the decision to make a "closed list" of persons who could receive reparation and decisions around and differentiation according to the severity or extent of need and/or financial status. Orr offers a critique of the RRC and says that "one of our failures was our inability to deliver some form of reparation or supportive intervention almost immediately. The fact that perpetrators felt the benefit of a positive amnesty decision at once, while victims have had to wait years [even for urgent reparation] has not facilitated healing" (247). She feels very strongly that the Commission (rather than the government) should have had the capacity to implement urgent interim reparation much more expeditiously, and she adds: "The concept of urgent reparation became a complete farce when its delivery only started shortly before the end of the TRC in October 1998."

Social pensions were provided by the government for members of the liberation armies, but thousands of members were excluded by the stipulations of the bill, for example, that a recipient had to be thirty-five or older in 1996. These terms, notably the age bracket, have since been altered.

7. South African Defence Force (SADF) and conscription. In 1967, all white men between the ages of seventeen and sixty-five were expected to serve for nine months of conscription in the South African armed forces, that is, the SADF. The length increased so that by 1977 men served for two years and thirty days per year for a period of eight years. In 1975, the SADF entered Angola as part of the "border war," and during that time men were forced to serve three-month tours of duty. By 1982, conscription totaled 720 days.

The SADF soldiers, the South African Police (SAP) members acting as soldiers, and soldiers of the liberation armed wings who were killed or seriously injured in armed combat (during, for example, the Namibian and Angola "border wars") were not viewed as victims of gross violations of human rights (GVHR) as defined in the Act that established the Commission. Those combatants who were killed or wounded while they were unarmed or out of combat, executed or wounded after they had been captured, or who had surrendered were held to be victims of GVHR as under the Geneva Conventions and Protocols (1:75–76). This protection had been bypassed under the apartheid regime in various ways

(Asmal et al. 1996, 55). There were uncertain areas in determining whom and under what circumstances a person can be said to have been a combatant (Burton 2000, 84–85). Burton calls for international clarification of the criteria of a combatant (ibid.).

In August 1984, the decision was taken to deploy the army in the townships (2:34). The Commission's findings on the SADF and the SAP are given in volume 5 (223–225). The SADF was renamed the South African National Defence Force upon the demise of the apartheid regime.

8. Liberation organizations. The African National Congress (ANC) was the largest liberation organization in South Africa and the one to which the young men in Zwelethemba with whom I worked belonged. It was founded in 1912 as the South African Native National Congress and in 1923 became the ANC. It was banned in 1960 under the Unlawful Organisations Act, and Oliver Tambo established it in exile. A year later, the military wing was instituted as Umkhonto we Sizwe (The Spear of the Nation). The ban on the ANC was lifted in 1990, and in 1994, as a political party, it won the first democratic elections held in South Africa.

In 1959, the Pan Africanist Congress (PAC) was formally constituted, and it formed an armed wing named the Azanian People's Liberation Army (APLA). The PAC was banned in 1960. The Communist Party of South Africa was banned in 1950 and was reconstituted as the SACP in 1962. The Azanian People's Organisation (AZAPO) was founded in 1978, and its armed wing was called the Azanian National Liberation Army. The organization was oriented toward the Black Consciousness Movement (BCM). The Black Consciousness Movement emerged in the 1970s, and it became renowned for the philosophical ideas of Steve Biko.

On February 2, 1990, at the opening of Parliament, the new president, F. W. de Klerk of the National Party, lifted the ban on the ANC, PAC, and SACP.

9. Umkhonto we Sizwe (MK). In June 1961, leaders in the ANC, including Nelson Mandela, "came to the conclusion that as violence in this country was inevitable, it would be unrealistic and wrong for African leaders to continue preaching peace and non-violence at a time when the government met our peaceful demands with force . . . the decision was made to embark on violent forms of political struggle, and to form Umkhonto we Sizwe" (taken from Mandela's statement in court on April 20, 1964, as accused of "treason" or of aiding "terrorists" in the Rivonia trial. Quoted in Westcott 1998, 76). On December 16, 1961, the manifesto of the armed wing of the ANC, the MK, was published.

The Commission states that the "MK engaged in acts of war from 1961 to 1990 when, following its unbanning on 2 February [1990] negotiations [toward a democratic dispensation] commenced. The armed struggle was suspended in August 1990" (2:326). The Commission's analysis of and findings on human rights violations committed by the liberation and mass movements can be found in 2:325–366.

In 1991, the MK was disbanded in accord with political change.

10. The Freedom Charter was adopted by the Congress of the People (ANC) on June 26, 1955, at Kliptown. It stresses the indivisibility of political, social, and economic rights. The text can be found in Asmal et al. (2005, 60–64).

11. Security forces. According to the *Report* (1:42), in the 1980s, when the state was in crisis, real rule-making power shifted from parliament and the cabinet to a nonelected administrative body, the State Security Council (SCC), which operated beyond public scrutiny. "Nominally a sub-organ of the Cabinet, in reality the SCC eclipsed it as the locus of power and authority in matters relating to security." Coleman (1998, 182) describes the security forces as including "the South African Police (SAP), South African Defence Force (SADF), homeland police such as the KwaZulu Police (KZP), homeland armies, municipal and council police and other parastatal law enforcement entities."

From 1949, "a formidable security network" was built up based on a security force, a network of undercover agents, and the recruitment of infiltrators. The overarching National Security Management Systems (NSMS) brought together the military, police, and national intelligence. It oversaw the "bloody repression of the 1980s . . . it was the true heart of the brute maintenance of apartheid, a vast structure led by those who planned, analysed and ordered the minions who carried out most of the violent acts which became the focus of the TRC" (Bell and Ntsebeza 2001, 191). See Sarkin (2004, 47) on security force indemnifications to escape prosecution.

Security force action "took place in the context of a nation wide state of emergency that effectively remained in place from June 1986 until mid 1990" (2:39).

12. There was an array of strong and important NGOs and institutions that stood on behalf of those adversely affected by the apartheid system. They included the following: The Black Sash Organisation was founded in 1955 as an independent political organization of women in South Africa committed to nonracism and parliamentary democracy. It aimed to secure the recognition and protection by law of human rights and liberties. Its opposition to human rights violations committed under apartheid earned it international and national recognition (Mary Burton, national president of the Black Sash, in Westcott 1988, 4). The Centre for the Study of Violence and Reconciliation (CSVR), launched in 1986, is a multidisciplinary institution involved in research, policy proposals, and lobbying for issues regarding violence, reconciliation, conflict management, and human rights violations in South Africa. In 1995, the Khulumani Support Group was founded in response to the Commission's activities to create a place for survivors and families of victims to talk about abuses and experiences under the apartheid regime and to find support; it developed into a powerful group

standing for the rights of people categorized as victims. The Catholic Welfare and Development Organisation was founded under the auspices of the Catholic Church in 1972 by two social workers. It is one of the largest and longest-established NGOs in the country. Their aim is to develop people to rise out of poverty, with the major focus being on development work. The Trauma Centre for Survivors of Violence and Torture was launched in 1993 in Cape Town, having been established in partnership with mental health organizations that had, in the 1980s, addressed the needs of victims of human rights abuses. It aims to provide healing and to respond to the changing face of violence, working toward a nonviolent society in which human rights are respected. In May 2000, following the end of the Commission's work, the Institute for Justice and Reconciliation (IJR) was established. It aims to consider the broader context of social concerns by using the insights that have been gained through South Africa's history to address the need for justice and reconciliation within and beyond South Africa's borders. The Detainees' Parents Support Committee (DPSC) became the Human Rights Commission, then the Human Rights Committee (HRC)—the latter was launched in September 1988. Over fifteen years, they monitored and compiled all the available evidence on repressive methods and practices used to sustain apartheid power. An invaluable historical resource was accumulated. In 1998, Max Coleman produced their findings as a reference work.

13. African National Congress Youth League (ANCYL). In 1943, the ANC Youth League (ANCYL) was founded by young professionals including Nelson Mandela, Walter Sisulu, and Oliver Tambo, who sponsored a "Programme of Action" that encouraged civil disobedience for the first time (Westcott 1988, 7). The militancy of the Youth League provided the impetus for the Defiance Campaign of 1952 and the drafting of the Freedom Charter (4:252–230).

The state's response to peaceful protest in the 1960s, especially against the pass laws, was mass repression, following which many youth left the country to take up arms and fight for liberation. On September 25, 1979, the Congress of South African Students (COSAS) was launched. It was formed as a national organization to represent the interests of black school students in the wake of the Soweto uprisings. During that time, the South African Student Movement (SASM) and other organizations of the Black Consciousness (BC) movement were banned. COSAS initiated the South African Youth Congress (SAYCO). It focused on organizing the nonstudent youth, unemployed youth, and young workers who shared the interests and aspirations of COSAS but could not belong to it. Individual townships and regions established their own youth congresses, and by 1983, twenty new youth organizations were launched. By the end of 1986, there were some six hundred youth congresses across the country, which was remarkable in its own right, as the youth congresses were established and operating during the time of the first state of emergency. The first youth congress was formed in the Western Cape in 1983. Known as the Western Cape Youth Congress (CAYCO), it brought together thirty-five youth groups. Worcester and Zwelethemba established congresses—WOYCO and ZWEYO. Some youth belonged to the South African National Civic Organisation (SANCO), a product of the community groupings that simultaneously fought for a qualitative change in people's social and community lives while tackling the overall political issues of apartheid. They called themselves "civics."

14. Soweto. On June 16, 1976, approximately ten thousand people, many of whom were schoolchildren, held a peaceful protest against the use of Afrikaans as a medium of instruction. Police opened fire on the gathering. The number of children killed or injured varies widely. Most were under the age of twenty-five; many were schoolchildren. The first pupil to be fatally wounded was thirteen-year-old Hector Zolile Pieterson. The journalist Sam Nzima took a picture that became famous. The photograph depicts Pieterson's body being carried away by another student, Mbuyiswa Makhubo, with his distressed sister alongside him (3:559–560). Details of the protest and testimony at the Commission's Soweto Day hearing can be found in volume 3 (557–562). Resistance spread across the nation, lasting for fifteen months. It was the beginning of mass action by the young against apartheid.

15. Many young men died during the years of apartheid, and their lives and fates became renowned, for example, Moeketsi (Stompie) Seipei. The abuse and killing of Stompie has been widely reported and examined. See the *Report* (2:567–570) for the Commission's account and findings. The findings point not to the security forces but to members of the ANC.

Siphiwe Mthimkulu was a political activist from the age of seventeen. He began, like so many others, with protests against Bantu Education. He was detained numerous times and subjected to severe forms of torture. He was shot in the arm and faced constant police harassment. In 1981, after his release from yet another arrest, his health deteriorated rapidly, and he was diagnosed as having been poisoned with thallium. Despite the poisoning, he fought to recover and began slowly regaining his health. Throughout his convalescence, Siphiwe continued with his political activities and filed a claim for damages against the police in connection with his poisoning. In 1982, he left his home for a check-up at the Livingstone Hospital. He never arrived, and it was later revealed that the security forces had killed him (4:260).

Hector Pieterson was one of the youngest persons shot by the police on June 16, 1976, during the Soweto uprising (see note 14).

The Gugulethu Seven killings. Seven young men (Zandisile Zenith Mjobo, Zola Alfred Swelani, Mandla Simon Mxinwa, Godfrey Jabulani Miya, Themba Mlifi, Zabonke John Konile, and Christopher Piet), members of the ANC, were drawn by security forces into a trap and shot (see 3:451–453). Lindy Wilson has made a powerful film, *The Gugulethu Seven* (2001), on the unraveling by the investigative arm of the Commission of the killings.

16. A short selection of works on children and armed conflict and on the situation of children in South Africa under apartheid: Beah (2008); Boyden and Berry (2004); Cohn and Goodwin-Gill (1994); Honwana (2006); Honwana and Dawes (1996); Human Rights Committee of South Africa (1990); Kuper (1997, 2005); Lawyers Committee for Human Rights (1986); Levine (2000, 2006); Machel and Salgado (2001); Pigou (2010); Straker (1992); Wessells (2006).

17. The Cradock Four. Four men, brave and effective activists from Cradock, a small farming town about 300 kilometers north of Port Elizabeth, Matthew Goniwe, Sparrow Mkonto, Fort Calata, and Sicelo Mhlauli, died on June 27, 1985. They had been abducted and assassinated outside Port Elizabeth. They became known as the "Cradock Four." The Report (3:112–117) gives details of their actions and consequences, noting that their treatment illustrates "the use of sophisticated covert operations by the security forces in the assassination of political opponents" (3:116). Testimony was given on April 15, 1996, at the first East London hearing of the Commission, by their wives Nyameka Goniwe, Sindiswa Mkhonto, Nomonde Calata, and Nombuyiselo Mhlauli and by the daughter of Mr. and Mrs. Mhlauli, Babalwa Mhlauli.

Two inquests were held, and at both of them it was found that the four men had been killed by unknown persons. In January 1997, the Commission received amnesty applications from the members of the Port Elizabeth security police for the killing of the Cradock Four.

I. THE GROUND ON WHICH THEY STOOD

1. One form of attack by community residents on people perceived to be informers was called "necklacing." A vehicle tire filled with gasoline was placed around the neck of the person under attack, then set alight. Burning was also used by police to cover up killings (2:386). Targets of necklace murders were frequently those suspected of being collaborators and informers. The *Report* estimates that seven hundred people were burned or necklaced, and of this number 191 were recorded in the Commission's database. During the mandate (1960–1994) years, there were a total of 5,707 (2,870 in the Commission database) deaths related to general public political violence (389). The figure is set in a context of security force tactics that included the widespread use of informers, some of whom had been turned during physical and psychological torture.

2. Detention refers to detention without trial. The *Report* (2:194–204) lists the security legislation that authorized detention during the mandate period. Torture of political detainees was reported as having begun in the early 1960s. Countries that trained South African security force members in methods of torture and third-degree harm are named (ibid.). The General Laws Amendment Act of 1963 extended from thirty to ninety days the initial period of detention that had been sanctioned before a detainee had to be brought to court. Any

commissioned officer was authorized to detain without a warrant any person suspected of political activities (dangerous to "law and order") and to hold such persons in solitary confinement without access to a lawyer. People were often released after having been held for ninety days only to be detained once more on the same day for a further ninety days. "The Minister of Justice said the intention was to detain uncooperative persons 'until this side of eternity'" (197). The period was later extended to 180 days, and subsequently the law allowed for redetention of a further 180 days. The old and the young, women and men, boys and girls were detained, as were persons of any "race" or ethnic group. The Terrorism Act (1967) authorized indefinite detention without trial, and the definition of terrorism was very broad. The security force members who interrogated detainees worked in teams. During the 1976 unrest, an amendment of the Internal Security Act (ISA) allowed for "preventive detention" that was not meant to exceed twelve months. Other acts followed, and in 1982 the ISA was altered in an attempt to consolidate security legislation. The men of Zwelethemba were frequently detained under Section 29 of that Act, which was chiefly used for those suspected of links with the underground. It was covered by the following clause: "Indefinite detention for interrogation, with detainees held in solitary confinement" (203).

State of Emergency regulations gave police wide-ranging powers, including extensive indemnity provisions that, with hardly any censure for excesses, "reinforced their understanding that they enjoyed impunity for extensive abuses committed in the interests of state security" (204). See note 3 in the introduction.

4. *IMFOBE*: THE REACH FOR MORAL PRINCIPLES

1. "Etymologically, 'attend' is a submerged metaphor. It comes from the Latin words *ad*, meaning 'to' or 'toward,' and *tendere*, 'to stretch.' 'When I attend to you, I stretch my ears toward you'" (Alvarez 2005, 16n).

2. At the time of the conversation, Fiona Ross and I were still working on the project on the TRC. She had completed her fieldwork for a doctoral thesis on young women activists in Zwelethemba under my supervision. She held the discussion with Nana, who was not a part of her study, to obtain his views on a number of issues. Their dialogue does not represent a formal interview between researcher and informant. Both have given me their permission to draw from the discussion. Fiona turned her thesis into a book (Ross 2003).

3. He is making the point that a woman as a potential mother—with all the weight of marriage that this implies—represents more than herself: she is the embodiment of the past for the future.

4. I remind the reader that in response to widespread unrest the government declared a State of Emergency in 1985. It was lifted later in the year, but another was declared in 1986. Wide legislative powers were given to the security forces

to reinstitute "law and order." Over forty thousand people were arrested during these years (see Foster et al. 2005, 116–119).

5. On the Cradock Four, see note 17 of the introduction.

6. In 1993, the senior ANC leader Chris Hani was assassinated. See Sarkin (2004) for details of the prosecution and refusal of amnesty for the two men accused of killing him.

APPENDIXES

1. Throughout the country, deponents implicated an average of 1.4 victims per statement and 1.6 violations per victim (Report, Volume Three: 3).

2. At the time of writing, statements are not public documents and details are not released. On 6th March 2000, I checked a list of names that I had obtained with Mirriam Moleleki, who had taken statements for the Commission in Zwelethemba. She was unable to identify five names on the list of twenty-six women and I have been unable to trace the women. Nine women made statements about their own experiences of gross violations of human rights; eight described violations committed against their sons, three were about husbands, and one about a father.

3. Numbers in brackets refer to statement case numbers.

4. In terms of the *Public Safety Act* No. 3 of 1953, magistrates had wide-ranging powers to limit the size and scope of funerals. By 1985, the Act had been amended to permit the state to limit the number of mourners, and to specify that there were to be no political speeches or political songs and no flags flown. If a number of people had been killed in the same incident, they could not be buried at the same time. In terms of the 1986 *Security Laws Amendment Act* No. 13, a person caught and charged with attending a restricted funeral could be imprisoned for up to ten years.

5. Amnesty was refused on the grounds that there was no political motive for Dyasi's killing. Decision no AC/2000/0005, TRC website, accessed 30th January 2002.

6. In a divide and rule strategy, policemen were brought from elsewhere in the country.

Adorno, Theodor. 1974. *Minima moralia*. Translated by E. F. N. Jephcott. London: Verso.

Alvarez, A. L. 2005. *The writer's voice*. London: Bloomsbury.

Arendt, Hannah. 2003 [1964]. Personal responsibility under dictatorship. In *Responsibility and judgement*, edited and introduced by Jerome Kohn. New York: Schocken.

Asad, Talal. 1997. On torture, or cruel, inhuman, and degrading treatment. In *Social suffering*, edited by Arthur Kleinman, Veena Das, and Margaret Lock, 285–308. Berkeley: University of California Press.

Asmal, Kader, Louise Kader, and Ronald Suresh Roberts. 1996. *Reconciliation through truth: A reckoning of apartheid's criminal governance*. Cape Town: David Philip.

Asmal, Kader, David Chidester, and Cassius Lubisi. 2005. *Legacy of freedom: The ANC's human rights tradition*. Johannesburg: Jonathan Ball.

Barrell, Howard. 1993. Conscripts to their age: ANC operational strategy, 1957–86. Ph.D. Dissertation, Oxford University.

Beah, Ishmael. 2008. *A long way gone: The true story of a child soldier*. New York: Harper Perennial.

Bell, Terry, and Dumisa Buhle Ntsebeza. 2001. *Unfinished business: South Africa apartheid and truth*. Cape Town: Redworks.

Benjamin, Walter. 1979. *One-way street and other writings*. Translated by Edmund Jephcott and Kingsley Shorter. London: Verso.

Boyden, Jo, and Joanna de Berry, eds. 2004. *Children and youth on the frontline: Ethnography, armed conflict, and displacement*. London: Berghahn.

Burton, Mary. 2000. Making moral judgements. In *Looking back, reaching forward: reflections on the Truth and Reconciliation Commission of South Africa*, edited by Charles Villa-Vicencio and Wilhelm Verwoerd, 77–85. London: Zed.

Butler, Judith. 2009. *Frames of war: When is life grievable?* London: Verso.

Canguilhem, Georges. 1989 [1951]. *The normal and the pathological*. Translated by Carolyn R. Fawcett. New York: Zone.

Cavell, Stanley. 1979. *The claim of reason: Wittgenstein, skepticism, morality, and tragedy*. Oxford: Oxford University Press.

———. 1981. *The senses of Walden*. Chicago: University of Chicago Press.

———. 1988. *In quest of the ordinary: Lines of skepticism and romanticism*. Chicago: University of Chicago Press.

———. 1995. *Philosophical passages: Wittgenstein, Emerson, Austin, Derrida*. Cambridge, Mass.: Blackwell.

———. 2002. *Must we mean what we say? A book of essays*. Cambridge: Cambridge University Press.

———. 2005. *Philosophy the day after tomorrow*. Cambridge, Mass.: The Belknap Press of Harvard University Press.

———. 2010. *Little did I know: Excerpts from memory*. Stanford, Calif.: Stanford University Press,.

Celan, Paul. 1999 [1983]. *Collected prose*. Translated by Rosemarie Waldrop. Manchester: Carcanet.

Coetzee, J. M. 1997. *Boyhood: Scenes from provincial life*. London: Secker & Warburg.

———. 2003. *Elizabeth Costello*. New York: Viking Penguin.

Cohn, Ilene, and Guy S. Goodwin-Gill. 1994. *Child soldiers: The role of children in armed conflict*. Oxford: Clarendon.

Coleman, Max, and Human Rights Committee of South Africa. 1998. *A crime against humanity: Analysing the repression of the apartheid state*. Cape Town: David Philip.

Das, Veena. 2007. *Life and words: Violence and the descent into the ordinary*. Berkeley: University of California Press.

Daudet, Alphonse. 2002. *In the land of pain*. Edited and translated by Julian Barnes. New York: Alfred A. Knopf.

Dawes, Andrew. 1987. Security laws and children in prison: The issue of psychological impact. *Psychology in Society* 8:27–47.

Dawes, Andrew, and C. de Villiers. 1989. Preparing children and their parents for prison: The Wynberg seven. In *Family therapy in South Africa today*, edited by J. Mason and J. Rubenstein. Cape Town: S.A.I.M.F.T.

Dawes, Andrew, and David Donald. 1994. *Childhood and adversity: Psychological perspectives from South African research*. Cape Town: David Philip.

De Boeck, Filip, and Alcinda Honwana. 2005. *Makers and breakers: Children and youth in postcolonial conflict*. Oxford: James Currey.

Deleuze, Giles. *Negotiations: 1972–1990*. 1995 [1990]. Translated by Martin Joughin. New York: Columbia University Press.

Derrida, Jacques. 1996. [1985]. *Archive fever: A Freudian impression*. Translated by Eric Prenowitz. Chicago: University of Chicago Press.

du Preez, Max. 2004. *Of warriors, lovers, and prophets: Unusual stories from South Africa's past*. Cape Town: Zebra.

du Toit, Andre. 2005. Experiment with truth and justice in South Africa: Stockenstrom, Gandhi, and the TRC. *Journal of South African Studies* 31(2):419–418.

Dyzenhaus, David. 1998. *Truth, reconciliation, and the apartheid legal order*. Cape Town: Juta.

Ellman, Maud. 2005. Introduction: Bad timing. In *On murder, mourning, and melancholia*, by Sigmund Freud. London: Penguin, 2005.

Foster, Don, Dennis Davis, and Diane Sandler. 1987. *Detention and torture in South Africa*. Cape Town: Juta.

Foster, Don, and Donald Skinner. 1990. Detention and violence: Beyond victimology. In *Violence and the struggle in South Africa*, edited by C. Manganyi and Andre du Toit. London: MacMillan.

Foster, Don, Paul Haupt, and Maresa Beer. 2005. *The theatre of violence: Narratives of protagonists in the South African conflict*. Cape Town and Oxford: HSRC Press and James Currey.

Foucault, Michel. 1999. *Religion and culture*. Edited by Jeremy R. Carrette. Manchester: Routledge.

———. 2003a [1994]. *The essential Foucault: Selections from the essential works of Foucault, 1954–1984*. Edited by Paul Rabinow and Nikolas Rose. New York: The New Press.

———. 2003b [1997]. *"Society must be defended": Lectures at the Collège de France 1975–1976*. Edited by Mauro Bertani and Alessandro Fontana and translated by David Macey. New York: Picador.

———. 2003c [1999]. *Abnormal: Lectures at the College De France 1974–1975*. Edited by Valerio Marchetti and Antonella Salomoni. Translated by Graham Burchell. New York: Picador.

Freud, Sigmund. 2003 [1933]. *An outline of psychoanalysis*. Translated by Helena Ragy-Kirby. London: Penguin.

———. 2005. *On murder, mourning, and melancholia*. Translated by Shaun Whiteside. London: Penguin.

Golding, William. 1959. *The Fall*. London: Faber & Faber.

Hamilton, Carolyn, Verne Harris, Jane Taylor, Michele Pickover, Graeme Reid, and Rasia Saleh, eds. 2002. *Refiguring the archive*. Cape Town: David Philip.

Handke, Peter. 2002. *A sorrow beyond dreams: A life story*. Translated by Ralph Manheim. New York: NYRB.

Hansard. 1960–1994. *House of Assembly questions and answers*. Cape Town: Government Printers.

Harris, Verne. 1999. "They should have destroyed more": The destruction of public records by the South African state in the final years of apartheid. Paper presented at a Conference on the TRC Commissioning the Past, University of Witwatersrand, Johannesburg, June 11–14.

Hastings, Max. 2010. Drawing the wrong lesson. *New York Review of Books* 57(4).

Honwana, Alcinda. 2006. *Child soldiers in Africa*. Philadelphia: University of Pennsylvania Press.

Honwana, Alcinda, and Andrew Dawes. 1996. Children, culture, and mental health: Interventions in conditions of war. In *Proceedings of the conference "Children, War, and Prosecution: Rebuilding Hope."* Maputo.

Human Rights Committee of South Africa. 1990. *Children and repression, 1987–1989.* Johannesburg: Human Rights Committee.

James, Wilmot, and Linda van de Vijver, eds. 2000. *After the TRC: Reflections on truth and reconciliation in South Africa*. Cape Town: David Philip.

Jay, Martin. 1994. *Downcast eyes: The denigration of vision in twentieth-century French thought*. Berkeley: University of California Press.

Kuper, Jenny. 1997. *International law concerning child civilians in armed conflict*. Oxford: Oxford University Press.

———. 2005. *Military training and children in armed conflict: Law, policy, and practice*. The Hague: Martinus Nijhoff.

Last, Murray. 1981. The importance of knowing about not knowing. *Social Science and Medicine* 1.5B(3):387–392.

Lawyers Committee for Human Rights (LCHR). 1986. *The war against children: Apartheid's youngest victims*. New York: LCHR.

Levinas, Emmanuel. 1989. *The Levinas reader*. Edited by Sean Hand. Oxford: Blackwell.

———. 1996. *Basic philosophical writings*. Edited by Adriaan Peperzak, Simon Critcheley, and Robert Bernasconi. Bloomington: University of Indiana Press.

———. 1998a [1974]. *Otherwise than being: Or beyond essence*. Translated by Alphonse Lingis. Pittsburgh, Penn.: Duquesne University Press.

———. 1998b [1991]. *On-thinking-of-the-other: Entre nous*. Translated by Michael B. Smith and Barbara Harshav. London: Athlone.

Levine, Susan. 2000. In the shadow of the vine: Child labour in South Africa. Ph.D. dissertation, Temple University.

———. 2006. The "picaninny wage": A historical overview of the persistence of structural inequality and child labour in South Africa. *Anthropology Southern Africa* 29(3–4): 122–131.

Lomax, Eric. 1995. *The railway man*. London: Jonathan Cape.

Lutz, Catherine. 2001. *Homefront: A military city and the American twentieth century*. Boston: Beacon.

Machel, Graca, and Sebastian Salgado. 2001. *The impact of war on children: A review of progress since the 1996 United Nations report on the impact of armed conflict on children*. London: C. Hurst.

Manganyi, N. C. , and Andre du Toit, eds. 1990. *Violence and the struggle in South Africa*. London: MacMillan.

Melville, Herman. 1992 [1851]. *Moby Dick.* New York: Penguin.

Mercier, Pascal. 2009. *Night train to Lisbon.* London: Atlantic.

Monk, Ray. 1991. *Ludwig Wittgenstein: The duty of genius.* London: Vintage.

Murdoch, Iris. 1993. *Metaphysics as a guide to morals.* London: Penguin.

———. 2001 [1970]. *Sovereignty of the good.* London: Routledge.

Neiman, Susan. 2002. *Evil in modern thought: An alternative history of philosophy.* Princeton, N.J.: Princeton University Press.

Nuttall, Sarah, and Carli Coetzee, eds. 1998. *Negotiating the past: The making of memory in South Africa.* Cape Town: Oxford University Press.

Nyezwa, Mxolisi. 2000. *Song trials.* Scottsville: Gecko Poetry, University of Natal Press.

Orr, Wendy. 2000. *From Biko to Basson: Wendy Orr's search for the soul of South Africa as a commissioner of the TRC.* Saxonwold: Contra Press.

Penn, Nigel. 2005. *The forgotten frontier: Colonist and Khoisan on the Cape's northern frontier in the eighteenth century.* Athens, Ohio: Ohio University Press.

Phillips, Adam. 1994. *On flirtation.* London: Faber and Faber.

Pigou, Piers. 2010. Children and the South African TRC. In *Children and transitional justice.* UNICEF. New York.

Posel, Deborah, and Graeme Simpson, eds. 2002. *Commissioning the past.* Johannesburg: University of Witwatersrand Press.

Rée, Jonathan. 1999. *I see a voice: A philosophical history of language, deafness, and the senses.* London: HarperCollins.

Reynolds, Pamela. 1995a. Youth and the politics of culture in South Africa. In *Children and the politics of culture*, edited by Sharon Stephens. Princeton, N.J.: Princeton University Press.

———. 1995b. Not known because not looked for: Ethnographers listening to the young in southern Africa. *Ethnos: Journal of the National Museum of Ethnography* 60(3–4):193–221.

———. 1998. Activism, politics, and the punishment of children. In *Childhood abused: Protecting children against torture, cruel, inhuman, and degrading punishment*, edited by Geraldine Van Bueren. Aldershot: Ashgate.

———. 2000. The ground of all making: State violence, the family, and political Activists. In *Violence and subjectivity*, edited by Veena Das, Arthur Kleinman, Mamphela Ramphele, and Pamela Reynolds, 141–170. Berkeley: University of California Press.

Rich, Adrienne Cecile. 1995a. Inscriptions. In *Dark fields of the republic: Poems, 1991–1995.* New York: W.W. Norton.

———. 1995b. *What is found there: Notebooks on poetry and politics.* London: Virago.

———. 1999. *Midnight salvage: Poems, 1995–1998.* New York: W.W. Norton.

Ross, Fiona. 2001. Speech and silence: Women's testimonies in the first five weeks of public hearings of the South African Truth and Reconciliation

Commission. In *Remaking a world: Violence, social suffering, and recovery*, edited by Veena Das et al. Berkeley: University of California Press.

———. 2003. *Bearing witness: Women and the Truth and Reconciliation Commission in South Africa*. London: Pluto.

Ross, Fiona, and Pamela Reynolds. 1999. Wrapped in pain: Moral economies and the South African TRC. *Context* 3(1):1–9.

———. 2004. Voices not heard: Small histories and the work of repair. In *To repair the irreparable: Reparation and reconstruction in South Africa*, edited by Erik Doxtader and Charles Villa-Vicencio. Cape Town: David Philip.

SAIRR (South African Institute of Race Relations). 1960–1994. *Race relations survey handbook*. Johannesburg: SAIRR.

Said, Edward. 2006. *Music and literature against the grain*. New York: Pantheon.

Sanders, Mark. 2007. *Ambiguities of witnessing: Law and literature in the time of a truth commission*. Stanford, Calif.: Stanford University Press.

Sarkin, Jeremy. 2004. *Carrots and sticks: The TRC and the South African amnesty process*. Antwerp: Intersentia.

Scanlon, T. M. 1998. *What we owe to each other*. Cambridge, Mass.: The Belknap Press of Harvard University Press.

Scarry, Elaine. 1985. *The body in pain: The making and unmaking of the world*. Oxford: Oxford University Press.

Sebald, W.G. 2003. *On the natural history of destruction*. Translated by Anthea Bell. New York: Random House.

Skinner, Donald. 1998. *Apartheid's violent legacy: A report on trauma in the Western Cape*. Cape Town: Trauma Centre for Victims of Violence and Torture.

Straker, Gillian. 1992. *Faces in the revolution: Psychological effects of violence on township youth in South Africa*. Cape Town: David Phillip.

Strathern, Marilyn. 2004. *Commons and borderlands: Working papers on interdisciplinarity, accountability, and the flow of knowledge*. Wantage, Oxford: Sean Kingston.

Suttner, Raymond. 2008. *The ANC underground in South Africa to 1976: A social and historical study*. Johannesburg: Jacana.

Thompson, Ginger. 2003. South Africa to pay $3,900 to each family of apartheid victims. *New York Times* (April 16).

Truth and Reconciliation Commission. 1998. *Truth and Reconciliation Commission of South Africa report*. Vols. 1–5. Cape Town: Juta.

———. 2003. *Truth and Reconciliation Commission of South Africa report*. Vols. 6–7. Cape Town: Juta.

Villa-Vicencio, Charles, and Wilhelm Verwoerd. 2000. *Looking back, reaching forward: Reflections on the Truth and Reconciliation Commission of South Africa*. Cape Town: University of Cape Town Press.

Weil, Simone. 2001 [1955]. *Oppression and liberty*. Translated by Arthur Wills and John Petrice. London: Routledge.

Wessells, Michael. 2006. *Child soldiers: From violence to protection*. Cambridge, Mass.: Harvard University Press

Westcott, Shauna. 1988. *The trial of the thirteen*. Cape Town: Black Sash.

Williams, Bernard. 2002. *Truth and truthfulness: An essay in genealogy*. Princeton, N.J.: Princeton University Press.

———. 2006. *The sense of the past: Essays in the history of philosophy*. Edited with an introduction by Myles Burnyeat. Princeton, N.J.: Princeton University Press.

Wilson, Francis. 2009. *Dinosaurs, diamonds, and democracy: A short, short history of South Africa*. Cape Town: Umuzi.

Wilson, Richard. 2001. *The politics of truth and reconciliation*. Cambridge: Cambridge University Press.

Wittgenstein, Ludwig. 1984 [1977]. *Culture and value*. Edited by E. G. H. von Wright with Heikki Nyman. Translated by Peter Winch. Chicago: University of Chicago Press.

Yeats, William Butler. 1951. The second coming. In *The Faber book of modern verse*, edited by Michael Roberts. London: Faber and Faber.

Žižek, Slavoj. 2009. *Violence: Six sideways reflections*. London: Profile.

forms of living

Stefanos Geroulanos and Todd Meyers, *series editors*

Georges Canguilhem, *Knowledge of Life*. Translated by Stefanos Geroulanos and Daniela Ginsburg, Introduction by Paola Marrati and Todd Meyers.

Henri Atlan, *Selected Writings: On Self-Organization, Philosophy, Bioethics, and Judaism*. Edited and with an Introduction by Stefanos Geroulanos and Todd Meyers.

Jonathan Strauss, *Human Remains: Medicine, Death, and Desire in Nineteenth-Century Paris*.

Georges Canguilhem, *Writings on Medicine*. Translated and with an Introduction by Stefanos Geroulanos and Todd Meyers.

Juan Manuel Garrido, *On Time, Being, and Hunger: Challenging the Traditional Way of Thinking Life*.

Catherine Malabou, *The New Wounded: From Neurosis to Brain Damage*. Translated by Steven Miller.

Pamela Reynolds, *War in Worcester: Youth and the Apartheid State*.

François Delaporte, *Chagas Disease: History of a Continent's Scourge*. Translated by Arthur Goldhammer; foreword by Todd Meyers.

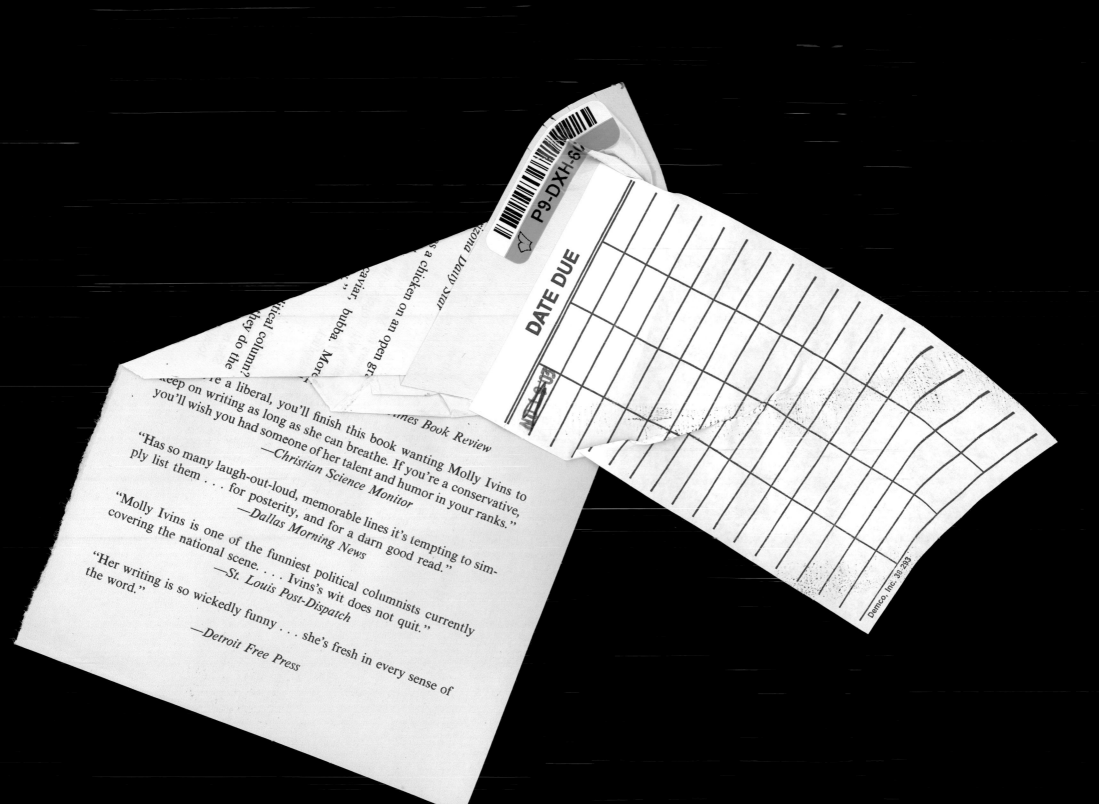

"If you're a liberal, you'll finish this book wanting Molly Ivins to keep on writing as long as she can breathe. If you're a conservative, you'll wish you had someone of her talent and humor in your ranks."
—*Christian Science Monitor*

"Has so many laugh-out-loud, memorable lines it's tempting to simply list them . . . for posterity, and for a darn good read."
—*Dallas Morning News*

"Molly Ivins is one of the funniest political columnists currently covering the national scene. . . . Ivins's wit does not quit."
—*St. Louis Post-Dispatch*

"Her writing is so wickedly funny . . . she's fresh in every sense of the word."
—*Detroit Free Press*

DATE DUE

Demco, Inc. 38-293